The Indian National Army and Japan

The **Institute of Southeast Asian Studies (ISEAS)** was established as an autonomous organization in 1968. It is a regional centre dedicated to the study of socio-political, security and economic trends and developments in Southeast Asia and its wider geostrategic and economic environment.

The Institute's research programmes are the Regional Economic Studies (RES, including ASEAN and APEC), Regional Strategic and Political Studies (RSPS), and Regional Social and Cultural Studies (RSCS).

ISEAS Publishing, an established academic press, has issued more than 2,000 books and journals. It is the largest scholarly publisher of research about Southeast Asia from within the region. ISEAS Publishing works with many other academic and trade publishers and distributors to disseminate important research and analyses from and about Southeast Asia to the rest of the world.

The Indian National Army and Japan

JOYCE CHAPMAN LEBRA

INSTITUTE OF SOUTHEAST ASIAN STUDIES
Singapore

First published in Singapore in 1971 by
Donald Moore for
Asia Pacific Press Pte Ltd
635-637 East Coast Road
Singapore 15

First reprinted in Singapore in 2008 by
Institute of Southeast Asian Studies
30 Heng Mui Keng Terrace
Pasir Panjang
Singapore 119614

E-mail: publish@iseas.edu.sg
Website: <http://bookshop.iseas.edu.sg>

All rights reserved. No part of this publication may be reproduced, stored in a retrieval system, or transmitted in any form or by any means, electronic, mechanical, photocopying, recording or otherwise, without the prior permission of the Institute of Southeast Asian Studies.

© 1971 Joyce Chapman Lebra
   2008 First Reprint

The responsibility for facts and opinions in this publication rests exclusively with the author and her interpretations do not necessarily reflect the views or the policy of the publisher or its supporters.

ISEAS Library Cataloguing-in-Publication Data

Lebra-Chapman, Joyce,
   The Indian National Army and Japan.
   1. Indian National Army
   2. World War, 1939–1945—India.
   3. World War, 1939–1945—Japan.
   4. India—Relations—Japan.
   5. Japan—Relations—India.
   I. Title.
DS442.6 L452   2008

ISBN 978-981-230-806-1 (soft cover)
ISBN 978-981-230-807-8 (PDF)

Typeset by International Typesetters Pte Ltd
Printed in Singapore by Photoplates Private Limited

Contents

Abstract		vii
Foreword		viii
Preface		xi
Acknowledgements		xii
Introduction		xiii
1	Mission to Bangkok	1
2	Malayan Jungle Meeting	16
3	Singapore Capitulates and the INA Blossoms	34
4	Tokyo Conference	43
5	Japanese Policy toward India	60
6	The Crisis of the First INA	75
7	Subhas Chandra Bose, Hitler, and Tōjō	102
8	Bose, the FIPG, and the *Hikari Kikan*	128
9	To India or Not?	149
10	The Rising Sun Unfurls; the Tiger Springs	174
11	A Plane Crash	194
12	A Trial in the Red Fort	200
13	Retrospect	210
Notes		220
Bibliographical Note		237
Bibliography		239
Index		246
About the Author		256

Illustrations and Maps

	facing page
"Harimao", or Tani Yutaka	50
Isoda Saburō	50
Fujiwara Iwaichi	51
Indian Independence League members at the Sanno Conference in Tokyo, April 1942—Fujiwara and Mohan Singh shaking hands, Goho in the centre and N. Raghavan on the right.	66
From left to right: N.S. Gill, Mohan Singh, and M. Akram	66
Shah Nawaz Khan and Staff Officer Okamoto discuss strategy during Imphal campaign.	67
Kawabe Masakazu	67

	page
Malaya and Thailand	13
Singapore	33
Imphal Setting—Terrain	148
Imphal Setting	152

Abstract

Overview

This is a reprint of *Jungle Alliance: Japan and the Indian National Army*, which was originally published in 1971 by Donald Moore for Asia/Pacific Press. It has long since been out of print and is unavailable. It covers the beginnings of the Indian National Army, as part of a Japanese military intelligence operation under Major Iwaichi Fujiwara, and moves forward to the arrival of Subhas Chandra Bose and the enlarged INA and Free India Provisional Government under his direction from 1943 until the collapse of Japan and the INA in August 1945.

Specific Aspects

Chapters relating to the origins of the INA in the interaction between Fujiwara and a young Sikh Major, Mohan Singh, are covered here as critical to the birth of the INA. The book also deals with the earlier career of Subhas Chandra Bose, including his stay in Berlin and the Indian Legion there.

How This Book Differs From Others

This is still the only volume dealing with the interaction between the Japanese Army and the Indian National Army that also deals with Japanese sources. No other book in English has replaced this book, which is why a reprint edition is required at this time.

Foreword

IT is a quarter of a century ago that Japanese armed forces left Southeast Asia, yet even now our knowledge about the occupation years can be likened to a jigsaw puzzle in which far too many pieces are still missing. Happily, the number of researchers devoting themselves to the study of wartime Southeast Asia is increasing. More than that, many if not most of them are better trained than the handful of scholars who preceded them. Thus, though there are entire countries about which we know as yet lamentably little, others, or parts of others at least, have emerged into ever-clearer perspective. This is particularly true of what might be called "macro-political" studies, which focus on the centres of political and administrative power, if not also on the largest, or dominant, population groups. Far less is known about regional and local developments beyond the capital cities, about smaller ethnic groups and, at least equally important, about racial minorities. It is surely remarkable that no monograph on the Chinese in wartime Southeast Asia has yet appeared, and that in spite of the highly complex relationships between Nanyang Chinese and Japanese.

The more fortunate, then, that we now have before us the first detailed study by a Western scholar of the second largest alien Asian minority in Southeast Asia, the Indians. It most ably supplements and complements K. K. Ghosh's *The Indian National Army: Second Front of the Indian Independence Movement*, published in India in 1969. Indeed, Dr Lebra's major concern is not with the Indian communities in Malaya, Burma and Thailand as such. Rather, it is with a peculiarly fascinating and turbulent chapter in modern Indian history—a history that happened for the greater part to take place in Southeast Asia (some of it of course also in Japan and one agonizing moment even in India proper). And though several prominent Indian residents in the region played a far from negligible part in the events of the 1940s, which also involved tens of thousands of their local compatriots, the real leadership lay with others. In order of appearance in the unfolding historical drama, there were, first, some of the officers of the British-Indian Army who went over to the Japanese and founded the Indian National Army as the Allied defences in Malaya crumbled; second, Rash Behari Bose, long-time Tokyo resident; and there was, finally, the towering figure of Subhas Chandra Bose, who, as soon as he reached Southeast Asia from self-imposed exile in Berlin, became the undisputed *Netaji*—head not only of the INA, but also of *Azad Hind*, the Provisional Government of Free India.

From rich published and unpublished sources in Japan and India, no less than from personal interviews, the author has distilled a story of absorbing interest. She knows how to hold her readers' attention by shifting from analyses of larger movements, policies and strategies to fascinating close-ups of incidents and major *dramatis personae*, especially those on the Japanese side. To mention the best example, Major (now Lieutenant-General) Fujiwara Iwaichi, the founder of the almost legendary *F Kikan*, up to now a dimly perceived marginal figure, emerges in Dr Lebra's pages as a full-blooded, dedicated—and in the end frustrated—"ugly Japanese" of the purest vintage. With the obvious exception of Dr Ba Maw's highly colourful autobiography, such portraiture is all too rare in the literature of occupied Southeast Asia. Almost equally rare is Lebra's objectivity. She takes both Japanese and Indians seriously, looks at them dispassionately and tries with success, as far as I am able to judge, to view their purposes and actions in the frameworks appropriate to their specific situations and personalities. We are at long last getting away from the stereotypes of evil, or at best clumsy, Japanese unsuccessfully trying to manipulate clever, patriotic, if not heroic, "subjects".

In at least one major respect the story told in these pages is, of course, unique: unlike the countries of Southeast Asia, India played at most a marginal role in Japanese thinking, for it was never envisaged as part of the Greater East Asia Co-Prosperity Sphere. Few at most were the Japanese enthusiasts who, like Fujiwara, wished to make the cause of Indian independence that of *Dai Nippon*; at no time did they succeed in converting high-level policy makers to their point of view. Nor was the ill-begotten foray into Imphal in 1944 planned as the opening act of a Japanese move into the subcontinent but as a defensive move to protect Burma against British counter-attacks. Thus the juxtaposition between Japanese and Indian aims was wide, indeed, and Bose's position far weaker than that of leaders representing peoples and lands actually occupied by Japanese forces. Dr Lebra rightly observes the very severe limitations which Tokyo imposed on such ostensible gestures of support as the pseudo-recognition of Bose's Provisional Government. True enough, yet one wonders whether any of the regimes "recognized" by Japan (and her Axis partners) enjoyed a much higher degree of real international stature in the eyes of the Imperial Government.

Be that as it may, the author makes us realize the fantastic personality of Bose, chief of state without a state and commander-in-chief of a token army, and hence a leader with virtually no bargaining power. But for him, Tōjō and his cabinet colleagues might never have done as much as they did to help the cause of Indian independence, albeit indirectly and symbolically rather than substantively. (How important Tōjō rated personalities and how deeply he, in turn, impressed some of the wartime spokesmen of the occupied countries can be gleaned from passages in the present book, as well as from Ba Maw's *Breakthrough in Burma.*) But for the *Netaji*, too, the Indian independence struggle in the *Nampō* might have completely disintegrated amidst debilitating personal and factional feuds and disputes. Had Subhas Chandra Bose not crashed to his untimely death four days after Japan's surrender to the Allies, Indian history might well have taken a somewhat different course. Ironically, the weakest of Japan's "collaborators" may well have been the strongest among her "allies", a man far less likely to have disappeared from centre stage than did, say, Ba Maw and Jose Laurel, who yet had seemed, for a few fleeting moments, to wield more real power than Bose.

Others, with special knowledge of Japanese and Indian history, will no doubt find even greater satisfaction in reading this fascinating book. Perhaps, too, they may find points of detail and interpretation to quarrel with. Whether this was the main reason why Dr Lebra preferred to entrust me with the writing of some introductory lines I cannot know. But let me, a specialist in modern Southeast Asian history, say that I have benefited from her account and that I hope others will emulate her painstaking research and graceful style.

New Haven, Connecticut   HARRY J. BENDA
October 1970

Preface

In the decades intervening between the publication of the first edition of this book in 1971 (*Jungle Alliance: Japan and the Indian National Army*, Singapore: Asia/Pacific Press) and this present edition, the outpouring of volumes on Subhas Chandra Bose and the Indian National Army has continued. None of these studies in English focuses on the relationship between the Imperial Japanese Army and the INA and also uses Japanese sources. For this reason this work is being reprinted.

With the exception of the book by Peter Fay (*The Forgotten Army*, 1993), most of these studies of the INA contain no more than a passing mention of the Rani of Jhansi Regiment, if that. This women's regiment, part of the Indian National Army, was composed primarily of teenage girls from Malaya and Burma who had never seen India, yet were eager to volunteer in response to Bose's summons, to donate not only their jewellery but also their lives in the struggle to liberate India.

A companion volume to this new edition of the 1971 publication will therefore be published, *Women Against the Raj: The Rani of Jhansi Regiment*. It is designed to address the academic vacuum on the subject.

JOYCE CHAPMAN LEBRA

Singapore
2008

Acknowledgements

For financial support of the research for this study I am indebted to a Fulbright grant to India (1965-6), and to a University of Colorado Grant-in-Aid (summer 1964 and 1968) for support of travel to Tokyo. Libraries which made their facilities available to me are: in India the *Netaji* Research Bureau, Calcutta; the Indian School of International Studies Library, New Delhi; the National Archives, New Delhi; the Historical Section, Ministry of Defence, Government of India; and in Japan the Foreign Ministry archives; the War History Library, Defence Agency; the National Diet Library; and the Keiō University Library.

Those who lent their advice, encouragement and suggestions over the four-year period of this research are too numerous to chronicle here. The names of a few without whom this study would not have been completed must be mentioned: Dr Girija Mookerjee, Dr Bimla Prasad, Dr K. K. Ghosh, Dr S. K. Bose, Dr S. N. Prasad, Mr Y. Horie, Mr N. Kurokawa, Professor Tanaka Toshio, Lieutenant-General Fujiwara Iwaichi, Mr Maruyama Shizuo, Mr Maruyama Makoto, Professor Mori Katsumi, Mr Nakano Keiji, Dr Charles Geddes and Dr R. P. Cuzzort. Thanks are due to my mother, Mrs Helen Chapman, for preparation of the maps. I am grateful also to Generals Fujiwara Iwaichi and Isoda Saburō for the loan of photographs.

It goes without saying that responsibility for errors of fact or interpretation is the author's alone.

Joyce Chapman Lebra

Boulder, Colorado
1968

Introduction

FOR over two decades following the end of World War II, Japan's goals and tactics in wartime Greater East Asia have remained buried in government and military archives and in the memories of wartime leaders still living. The image, fostered through the proceedings of the International Military Tribunal in Tokyo, of Japan as one of the world's most rapacious militarist powers has long prevailed on both sides of the Pacific. Difficulty of access to private and official archives of the war years has helped perpetuate the darkness which still obfuscates many aspects of the Pacific War. Japanese historians still remain reluctant to scrutinize the concepts, goals, and implementation of Japan's Greater East Asia Co-Prosperity Sphere in Asia.

American scholars have only recently pioneered in re-examining Japan's war aims and have begun the work of revising earlier assumptions. This task has been facilitated by the appearance of the first volumes of the Japanese official history of World War II, edited by the staff of the War History Office of the Defence Agency.

The war, according to some American revisionists, was not simply a Japanese version of the capitalist pattern of imperialism described by Lenin and demonstrated by Western powers. It was more significantly a war for preservation and defence of vital interests threatened by the advance of Western imperialism in Asia. Similarly, the traditional image of the Greater East Asia Co-Prosperity Sphere as the grand design for Japanese empire in Asia can also be questioned. For one thing, the borders of the Greater East Asia Co-Prosperity Sphere were nebulous and elastic. The concept crystallized in the minds of various individuals, some civilian but mostly military, by late 1940. But the forerunners of the Sphere—the East Asia Co-operative Body and the New Order in East Asia—were advanced even earlier, during the Manchurian Incident. For some, by early 1941, the Greater Sphere, or sphere of influence, would sweep across Asia to embrace India, Australia and New Zealand within its compass. The goal of economic self-sufficiency provided the rationale for political and cultural arrangements. The concept of the Sphere grew as more of Southeast Asia fell under Japanese military occupation.

In actuality, military strategy was never devised to push the boundaries of the Sphere much beyond Burma. Protection of the Burma border and disruption of China-India lines of communication took the Japanese Army in 1944 into Imphal in the state of Manipur, India. Militarily, the campaign was ill conceived; it was a fiasco in execution.

Politically, however, India was included in the vision of the Japanese sphere of influence, even before the outbreak of hostilities in the Pacific. The propaganda goal of "Asia for the Asiatics" served Japan well in Southeast Asia. Japan adopted a policy aim of encouraging anti-British sentiment throughout Southeast Asia and particularly in Burma, Malaya and Thailand. Intelligence missions were sent inside the borders of India. The Imphal campaign of 1944 was designed in part to encourage Subhas Chandra Bose and the Indian National Army, and thereby to incite revolution within India. In Japan's military fiasco at Imphal the immediate political goal was also defeated.

From the Indian viewpoint, the struggle throughout Asia was for independence. The roots of Indian nationalism extend back into the nineteenth century under the British Raj. During the early decades of the twentieth century the political mainstream of Indian nationalism followed the Gandhian doctrine of non-violent disobedience. But there was another tradition, a heterodox political vision with equally ancient roots, which turned toward violence. Subhas Chandra Bose became leader of this militant wing of the nationalist movement, splitting with Gandhi and Nehru over the issue of the use of force against the British. Despite the opposition of Gandhi, however, Bose was elected President of the Indian National Congress in 1938 and again in 1939.

Bose was a Bengali revolutionary. Nurtured in a Kshatriya family on reformist doctrines prevalent in Bengal at the turn of the century, he advocated the use of force as the only means to rid the motherland of the British imperial power. Placed under house arrest in 1940, he eluded the authorities, escaping to Afghanistan and then to Nazi

Germany, where he sought aid in his campaign to liberate India from without. With the German defeat at Stalingrad, Bose turned east to Japan for help. Coming to Southeast Asia in the summer of 1943, he assumed leadership of the Indian National Army and Indian Independence League, which had already rallied civilians and Indian POWs to the struggle for independence.

This study is concerned with the interaction between Japan and the Indian independence movement in Southeast Asia. The logic of the alliance was the existence of a common enemy, Britain. A limited co-operation evolved from the confrontation between Japan's pan-Asian push southward and Indian nationalism. There was some initiative on both sides: on the Indian side by Subhas Chandra Bose and his revolutionary predecesssors, Mohan Singh and Pritam Singh, and on the Japanese side by a young major sent by Imperial General Headquarters to Bangkok on an intelligence mission. Major Fujiwara brought India to the attention of IGHQ and helped organize the INA. Fujiwara established the initial sincerity and credibility of Japanese aid for the Indian independence struggle. Captain Mohan Singh, a young Sikh POW from the British-Indian Army, co-operated with Fujiwara in the inception of the INA.

Disagreement and a disjunction in aims also became apparent between the Japanese and Indians. For Japan there were strategic considerations of a total war in which her resources were proving deficient and in which India was a peripheral concern. For the Indian National Army and *Azad Hind* (Free India) Government there was the single goal of independence which took precedence over all other considerations. From these divergent viewpoints arose obstacles to the working out of effective co-operation. Japan was willing to grant the form but not the substance of independence to the *Azad Hind* Government. Japan was ready to assault Imphal together with the INA, but with the INA only as guerrilla or special services units ultimately under Japanese command. The INA co-operated because without Japanese aid there was no real hope for effective military action against Britain. But Japan could not satisfy INA pressure for material and military support. It was an uneasy alliance, but some of the Japanese who activated it were alert to the need to maintain the delicate balance.

The political repercussions of the wartime struggle of the INA are still being felt within India today. British withdrawal in 1947 was in part precipitated by the trial of INA officers for treason and the popular protest against the court martial of INA patriots. Nor did the story of the INA end with India's independence. Out of the legacy of the struggle of the INA and *Azad Hind* Government an attempt was made to create a new political party dedicated to Bose's ideals, the *Azad Hind Sangh.*

The lessons learned during World War II provided the groundwork for Japan's extraordinary success today (1970) in Southeast Asia. In the words of one former general, Japan has quietly achieved in the "new Greater East Asia Co-Prosperity Sphere" the goals she sought by other means in World War II.

CHAPTER ONE

Mission to Bangkok

I   THE ASSIGNMENT

1 OCTOBER 1941 was a hot, muggy day in Thailand. A young Japanese major stepped from a Douglas Dakota and was momentarily blinded by the rays of the Bangkok sun. He was tense and, in his nervousness, felt certain the eyes of the airport employees were fixed on him—curious about the nature of his mission. His shirt had wilted in the humidity, and he thought briefly of the autumn air of Tokyo. As he sank into the back seat of the Embassy car which drove him to the Thailand Hotel he worried about his lack of experience in international intelligence. Although the hotel was Japanese managed, the major, travelling under the civilian alias Yamashita Hirokazu, was unable to relax—it would be better, he thought, to avoid questions from inquisitive Japanese. At the same time he was lonely and thought of the lieutenant assigned to him who was forced to remain in Taiwan with an attack of acute appendicitis.

In the solitude of his room Yamashita—in reality Major Fujiwara Iwaichi—was awed by the importance of his mission and his own lack of experience for it. Of course, a young major in the 8th Section, Second Bureau, Imperial General Headquarters had no choice. This was his duty and he would do his best. The Imperial Japanese Army assigned important missions to middle-ranking officers and gave them plenty of leeway to use their own initiative in executing their tasks. In this respect the Japanese Army differed from the British or American armies and the army of the Third Reich. And because of this difference Fujiwara was now involved in ideological warfare in Bangkok, unable to speak any Malay or Hindi and with only a smattering of English remembered from high school.

Fujiwara was not a complete stranger to Bangkok. He had been sent down on a brief secret mission about eight months ago in late March. He was, after all, in propaganda broadcasting affairs in the 8th Section at Headquarters. Even earlier, in December 1940, Fujiwara had been responsible for three Indian escapees from a British prison in Hong Kong who were given safe passage on a Japanese ship bound for Bangkok. Once there, the exiles contacted leaders of the Indian independence movement in Southeast Asia and the Japanese military attaché. The mission had been accomplished so quietly that the names of the three Indians were not even recorded at Headquarters.

Still, Fujiwara's assignment had come as a surprise to him. It was a logical enough policy for Japan to step up intelligence operations in Southeast Asia, as it looked increasingly like war in the Pacific. Japan already had Indochina, and the British-American-Dutch economic blockade had tightened when Japan entered the alliance with Germany and Italy. Doubtless Bangkok was already infested with British, American, Chinese and German intelligence agents. Japan could not afford to fall behind. Further, Southeast Asia was a source of tin, rubber and oil supplies that were vital for Japan. Bangkok was a key listening post for all of Asia.

In the event of war in the Pacific, the Indian, Burmese and Malayan (Malaya is now West Malaysia) independence movements would assume great importance for Japan. Japan could recognize the aspirations for independence in Southeast Asia and weaken Britain at the same time. Headquarters knew of these movements. And Fujiwara had some ideas of his own. Convinced from the beginning that political warfare had to be waged without pushing one's own interests too hard, he felt Japan must show genuine sympathy for the liberation movements. Others in the Second Bureau, however, deprecated Fujiwara's views, and this shook his self-confidence. He had asked for one night to think over the new assignment before accepting.

Fujiwara now reflected on his decision. That afternoon in Tokyo he had walked with his small daughter to the shrine of Yoshida Shōin, the super-patriot who had influenced many loyalist leaders of the Meiji Restoration and then become a martyr for his nation. This afternoon visit gave Fujiwara the courage to undertake his assignment. Before leaving Tokyo Fujiwara also visited the shrine of the Emperor Meiji.

Courage was no substitute for knowledge, and Fujiwara was dismayed on looking through the library of General Staff Headquarters to find only an Indian travelogue by a Japanese and scattered references to India. Clearly, in the push into Manchuria and China, Headquarters had neglected India and also slighted Southeast Asia. This was the beginning of Fujiwara's sense of mission toward India and the Indian independence movement.

Chief of General Staff Sugiyama on 18 September called in Fujiwara and five commissioned officers assigned to him. General Sugiyama handed Fujiwara a typed directive: "You will assist Colonel Tamura in aiding movements in the Malayan sector and particularly in maintaining liaison with the anti-British Indian Independent [later Independence] League and with Malays and Chinese." As Fujiwara looked up from the typed sheet, General Sugiyama said, "Apart from your official duties, if an Anglo-Japanese war should break out, you will prepare to facilitate military strategy and encourage friendship and co-operation between the Japanese Army and the Malayan people. I want you also to look at the total Indian situation and to consider future Indo-Japanese relations from the standpoint of establishing the Greater East Asia Co-Prosperity Sphere. Further, I hope that you will study the skilful organization and leadership of the British-Indian Army which is designed to restrain any anti-British movements among the Indians."[1] As Sugiyama finished, Fujiwara stood in stunned silence for a moment. Quickly collecting himself, he replied, "In order to realize the great concept of a New Asia we will encourage Indian independence and Japanese-Indian co-operation, beginning with operations in the Malayan sector."[2]

II INDIANS IN BANGKOK

Now Fujiwara was thrust into the midst of it. His intelligence operation would spread from Thailand to Malaya and then to Burma. He was to maintain liaison with Chinese, Malays, and especially with the Indian independence movement. Thailand was the crucial foothold in working with these movements. Japanese military strategy would not succeed in Malaya and Thailand unless Fujiwara did his job well. This was the task of a thirty-three-year-old major, a staff of five commissioned officers, and a Hindi-speaking interpreter.

Next morning Fujiwara took a taxi, past orange-robed priests holding up their begging bowls in the morning rain, to the quarters of the military attaché. Colonel Tamura greeted Fujiwara with an invitation to breakfast, which included a whisky and soda. But Colonel Tamura was serious and went straight to the point. He gave Fujiwara instructions for contacts with three projects: the Indian independence movement, the overseas Chinese merchants, and Malay organizations and sultans. Another project called *Harimao*[3] involved a Japanese contact in Malaya.

Tamura warned Fujiwara of the sensitivity of the Thai Government to intelligence activities of the competing powers. Part of the Thai Government was friendly to Britain, part of it to Japan; the political balance was delicate. Tamura also cautioned Fujiwara to avoid contact with the many Japanese working in Bangkok. Some were training the Thai Army, some were businessmen with the Mitsui Trading Company, some were on political assignments such as arbitrating a Thai-Indochinese boundary dispute. Fujiwara apologized for his lack of knowledge and experience, but Tamura assured him that the important ingredient was enthusiasm. Fujiwara went to work immediately. His staff included a "boy" in the Thailand Hotel who had to visit Fujiwara stealthily at night.

Fujiwara had a memorable first meeting with a leader of the Indian independence movement. He went secretly to the quarters of the military attaché on 12 October at noon. He was as impatient as if going to a midnight tryst with a lover. Fujiwara anticipated a robust revolutionary; he met a young, turbaned Sikh of delicate physique. Pritam Singh greeted Tamura and Fujiwara with the Indian salutation of hands clasped before him. Fujiwara was overcome by the Sikh's idealism, sincerity and enthusiasm for Indian liberation from British rule. Fujiwara offered, "I have come to help you realize your lofty ideal and I look forward to co-operating. I have confidence that Indian independence will be achieved through devotion and friendship." Colonel Tamura interpreted. Fujiwara then inquired after the three Indians who had been sent to Bangkok aboard a Japanese ship the previous year. Pritam Singh's face lit up at this: "Oh, was it you who sent the three men? Then we're already old comrades, aren't we?"[4] He told Fujiwara then of his own escape from India in 1939, his experience teaching the Sikh religion to Indians in Bangkok, and of the hopes of Indians for independence while Britain was fighting in Europe. It was an appropriate beginning for Fujiwara's mission and for Indo-Japanese co-operation in Southeast Asia.

In the interests of security Fujiwara moved out of the hotel into a modest house near the Bangkok railway station. He next met Pritam Singh in an out-of-the-way place—the house of an Indian cloth merchant over a Japanese pickle factory on a back alley. It was a sweltering evening and the mosquitoes were persistent. Fujiwara half-heartedly quenched his thirst with water. Pritam Singh told Fujiwara that there were two Indian organizations in Bangkok: the Indian Independence League composed mostly of Sikhs, and an Indo-Thai cultural organization centring around a swami and a man named Das. Fujiwara felt a premonition about the apparent antagonism between the two organizations and inquired about the possibility of a reconciliation. He also worried lest the co-operation between himself and Pritam Singh's faction be revealed by someone in the opposing faction.[5]

Fujiwara decided Pritam Singh's faction was the group he must work with most closely. Pritam Singh's organization already had men scattered through South Thailand and north-east Malayan coastal cities, whereas the Swami-Das group was an organization of intellectuals interested primarily in things cultural. The Sikh and his cohorts were already distributing propaganda leaflets among Indian officers and men in the British-Indian Army in the border states of Malaya. According to Pritam Singh, Indian soldiers in the British-Indian Army harboured anti-British feelings. These men were fertile ground for Pritam Singh's propaganda; why not try some Japanese propaganda on them? Fujiwara was excited by Pritam Singh's ideas but also had to avoid giving him any hint of Japan's military plans.[6]

Pritam Singh suggested anti-British broadcasts beamed to India from Tokyo. The audience would be limitless: not only soldiers in the Army but all of India! Pritam Singh already had contact by telegraph with Indians in Shanghai and Tokyo. With a bit of Japanese help the whole movement could be unified. An electrifying idea! Pritam Singh's statements were punctuated by coughing, and Fujiwara saw by the dim light of the single bulb that the Sikh's face was pallid. When Fujiwara asked about his health Pritam Singh replied that he had respiratory trouble but that he wouldn't die before completing the mission entrusted him by God. The two men parted after promising to meet again. Fujiwara transmitted a report of his meetings through Tamura to Imperial General Headquarters.[7]

Fujiwara's staff members arrived in Bangkok and were given assignments, some to trading firms, some to the military attaché. Fujiwara briefed his men daily, through the night and early morning hours. Fujiwara often worked all night, as his Indian colleagues later complained. He constantly dwelt on the theme that the Japanese should not appear as conquerors, that all Asian peoples should work together in mutual respect and harmony. For Fujiwara this was an article of faith. Japan had little experience or skill in ruling other peoples compared with Britain; caution and sincerity should be the order of the day. Japan would encourage independence movements but with no hint of constraint. Fujiwara and his men would mediate between the Japanese Army and the local inhabitants to avoid cruelties like those perpetrated in China. Pritam Singh had warned Fujiwara of Indian antagonism toward Japanese actions in China.[8]

Fujiwara and Pritam Singh planned another secret meeting. Fujiwara reminisced that it was the eve of the anniversary of the Meiji Restoration and the chrysanthemums would be blooming in Japan. Pritam Singh brought with him a white-bearded, white-robed old Sikh, Amar Singh. He approached Fujiwara softly and stood still as a clay image, hands clasped before him. His flashing eyes met Fujiwara's directly, as he recited a soft incantation from the Sikh holy scriptures. Fujiwara intuitively felt the strength of the venerable Sikh; here was a man who could be trusted. The prayer ended, and the old priest was led to a chair. He began to speak with revolutionary fire of the inhumanity of British rule of India. He had been imprisoned for ten years in the Andaman Islands and in Rangoon. In British prisons his fighting spirit had been incubated. Fujiwara was deeply impressed but also beset by doubts. Amar Singh was obviously a man of emotion rather than reason. How suited would he be to lead a vast independence movement? Perhaps Amar Sihgh and Pritam Singh together could lead. Fujiwara described to the two Sikhs Japan's ideal of mutual existence and prosperity for all Asia. Finally Amar Singh stood and prayed for Divine protection. Fujiwara heard a cock crowing in the distance and realized it was 4 a.m.

III A VISION OF REVOLUTION

Fujiwara and Pritam Singh continued their secret meetings. In mid-October from Tokyo came news of the fall of the Konoe Cabinet and formation of the Tōjō Cabinet. The Hull-Nomura peace negotiations in Washington were deadlocked. Uneasiness spread through Bangkok. Japanese plans for the occupation of Thailand and the capture of Malaya and Singapore were laid, but intelligence reports told of Singapore's defences being strengthened. Fujiwara had to conceal information of Japanese preparations but at the same time give Pritam Singh some inkling of what Fujiwara hoped the Indian group would do when war broke out. It was a delicate position. Headquarters did not anticipate co-operation from the Indian soldiers or Pritam Singh's group; Fujiwara would have to surprise and convince Tokyo. Fujiwara and Pritam Singh concocted their own plan: as soon as war erupted they would dash behind enemy lines to reach Indian soldiers in the British-Indian Army. The propaganda activities of Pritam Singh's Indian Independence League would be expanded in the British-Indian Army and among Indian civilians as well. Fujiwara's staff would protect Indian prisoners and inform them both of Pritam Singh's organization and of Japan's aims. These prisoners would form a revolutionary army to fight for Indian independence. Eventually all Indians in the British Army would be drawn to it. Indians all over Asia would volunteer. Fujiwara's staff would protect Indian lives and property. It was a bold design. Fujiwara and his staff would work and fight for Indian independence side by side with Indians.[9]

Fujiwara's group were also assigned to Chinese merchant groups and to anti-British Malay organizations such as the Malay Youth League. Fujiwara had to arrange co-operation with all these groups in short order. His staff was now a small, close-knit unit of twelve members, who worked well together with a feeling of camaraderie among them. Fujiwara named his group the *F Kikan*[10] or *Fujiwara Kikan*. Fujiwara preferred "F", for it stood also for freedom and friendship.

Fujiwara's operation encompassed several projects besides the India project—the Sumatra project, the Malay Youth League project, the overseas Chinese merchant project, and the *Harimao* project. Fujiwara was to make contact and co-ordinate co-operation with all these groups to facilitate the military offensive in Singapore.

Fujiwara's staff members went under a variety of guises—as businessmen, watchmakers, druggists, hotel boys, mining engineers in mountain areas, and rubber merchants and brokers on plantations. For all the major objective was the same—gathering intelligence. *F Kikan* members also became scouts for Japanese units and engaged in espionage, disrupting communications, collecting provisions and military *matériel*. Malays, Thais, Chinese, and Indians worked under *F Kikan* staff members, multiplying by several times the effectiveness of the operation. The network spread from Bangkok through Thailand and Malaya and south toward Singapore.[11]

IV "TIGER OF MALAYA"

Fujiwara found a ready-made agent in Tani Yutaka, the "Tiger of Malaya". The *Harimao* project revolved around a fanatic young Japanese whom Fujiwara came to respect. Tani had been brought to Malaya from Japan as an infant by his parents in 1911. They opened a barber shop in Kota Bahru and grew prosperous. At the time of the Japanese takeover of Manchuria in 1932 anti-Japanese sentiment spread not only among the Chinese merchant community but among the Malays as well. Chinese merchants seized the chance to organize boycotts and to harass customers of Japanese shops, with police support. Anti-Japanese sentiment ran so high that mobs killed Japanese on sight, including children. One of the victims in November 1932, was the eight-year-old sister of Tani Yutaka. Enraged, Tani, by now twenty-one, took the name "Tiger" and began a rampage of revenge. He organized a group of Malays and Thais who returned violence for violence. The legend of *Harimao,* the gangster chief who spoke Malay and Japanese, spread throughout Malaya.

By November 1941 the name *of Harimao* came to the attention of *F Kikan* members. Kamimoto of the *F Kikan* rescued Tani from a jail in South Thailand. Kamimoto showed Tani some weapons of the Japanese Army, and Tani's eyes betrayed his delight.[12] Kamimoto told Fujiwara about Tani. Fujiwara looked at the picture of the unshaven figure in torn clothes with some dismay. There was no visible difference between the Tiger and the Malay members of his robber gang. But through a few probing questions Kamimoto convinced Fujiwara that Tani was patriotic to the point of fanaticism. The Tiger looked like an ideal operative.

There was a hitch. Fujiwara and *F Kikan* members discovered Tani was constantly being tailed by Japanese-speaking Thai police disguised as Chinese coolies. By day he was immobilized in hiding. But by night he became a fish vendor peddling his bucket of fish. Below the fish Tani hid hand grenades and explosives. Once he was caught by vigilant Thai police. Armed with only a pistol he broke through the border of south Thailand into Malaya by bicycle as far as Kota Bahru and the Jitra line. Tani and his tough followers supplied the *F Kikan* valuable information on local terrain and routes into north Malaya. This intelligence speeded up the whole Malaya operation. Tani's group fanned out through the central mountain range, through jungles and rivers infested with wild animals and poisonous snakes and insects. Malaria caught members of Tani's gang and finally the Tiger himself. Tani continued his work from a stretcher with a fever of 104°F. When his fever abated the Tiger continued to strike, sometimes as an Indian merchant, sometimes as a Chinese banker, sometimes as a Thai official. Fujiwara's first meeting with Tani on the battlefield in January convinced Fujiwara that his earlier assessment of the zealous young patriot had been correct.

One of Tani's last jobs was to destroy a huge dam on the Perak River. The dam was guarded by a British platoon. Before the job was under way a counter-order arrived to save the dam. Tani's party, dressed as Malays, approached the dam from upriver in a local craft. They were to remove the explosive fuses. As they neared the dam it exploded before their eyes. The British platoon had counter-orders too and had beaten Tani to the dam.

At Ipoh the Tiger struck again, this time in the midst of the British-sponsored Malay Volunteer Army. The army of young Malays was acting as railway guards for the British Army. Tani in Malay guise encouraged the volunteers to return home, disrupting the army. It was later reorganized to help the Japanese Army in defence of occupied areas. The Tiger derailed British trains and cut British communication lines.

Neither Tani's zeal nor his fever abated. Arriving at Johore Bahru at the rear approach to Singapore he collapsed. Tani had written his mother telling of his love for Japan and his family. He felt he had been redeemed in both in his work for the *F Kikan* after his earlier gangsterism. Fujiwara brought Tani on his death-bed a letter from home. Fujiwara praised Tani's work and assured him he would go on to the secret police of the Southern Army. The Tiger had become a legend in the Japanese Army before he died while yet a very young man. A wartime song, "*Harimao*", carried the legend through the Japanese fighting forces. Fujiwara made no attempt to check his tears as he clutched Tani's letter from home.

V   BANGKOK WATCH

At the end of November Colonel Tamura told Fujiwara that when war broke out the *F Kikan* would operate under General Terauchi, commander-in-chief of the Southern Army, through Lieutenant-General Yamashita, commander of the 25th Army. Fujiwara and Pritam Singh met several times to devise plans to meet the eventuality. Fujiwara repeated his promises of Japanese help in the struggle for Indian independence from Britain. Fujiwara still had to forbear informing Pritam Singh of Japan's specific plans for an offensive in Burma and Thailand; their discussions remained somewhat abstract. Pritam Singh did agree that the Indian Independence League would advance with the *F Kikan* (aboard Japanese planes), following the Japanese Army into south Thailand and Malaya. There League members would contact Indians in the British-Indian Army. The Japanese Army, through the *F Kikan,* would help the League. Further, the Japanese Army would respect the lives, property, freedom and honour of Indians. Pritam Singh's group would wear the designation "F" for identification by the Japanese Army. This agreement was put into writing and signed on 1 December by Pritam Singh and Colonel Tamura.[13] Copies of the agreement were forwarded to 25th Army Headquarters, Southern Army Headquarters, and Tokyo. Fujiwara was satisfield that all was in readiness. Both the Fujiwara and Pritam Singh groups would wear khaki riding habits rather than regular Japanese Army uniforms. *F Kikan* members would not carry arms.

On 4 December a telegram from Tokyo announced war would begin 8 December. The attitude of the Thai Government was still in doubt. Fujiwara sent messengers to strengthen contacts and cooperation with the Malay Youth League and the sultans of the Malay states. Late on 7 December (6 December in the US) the military attaché handed the Thai Cabinet a notice that a Japanese Army of occupation would pass through Thailand; immediate approval of the Government was requested. Tamura thought Premier Phibun Songgram's approval a ninety per cent certainty, but there was the danger that news of Japan's plans might reach Britain and the United States. If the Cabinet refused, the Japanese Army would probably be in Bangkok by noon 8 December anyway. If this happened, Japanese residents in Bangkok would be in danger. The atmosphere in Colonel Tamura's office was tense all through the day. Fujiwara kept glancing nervously at his watch.

About 9 a.m. the morning of 7 December a member of the Thai Cabinet had unexpectedly rushed into the room and said to Colonel Tamura without preliminaries: "Premier Phibun Songgram says the Japanese Army has inflicted an outrageous humiliation on the Thai Foreign Ministry and is advancing on the border of Thailand and Indochina. He's indignant and disappeared last night without reporting his whereabouts to anyone. Here is his letter."[14] The Thai cabinet minister abruptly left the room without waiting for any response.

According to the letter, on 5 December a section chief of the Thai Foreign Ministry had been sent to the border. Caught by an officer of the crack Konoe Division, he was beaten as a spy and released the next day without being given a chance to explain his mission. This senseless act had infuriated Premier Phibun Songgram and the rest of the Cabinet. Fujiwara was apprehensive that such stupidity might antagonize the people of Thailand and destroy his own work. Colonel Tamura lost no time in sending a report of the incident through channels to Tokyo, meanwhile apologizing to the Thai Government. Fujiwara asked Japanese Ambassador Tsubokami to try to find Premier Phibun Songgram before the deadline of the Japanese ultimatum expired. Meanwhile a telegram from Tokyo Headquarters demanded punishment of those responsible for the incident and authorized an apology and guarantee against such incidents in the future. The Thai Cabinet secretly told Ambassador Tsubokami that in the absence of the Premier it could not reply to the ultimatum. Arrangements were accordingly made for all Japanese residents to gather in the Japanese primary school. The situation looked bad for them.

Fujiwara could no longer postpone reporting to Pritam Singh. He sent two members of the *Kikan* to ask Pritam Singh to leave for south Thailand on 9 December because fighting was about to begin.

Colonel Tamura was faced with a dilemma: should Japan count Thailand an enemy or ally? Japanese reconnaissance planes were already overhead looking for a signal from the Embassy. Tamura rushed men to the race track with orders to display the "unclear" signal. The men were immediately surrounded by vigilant Thai police, but the planes had already seen the signal and headed east. Simultaneously a news broadcast announced the successful attack on Pearl Harbour, the Imperial Edict declaring war, and the arrival of the Konoe Division on the outskirts of Bangkok. Premier Phibun Songgram unexpectedly cleared the air with a radio announcement of co-operation between Thailand and Japan. The Japanese Army was already dashing across south Thailand toward Malaya, securing airports en route.

Pritam Singh and Amar Singh met the commander of the 15th Army, Lieutenant-General Iida Shōjirō, who promised help to all Indian patriots in Thailand. Fujiwara, Pritam Singh and part of their staffs emplaned on 10 December for Singora airport in south Thailand. Aboard the plane Fujiwara was moved when Pritam Singh tried to present the Japanese pilot with a monetary token of thanks, only to have the pilot return it to Pritam Singh for use in the fight for Indian freedom. When the plane arrived over the Singora airfield, overturned and burning fighter planes on the ground bore fiery witness to a recent British attack. The veteran pilot brought the plane down on a muddy runway, despite airport signals warning of another British attack.

Fujiwara immediately reported to 25th Army Headquarters. He learned that the main force of the 5th Division had landed on the coast of Singora and was advancing with lightning rapidity in the face of faltering opposition. Other units of the 5th Division had landed at Pattani and were also advancing steadily. Part of the 18th Division had landed at Kota Bahru. All three landings had surprised the British. While Fujiwara was being briefed on the military situation a report came in that the two British battleships, the *Prince of Wales* and the *Repulse,* had been sunk attempting to foil the landing at Kota Bahru. Shouts of *"Banzai!"* greeted this report to the group in 25th Army Headquarters.

Fujiwara was ordered to send a liaison unit with the League group into every military operation at the front. He was ordered also to

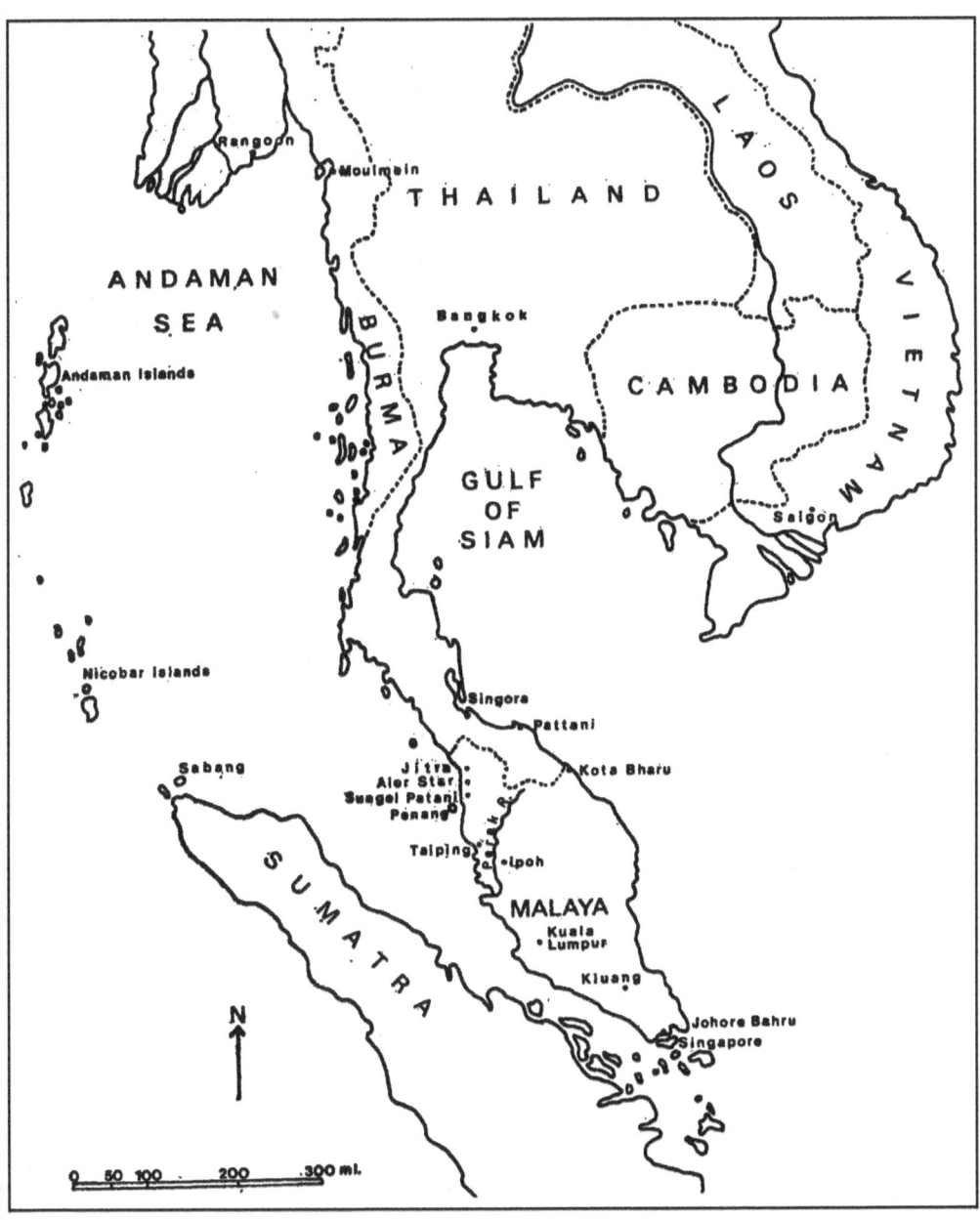

Malaya and Thailand

continue propaganda *vis-à-vis* Chinese and Malay organizations. He was to protect the sultans as the British Army retreated.[15] The *F Kikan* had eleven men and two cars on the spot. Fujiwara allotted one of the cars to Pritam Singh. The first joint party of the *F Kikan*-IIL left for the Alor Star battleline in high spirits in the midst of torrential tropical rain.

Fujiwara in rapid succession met with Pritam Singh's group, called a meeting of the Singora Indian Association, helped found the south Thailand branch of the Indian Independence League, and arranged to send an IIL propaganda unit to the Kota Bahru battleline. Pritam Singh's headquarters were established in an elegant two-storey house in a small border town. Fujiwara watched Pritam Singh unfurl atop the house a large Indian tricolour national flag which he had brought from Bangkok. The Sikh's hands trembled as he let go of the flag and stood in silent prayer. *F Kikan* headquarters were more modestly ensconced in a small shop. During the night a steady stream of Japanese units slogged along the muddy road to Alor Star.

Next day Fujiwara and Pritam Singh went together by car along a jungle road to a hut where a dishevelled Sikh greeted them and served them tea. The tentacles of Pritam Singh's network had already reached the border area. Pritam Singh handed out propaganda leaflets as the car made its way back to town. In front of IIL headquarters about two hundred Indians had gathered. Pritam Singh spoke to them passionately of the fight for freedom. Fujiwara felt plunged into a revolution in the making.

F Kikan members coming in from the front reported the 11th Division of the British-Indian Army falling back rapidly from the Jitra line under attack by the 5th Division. Fujiwara guessed that the lightning attack had caught the British completely by surprise and that their defences would not hold. On the morning of the 13th Fujiwara and Pritam Singh left by car with a lorry for the Alor Star battleline. The road threaded through a forest of rubber trees. Abandoned British equipment and cars were scattered about. South of the rubber forest Pritam Singh suddenly said, "It's the national border." He jumped from the car and walked a few steps facing west, toward Malaya and India beyond. Again he clasped his hands in prayer. Fujiwara was impressed again by the combination of patriotic fervour and monk-like devotion in his Indian colleague. Fujiwara got out of the car and stood silently, head bowed, as Pritam Singh's prayer continued for ten minutes. Pritam Singh turned to Fujiwara and said simply, "I've kept you waiting a long time." The car sped on past the border and arrived at Alor Star half a day behind the 5th Division of the Japanese Army. Fujiwara and Pritam Singh immediately set up joint *F Kikan* and IIL headquarters in the police station at Alor Star, hung out flags, and sent parties into the jungle.

CHAPTER TWO

Malayan Jungle Meeting

I CAPTAIN MOHAN SINGH

IN 1941 Mohan Singh was a captain,[1] aged thirty-three, second in command of a battalion of the 15th Brigade, 1/14 Punjab Regiment of the British-Indian Army. Like many Indian officers, Mohan Singh felt a mixture of pride at being a viceroy commissioned officer and annoyance at British discrimination against Indian officers. In March the brigade landed at Penang Island and from there pushed inland to Ipoh in Perak state, Malaya. After two months the brigade moved to Sungei Patani, seventy miles south of the Malayan-Thai border. Then in September the brigade advanced to Jitra, north of the Alor Star defences and just sixteen miles south of the Malayan-Thai border. It was marshy jungle country and the going was painfully slow. The British strategy was defensive; there was little eagerness to fight the Japanese in Malaya.

Captain Mohan Singh got three weeks' leave in late November, but the situation became tense and he was recalled to his battalion in early December. He celebrated the last night of his leave at a party where libations flowed. Before the party broke up Mohan Singh surprised his friends and himself when, with Punjabi ebullience, he cried, "I don't know what will happen, but one thing is certain: I'm not going to die, and mind you, don't be surprised if you see me as your liberator coming down fighting the very British whom I'm going now to defend."[2] Everyone was surprised because Mohan Singh was actually a rather apolitical young man; later he could not explain to his friends what had prompted these words.

On 4 December Mohan Singh rejoined his battalion near Alor Star. They were digging in for a Japanese landing at Singora. The 15th Brigade was to spearhead the British advance into Thailand from Malaya. On the night of 7 December orders came for the brigade to occupy Singora; but, according to intelligence reports, the Japanese already had Singora. On 8 December twenty-seven Japanese bombers bombed the Alor Star airport and rail lines to Thailand. This became a pattern of Japanese attack: bomb the rail lines, then take the airport. The British defences became confused. The 15th Brigade was ordered to dash from Jitra to the Thai border. They reached the border just before Japanese troops rushed in from the opposite direction across Thailand. Mohan Singh's battalion was detailed to stop the Japanese at the border near Jitra. The Japanese advance took Mohan Singh and his battalion by surprise. The Japanese had tanks. The British division commander had said Malaya was not fit for tank warfare, so the British Army had no tanks and did not expect the Japanese to use them. There were none to spare for the Malaya battle anyway. It was now impossible for Mohan Singh's battalion to cross the border. The aggressor chose the time and place of attack; the Japanese had a double advantage. Advance units of both sides met on 9 December. Mohan Singh was ordered to brigade headquarters by his commander, Colonel Fitzpatrick. A Gurkha brigade had arrived and Mohan Singh was ordered to position it. On 10 December he returned to the front.[3]

Fighting was limited to the road and the area along both sides of the road. Everything beyond was thick impenetrable jungle and marsh where it was impossible to move. On 11 December Japanese reconnaissance planes pinpointed the British-Indian position. The Japanese immediately opened up with mortar fire on the road. Mohan Singh's battalion withdrew along both sides of the road. There followed silence for two hours. By 5 p.m. the Japanese brought their tanks into position and made a tank attack on the battalion. The battalion had ten ammunition trucks; these were the first targets blown up by the advancing Japanese. Ammunition exploding everywhere dispersed Mohan Singh's battalion in a mêlée of mud and shouting figures. This was the last glimpse Mohan Singh had of his battalion as a unit. The Japanese had the road; the Indian troops took to the jungle on both sides.

Relations between Mohan Singh and his commanding officer were already somewhat strained because of discriminatory promotion policies. Mohan Singh was covered with mud and was surprised to see his commanding officer stumbling toward him. The colonel's uniform was torn and blood was oozing down his back. He took out his revolver and handed it to Mohan Singh, saying, "I'm wounded, I entrust myself to you." Mohan Singh tossed the revolver into the mud. He ducked behind a huge tree just as a Japanese tank rolled by. Mohan Singh peered around the tree, grinning and waving at the Japanese gunner; gun-fire returned the greeting. It was a gesture of Punjabi verve and defiance, though Mohan Singh knew the fight was over for his battalion. It was every man for himself, and Mohan Singh lost track of his colonel.[4]

For the next three days in the jungle of the rubber plantations near Jitra Mohan Singh had time to think. It didn't seem likely that Britain would ever give India freedom unless compelled by force of circumstance. But Indians would have to create the circumstances. Britain would never let go so long as Indian officers in the Army remained loyal. And if the Army did not remain loyal, what was to guarantee the security of the British in India? Why were Indians fighting in the British Army? The only answer Mohan Singh could give himself was that they were hoodwinked mercenaries fighting at the expense of India to help Britain keep India in subjugation. What kind of patriotism was this? To whom did Indians owe loyalty and honour anyway? Even in the Army the Indian officer never had an equal chance with the British officer, rarely got a chance to go to Sandhurst and get a King's Commission, could not join the same officers' clubs, and didn't get an even break in promotion. Mohan Singh knew most Indian officers felt these grievances keenly. But he had never even seen a Japanese and had no idea what to expect when he surrendered.[5] All he had to go on was British propaganda.

II FUJIWARA AND MOHAN SINGH

By 5 p.m. on 12 December a crowd of Indians had gathered under the Indian national tricolor at IIL-F *Kikan* headquarters at the Alor Star crossing. There were Malays scattered through the crowd too, including a member of the Sultan's family. Pritam Singh, drawn to the balcony by cheers and applause, spoke in Hindi about the plans to fight for Indian independence with Japanese assistance. Each sentence was translated into Tamil and met by thunderous applause.

Pritam Singh was followed by a representative of the Sultan's family, who called on Indians, Malays, and Chinese alike to co-operate jointly for their respective freedom and prosperity. Fujiwara next stepped onto the balcony and explained Japan's desire for peace in East Asia based on freedom, equality and co-operation. When he had finished speaking it was already dusk, but the crowd continued to stand in the square around the police station, as if unwilling to break the spell.[6]

After the meeting Pritam Singh brought several Sikhs from the crowd to see Fujiwara in his room. The men were wealthy rubber plantation owners in the vicinity. They brought news of a retreating battalion of the British-Indian Army, lost in the jungle and unable to find a new path of retreat. The men were exhausted, hungry, and demoralized to know of the Japanese occupation of Alor Star. There was an English lieutenant-colonel in command; all the rest were Indians. The Indians were trying to get news from the Sikh plantation owners. The plantation owners in turn told Fujiwara the Indians were ready to surrender. Fujiwara and Pritam Singh decided to go to talk to the Indian officers and men directly.

Fujiwara and Pritam Singh, following the directions of the Sikh plantation owners, reached the plantation the next morning. Fujiwara met the wounded English commander, Lieutenant-Colonel Fitzpatrick. Fitzpatrick turned to his second-in-command, Mohan Singh, and gave an order which Fujiwara could not catch. The captain immediately lined up all the officers and men, spoke to them, and had them place their weapons and ammunition on the ground before them. Their pockets were searched. Fujiwara was impressed at the efficiency of the handsome Sikh captain. Pritam Singh invited all the officers to the plantation house and explained to them his plans for the independence struggle with Japanese support. Fujiwara in turn described the aims of the Japanese Army. The Indian officers seemed pleased and surprised. The officers and men jumped aboard lorries loaned by the plantation owners, and Fujiwara and Pritam Singh directed them back to Alor Star headquarters. Captain Tsuchimochi of the *F Kikan* had made Congress flags, and they now flew on the trucks. Indian stragglers jumped onto the road, halted the lorries, and jammed into the already packed trucks. Fujiwara was dog-tired and found his head drooping on the shoulder of an Indian crammed into the truck beside him. At Alor Star Lieutenant-Colonel Fitzpatrick was treated for his wounds, bade farewell to

Fujiwara and Mohan Singh, and was sent to Japanese Army Headquarters.

The Japanese Army chasing the British Army toward the Perak River had created a political vacuum in Alor Star. Chinese merchants, fearing the Japanese Army, had closed their doors. Malays and Indians, expressing annoyance at Chinese economic exploitation took advantage of the situation to attack and loot Chinese property in broad daylight. Fujiwara found the town in chaos. There was not a single armed soldier in the *F Kikan* to restore order in Alor Star. Suddenly the image of the Sikh captain came to Fujiwara. He called Pritam Singh and told him he had found the answer: entrust the job to the Indian officers and men who had just surrendered. To gain absolute trust you must first show it. Fujiwara asked Mohan Singh and his men to take charge, using police clubs and handcuffs rather than arms. Mohan Singh, surprised, agreed to assign eighty men to the job, and within an hour order had returned to Alor Star. Fujiwara told Mohan Singh he would be treated as a friend, not a prisoner; it seemed he meant it.[7]

Indian stragglers, learning of Japanese Army protection for men under Mohan Singh's command, trickled into Alor Star in small, dishevelled groups, adding to the growing numbers. There were no Japanese guards and no escapees. Mohan Singh quartered the Indians in the police barracks and maintained discipline and order. The residents of the town returned and life returned to normal.

With the surrender accomplished and order maintained, Fujiwara and Pritam Singh began discussions with Mohan Singh. Fujiwara explained the aims of the Japanese Army in aiding Indian independence and his own personal views on achieving independence. He was convinced independence would come only from a struggle of the Indian people themselves. The Pacific War was a chance for the Indians to rise and win freedom with Japanese help. Fujiwara pointed out Japan and India had several things in common: 1) a common enemy; 2) historical ties, for India was the home of the Buddhist faith; 3) geographic and ethnic ties; and 4) common indignation at India's subjugated position.[8]

This was not what Mohan Singh expected to hear on surrendering. Encouraged, he expressed his own and India's indignation toward Britain. He told Fujiwara he agreed that Indian freedom depended on the Indian people. Mohan Singh was impressed but not completely convinced by Fujiwara's words. Indians should be suspicious of Japanese help because of Japanese actions in Korea, Manchuria and China. This reinforced what Pritam Singh had already told Fujiwara earlier. Furthermore, Mohan Singh continued, Indian independence would never succeed without the support of the Indian Congress Party; it would be divorced from the mainstream of Indian politics. He explained to Fujiwara the effectiveness of the non-violent posture of Gandhi and of Congress within the Indian political context. Mohan Singh's ideas were taking shape as he talked. Fujiwara pointed out that the Congress Party would have to recognize Pritam Singh's League and its role in the struggle. The discussion continued until after 3 a.m. before Fujiwara realized that they were all exhausted by the events of the past twenty-four hours. He was satisfied to learn that Mohan Singh was a patriot and indignant at British control. It had been a fruitful first conversation.

British defences at the Jitra line had fallen, and the British 11th Division had dashed south of the Perak River leaving behind vast quantities of equipment. Nor was there any sign of British resistance at Sungei Patani. The work of the *F Kikan* had to be expanded on all fronts simultaneously. Meanwhile, Indian soldiers already captured at Alor Star and Sungei Patani had to be protected, quartered and fed. And contact had to be maintained with the Malays, including the Sultan of Kedah state and the Malay Youth League. One of the *F Kikan* members had been killed, and Fujiwara felt pressed for personnel. Local workers had to be enlisted. This was arranged sometimes through the IIL; sometimes workers appeared spontaneously. Two Japanese newly joined the *F Kikan*: Second Lieutenant Kunizuka, an interpreter with the 5th Division, and Mr Itō Keisuke of the Singora Consulate. The two members were assigned to the care of all Indians captured at Alor Star and Sungei Patani, now about seven hundred men. The two young members ate with the Indians and spoke with them in Hindi. These two remained with the *Kikan* throughout the war.

Fujiwara gave a dinner on 17 December for all Indian officers. Indian food was prepared and there was music. The vibrant Mohan Singh, speaking after the banquet, pointed out emotionally that in the British Army a staff officer would never share a meal with officers of a defeated army or even with fellow Indian officers. Fujiwara was delighted, and felt his new Indian associates had become friends. It was worth the effort and embarrassment of trying to eat the hot, greasy curry with his fingers.[9]

III FUJIWARA PERSUADES MOHAN SINGH

By day Fujiwara directed the activities of the *F Kikan* in co-ordination with Pritam Singh's group, by night he met with Mohan Singh, five nights running. Fujiwara and Mohan Singh were each impressed by the sincerity and devotion of the other. Mutual respect began to grow between them as they continued their exchange of views far into the early morning hours. Mohan Singh recorded his impressions of the meetings in an essay titled "The First Japanese Officer I Met", which he showed to Fujiwara. The manuscript was later lost in the crash of a plane en route to Tokyo. The energy and enthusiasm of Fujiwara were matched by Mohan Singh, who seemed to personify Punjabi vitality and the Sikh martial tradition. The two men found accord on many things. Mohan Singh told Fujiwara about the Indian revolutionary leader and former Congress president Subhas Chandra Bose, who was an exile in Berlin. If Bose were brought to the East all Indians in Asia would rise against the British. Fujiwara was impressed that every Indian he talked with seemed to worship Bose. Fujiwara reported this observation to Imperial General Headquarters again and again, hoping the Japanese Government might approach Berlin to bring Bose to Asia. But the matter was out of Fujiwara's hands, and there might be opposition to the idea in Tokyo. Mohan Singh knew many Japanese felt Congress leaders were anti-Japanese. Meanwhile Fujiwara urged Mohan Singh and Pritam Singh to work to develop the movement among Indians in Asia.[10]

Five nights of discussion were inconclusive. Mohan Singh's determination to fight for the liberation of his country had crystallized, but he asked Fujiwara for a clear-cut assurance that Japan had no designs on India. Fujiwara tried in the strongest possible terms to assure Mohan Singh. Finally Fujiwara decided to arrange a meeting of Mohan Singh and Pritam Singh with Lieutenant-General Yamashita, commander of the 25th Army. Perhaps Yamashita could convince the Indian leaders of Japan's sincerity. On the afternoon of 20 December the stout, energetic lieutenant-general ushered Fujiwara and the two Indians into his staff room. Pointing to his operations map he explained the progress of operations. With an air of friendliness he stated he was prepared to give unconditional aid to the Indian independence movement through Major Fujiwara. Fujiwara hoped the interview had had its effect.

But for Mohan Singh there were still three matters to be confirmed through discussions with his officers before he could commit himself to working with Fujiwara and the Japanese: 1) Japanese sincerity in offering aid, 2) support of India, including the Congress Party, for the idea of co-operation with the Japanese, and 3) the solid agreement of Indian officers and men. Unless Mohan Singh could satisfy himself on these points, he could not lead his men in the struggle. He needed time to think and to talk with his officers, especially his Muslim aide, Captain Mohammed Akram. The first point was the most difficult. It was practically impossible to decide from talking with Fujiwara whether Japan had designs on India. Sincere as Fujiwara was, he was one man, and a major at that, though of course Yamashita had promised too. Besides, stories of Japanese atrocities on prisoners of war and civilians were rife. But even if Japan proved insincere toward Indian freedom, it might be worthwhile to work initially with the Japanese in an effort to spare Indian soldiers and to protect Indian civilians and property from Japanese exploitation.[11] The Congress Party, as Mohan Singh explained to Fujiwara, had taken a stand on non-violence. There was no certainty that Gandhi and Nehru would support an armed struggle against Britain. They had already split with Subhas Chandra Bose on this issue. But if Japan proved sincere, then the joint effort would be justified. It was worth the gamble.

After discussing these considerations for several days with his officers, Mohan Singh decided in favour of fighting together with the Japanese. He credited Fujiwara with the deep mutual trust and confidence that had been generated. Fujiwara's sincerity, persuasiveness, and lack of artifice impressed Mohan Singh. Yes, he would lead an Indian army of liberation, fighting beside the Japanese against the British.

IV   THE INA IS BORN

On New Year's Eve, 1941, Mohan Singh left Alor Star and rejoined Fujiwara at Taiping in Perak state, where Fujiwara had gone to expand his work into Sumatra. Fujiwara instantly saw that Mohan Singh was trembling with a chill and a high fever. Fujiwara scolded his friend for travelling in such a state, but saw the determination in the bloodshot eyes of the Sikh. When Mohan Singh had rested and his fever subsided, he came to Fujiwara with a six-point proposal: 1) the Indians would organize an Indian people's army; 2) the Japanese Army would give it whole-hearted aid; 3) the Indian army and IIL would co-operate for the time being; 4) the Japanese Army would recognize Mohan Singh as leader of the Indian captives; 5) the Japanese Army would treat Indian captives as friends and liberate those who wished to join the Indian army; and 6) the Indian army would be recognized as a friendly allied army by the Japanese Army. Fujiwara and Mohan Singh chose the name Indian National Army for the new revolutionary army. They talked for two days about how they would co-operate. They discussed the relationship between the IIL and the INA. Mohan Singh wanted a stronger man than Pritam Singh to lead the political arm of the struggle. Mohan Singh was surprised by Pritam Singh's silence during discussions with Fujiwara. Pritam Singh kept silent when Mohan Singh felt a vital point needed clarification. Pritam Singh's passive attitude made Mohan Singh seriously doubt the sincerity of his Sikh colleague.[12] Pritam Singh's quiet, religious nature was indeed unlike Mohan Singh's ebullience and verve. The two men would not have been successful colleagues for long.

Again Mohan Singh raised the name of Subhas Chandra Bose and asked that the Japanese Government bring him East. Mohan Singh agreed to co-operate with Pritam Singh on a temporary basis. Units of the INA would infiltrate behind the lines of the British-Indian Army as Pritam Singh's group was already doing. Mohan Singh insisted that the INA would fight only on the Indo-Burmese border, not elsewhere in Asia. As soon as the INA reached India, Indians would surely join and light the spark of revolution within India. He requested the same training and equipment that the Japanese Army got, if they were to fight together.[13]

Fujiwara gave Mohan Singh his personal consent but said recognizing the INA as an allied army might create technical difficulties for the Japanese. The INA was a small, new revolutionary force starting with a handful of men. It expected to be recognized as equal by the Japanese; agreement was never reached on this issue, and it caused difficulties until the end of the war.

Fujiwara rushed to Lieutenant-General Yamashita's headquarters with Mohan Singh's proposal. Lieutenant-General Yamashita and his chief of staff both approved but with the reservation Fujiwara had already made about the allied status of the INA. Fujiwara hurried back to Mohan Singh and Pritam Singh with the good news. Mohan Singh gripped Fujiwara's hand firmly and said, "I'm slow in reaching a decision, but once I reach it I carry it out to the limit. I want you to understand the officers and men who have reached this decision to rise with me on behalf of India and whose families are left behind to suffer in India. This devotion to the high moral duty of liberating India will give a completely new picture to the men in the British-Indian Army."[14] Fujiwara, moved, vowed to cooperate with the INA to realize its revolutionary aims. An army had been born and a revolution begun.

Mohan Singh, still suffering from malaria, left that night with Captain Akram and Lieutenant Kunizuka for Alor Star. As Mohan Singh disappeared into the darkness Pritam Singh turned to Fujiwara, shook his hand and said quietly, "Thank you."

Next morning was 1 January 1942. Colonel Tamura and all *F Kikan* members gathered and hung the Japanese flag from an acacia tree. As the men faced east toward Japan the rays of the sun seemed especially bright on the rising sun of the flag. It seemed to Fujiwara to augur well for the future of the New Order.

Fujiwara moved his headquarters to Ipoh as the British Army fell back before the Japanese advance everywhere in Malaya. Headquarters in a school building were shared with the IIL, INA, YMA (Young Malays Association) and now the Sumatra Youth League as well. IIL propaganda units had already gone to the front with members of the *F Kikan*. As soon as headquarters opened and flags were hung, Indian citizens of Ipoh began assembling. Word of Japanese help for Indians had spread throughout Malaya.

V THE INA GETS SET

Mohan Singh and his first propaganda team appeared unexpectedly at Ipoh headquarters. He showed Fujiwara a history of the French Revolution he had been reading. The Sikh patriot was becoming a real revolutionary before Fujiwara's eyes. Fujiwara felt the pride of a midwife who had safely delivered a first infant.

Mohan Singh personally chose volunteers for his propaganda unit. He lectured them on the ideology of independence, infiltrating behind enemy lines, and bringing men out of the British Army. The men wore regular uniforms and carried *F Kikan* passes and "F" insignia to get through Japanese lines. They were joined by *F Kikan* members who escorted them behind enemy lines and collected Indian soldiers at the rear of each propaganda group. The first sortie threaded through the rubber trees beyond the roads and observed the enemy position and topography. INA and IIL teams went back and forth through enemy fire, bringing in Indians, returning again to the front for more.[15] It was an effective shuttle operation. Japanese Army commanders, mistaking the INA teams for members of the British Army, had to be reassured by *F Kikan* liaison men. Japanese commanders feared the INA propaganda teams would report back to the British Army on Japanese positions. The fear proved groundless but gave Fujiwara some anxious moments. If any Indians were accidentally shot by Japanese guards the whole project might collapse. The success of the teams passing through front lines of two armies in the dense forest reassured Fujiwara and Mohan Singh. The teams hunted for Indian soldiers without English officers and encouraged them to leave the British Army.

With a hand-printing press and Hindi and Urdu moveable type, Mohan Singh and Pritam Singh worked day and night printing the first propaganda leaflets. They were distributed over the Slim battleline by the 3rd Airborne Division, whose commander was a former teacher of Fujiwara in the General Staff College.[16]

As fighting spread through Malaya and the Slim battleline fell under Japanese assault, increasing numbers of Indians were brought into Ipoh by the propaganda teams. Fujiwara believed the time had come to advance headquarters to Kuala Lumpur as the Japanese front line pushed south toward Singapore.

VI   FUJIWARA PROPOSES AN INDIA POLICY

Before Fujiwara could accomplish the move, he was visited on 8 January by Major Ozeki from the 8th Section of IGHQ, who had come to discuss with Fujiwara the progress of his mission. By this time Fujiwara had clearly delineated his convictions. He expressed his views to the major as follows: 1) Japan should adopt a policy of cutting India adrift from England, not through military means or a Machiavellian policy but through genuine assistance to the Indian independence movement; 2) Japan's basic policy toward India and the Indian independence movement must be clarified; 3) the Government and Imperial General Headquarters must be united in policy toward India; 4) the work of the *Fujiwara Kikan* in Malaya and Thailand must be expanded into all areas of Asia, and India must be appealed to directly; 5) Japan's policy toward India must be based on world-wide considerations, which would include an invitation to Chandra Bose to come to East Asia; 6) Japan's policy toward India in East Asia should be to assist the independence movement both through its political arm, the Indian Independence League composed of Indian civilians, and its military arm, the Indian National Army composed of captured Indian soldiers in East Asia; 7) Japan should prove by personal example to watching Indians in Burma, Penang, and occupied areas the ideals of the New Order; and 8) the *Fujiwara Kikan* should be reorganized in structure and scope to accomplish these fundamental aims.[17]

Fujiwara hoped that the visiting major would report his views to Imperial General Headquarters. He hoped to force Tokyo to pay attention to its India policy and to the Indian independence movement. So far his mission was the only sign that IGHQ was cognizant of India. Fujiwara had no direct communications or instructions from Tokyo until the visit of Major Ozeki. He hoped the visit meant more awareness in Tokyo now that Japanese forces were advancing through Malaya. It was Fujiwara's long-awaited chance to deal with Tokyo directly rather than through 25th Army and Southern Army Headquarters.

When Fujiwara finished talking with Major Ozeki he sat up all night making plans for the expansion of the *F Kikan* propaganda work in Sumatra and Penang and for headquarters to move from Ipoh to Kuala Lumpur. The success of Fujiwara's work was temporarily checked following the fall of the Slim battleline when the British Army transferred Caucasian troops to north Malaya and Indian troops to the south in preparation for the defence of Singapore. Further, Japanese Army reports indicated British Army intelligence was aware of the work of the *F Kikan* and would probably take positive defensive measures against the unit.[18] Fujiwara knew that Lieutenant-General Yamashita was deploying Japanese troops for the decisive battle of Singapore, and he discussed with Mohan Singh and Pritam Singh plans to move to Kuala Lumpur on 9 January.

In spite of these problems, during the move to Kuala Lumpur, Indian officers and men holding white flags and propaganda handbills joined the growing procession to Kuala Lumpur on foot and in trucks, mingling with the pursuing Japanese troops. Fujiwara marvelled at the strange spectacle. By the time the procession reached Kuala Lumpur about one thousand Indians had surrendered. They were quartered in Kuala Lumpur in barracks and billets occupied until a few days before by the British Army. Mohan Singh told Fujiwara of his plans to expand and train the growing army of independence. Mohan Singh had a three-point plan for the INA: 1) the INA be given armed drill, 2) a large propaganda unit be trained to canvass Indians in the British Army as it approached Singapore, and 3) propaganda broadcasts be beamed from Saigon to India.[19] Fujiwara and the chief of staff of the 25th Army both concurred.

The number of surrendered Indians was now about two thousand five hundred, and Mohan Singh began to reorganize and educate them in the ideals of the revolution, and to create an *esprit de corps.* He told them if they were not convinced of his sincerity they would be given safe conduct back to the British lines. Among the officers were about a dozen Indian commissioned officers, a hundred viceroy commissioned officers, and several hundred non-commissioned officers. Within a week of arrival at Kuala Lumpur Mohan Singh organized the whole army into five battalions with a single class of officers. The lower ranks of officers were all promoted. The Indian commissioned officers were assigned top staff jobs. Common kitchens were opened in place of the separate kitchens for different ranks. Common slogans and songs were adopted.[20]

By the end of January Mohan Singh decided the time had come to assign small parties of the INA to various propaganda tasks away from headquarters and even to send token units into action with the Japanese Army. Some officers were sent to the Saigon radio station and some to Penang radio station to broadcast to India. A volunteer force of about fifty officers under command of Captain Ram Swarup was sent with Captain Tsuchimochi and three others from the *F Kikan* to help Japanese propaganda operations in Burma.

In Burma the Thakin Party, a group of young nationalists under the leadership of Aung San, was agitating for independence. Some of the men had escaped from Burma and were receiving military training under the Japanese Army on Hainan Island. The Thakin Party in Burma came under the protection of the ten-man *Minami*

Kikan (Southern Agency), a joint army-navy venture whose work paralleled the *F Kikan*'s. At the outbreak of fighting in December 1941, Aung San and others had gone with *Minami Kikan* members to Thailand, where they organized a corps of Burmese volunteers called the Burma Independence Army. The BIA became the spearhead of pro-Japanese and anti-British sentiment in Burma. Japanese Army authorities were apprehensive about the antagonism that existed among Burmese toward Indians. For this reason Fujiwara was ordered to send part of the *F Kikan* with a party of Indian followers of Mohan Singh into Burma to promote goodwill between the BIA and INA.[21]

Mohan Singh decided that the morale of the INA was so high that it could be tested in propaganda operations and actual battle. Fujiwara and the 25th Army Headquarters staff agreed and encouraged Mohan Singh's plans. It was decided to send a token force of selected volunteers. Mohan Singh selected and trained two companies of one hundred men each. The companies were put under command of Captain Allah Ditta. In early January they were sent to accompany the Konoe Imperial Guards Division in the Singapore operation.[22] The Japanese estimated that eighty per cent of the British forces at Singapore were Indians. These men were the target of the Allah Ditta party.

VII VISITORS FROM TOKYO

By 24 January Japanese forces had control of the Philippines, the Celebes Islands, and New Britain. Fujiwara decided the time had come to make his report on Japan's India policy to IGHQ and to recommend its adoption. Just as Fujiwara reached this decision, he was called by a Southern Army Headquarters staff officer and ordered to report to 25th Army Headquarters in Kluang with a report on India policy in document form. Elated, Fujiwara worked on his draft through the night. The final copy of the draft was completed by three of Fujiwara's assistants the following day. Fujiwara left for the Kluang headquarters with copies of the plan for Lieutenant-General Yamashita, General Terauchi, and IGHQ. By the time Fujiwara arrived at Kluang he had lost two nights' sleep. There he was greeted by staff officers of the 25th Army, the Southern Army, and IGHQ who had assembled to draft final plans for the assault on

Singapore. Among them were General Tominaga, head of the Personnel Bureau, Army Ministry, and General Tanaka, chief of operations, IGHQ, representing General Tōjō, War Minister, and General Sugiyama, chief of general staff.[23]

Fujiwara felt luck was with him and his report would be heard where it counted. Strictly speaking, he was only entitled to report to 25th Army Headquarters staff. But Fujiwara was aware of the tension between 25th Army Headquarters and Southern Army Headquarters, and between Terauchi and Tōjō, which might delay the transmission of his plan through channels. Further, the India problem was so broad that it was really a matter for IGHQ. Fujiwara's proposals involved all of Greater East Asia.[24]

Fujiwara, after talking with the appropriate staff officers, was unexpectedly accosted by Generals Tominaga and Tanaka. Assailed by a momentary sinking sensation, he summoned his courage and explained to the generals his project in Malaya and Sumatra. He told them of the Indian independence army and Indian Independence League and made suggestions for a Japanese policy toward India. General Tanaka asked, "What do you say, Fujiwara? Will you let us see this Indian National Army you are supporting? What do you think, General Tominaga?" General Tominaga said brusquely, "Let's go!" Staff officers of the 25th Army were open-mouthed that Fujiwara had got the consent of the two generals from Tokyo to visit the INA at Kuala Lumpur.

At Kuala Lumpur Fujiwara's aides were beside themselves with enthusiasm but at the same time had some misgivings about the reaction of the generals to the INA. Fujiwara rushed to find Mohan Singh and Pritam Singh and explained what had transpired. The generals toured the INA camp and reviewed the troops. Fujiwara felt the INA had made a good impression. The generals and their staff officers met Mohan Singh and Pritam Singh. Staff officer Lieutenant-Colonel Okamura, who had met Fujiwara earlier, was left to question Mohan Singh closely. Lieutenant-Colonel Okamura asked: "This is a blunt question, but some people claim it will be difficult to promote an Indian independence movement because of religious differences, the bondage of the caste system, and discord between the various communities. I'd like to know what you think about it?" Mohan Singh answered, "I believe love of one's country should transcend attachment to a particular religion, community or race. The caste system is an inhuman residue of the old tradition and is gradually being rectified. Not a single incident has occurred in the INA because of religious or racial differences."[25] There was evidence that in the INA the traditional divisive influences of religion, caste, language and culture had been transcended.

When the interrogation of Mohan Singh was finished, Fujiwara was called in to talk with the two generals. General Tanaka challenged: "Fujiwara, you've brought us here with great confidence, but according to the report we have just had from the staff officer. Captain Mohan Singh, whom you have been praising so generously, is not that great." Fujiwara was taken aback, but then remembered the expression of approval on the faces of both generals as they had reviewed the INA troops earlier. Possibly they were testing his own convictions. He replied, "What you say is incorrect. If a staff officer has such a misunderstanding I'd like to hear the reasons directly from him." General Tanaka reddened and shouted, "It's a report of a staff officer! Do you say you disagree?" Fujiwara said, "Yes. The report is wrong so far as this issue is concerned. There is absolutely no mistake in my observations of the past fifty days of crisis." General Tanaka pressed, "That may be so, but Captain Mohan Singh is neither a statesman nor an experienced revolutionary." Fujiwara felt he had to persist and not be cowed. He countered, "Famous revolutionaries were all once unknown youths. If a man has unselfish affection for his country, passion for revolution, strong capacity for action, intelligence, and popularity, no matter how unknown he may be, he will become a great revolutionary. The independence of India and co-operation between Japan and India are essential for completing the East Asia War and establishing the New Order in Greater East Asia. Japan hasn't formulated any policy or made any effort to co-operate with the leaders of India." Fujiwara spoke of the formation of a huge Indian revolutionary army of one hundred thousand men. He mentioned the Indian request to bring Subhas Chandra Bose to Asia to unite all Indians. Finishing his explanation, Fujiwara recommended an expanded agency to replace the *F Kikan* which could not handle all the functions which Fujiwara envisioned. General Tominaga asked for Fujiwara's recommendation of the type of man who should replace him; this suggestion of confidence encouraged Fujiwara. General Tanaka said non-committally, "I shall keep in mind what you have reported."[26]

Fujiwara had expected a more positive response. Had he succeeded or failed? Fujiwara was not sure. General Tanaka may have been only testing his convictions. He was an adroit politician. It was only as the generals were leaving that a staff officer told Fujiwara that General Tanaka was delighted with his success in a significant project and valued his views. Fujiwara felt he had made Tokyo listen.

The British Army was retreating rapidly toward Singapore across the Johore Strait from Johore Bahru and the fall of Johore Bahru was imminent. General Yamashita's headquarters in Kluang was preparing for the advance on the century-old British bastion at Singapore. The Japanese Army had made a lightning fifty-five-day dash across the jungles of south Thailand and the Malay peninsula, a distance of some six hundred miles. Small unarmed boats had carried out landings up to three hundred miles behind enemy lines on the west coast of Malaya. Japanese forces numbering thirty-five thousand had succeeded against eighty thousand British troops. The Japanese flag fluttered in the sea breeze atop the Sultan's palace at Johore Bahru which commanded an excellent view of Singapore across the Johore Strait.

The Seletar Naval Base[27] protected the east end of the strait which was patrolled constantly by British planes. Reinforcements had recently arrived from England and Australia. Anti-aircraft guns and an unlimited supply of ammunition awaited the Japanese attack.

Generals Tanaka and Tominaga from Tokyo were working on plans for the final assault on Singapore with the staff of 25th Army Headquarters. A mood of elation pervaded Headquarters as plans were completed to take the fortress by 11 February, legendary anniversary of the coronation of Emperor Jimmu in 600 B.C.

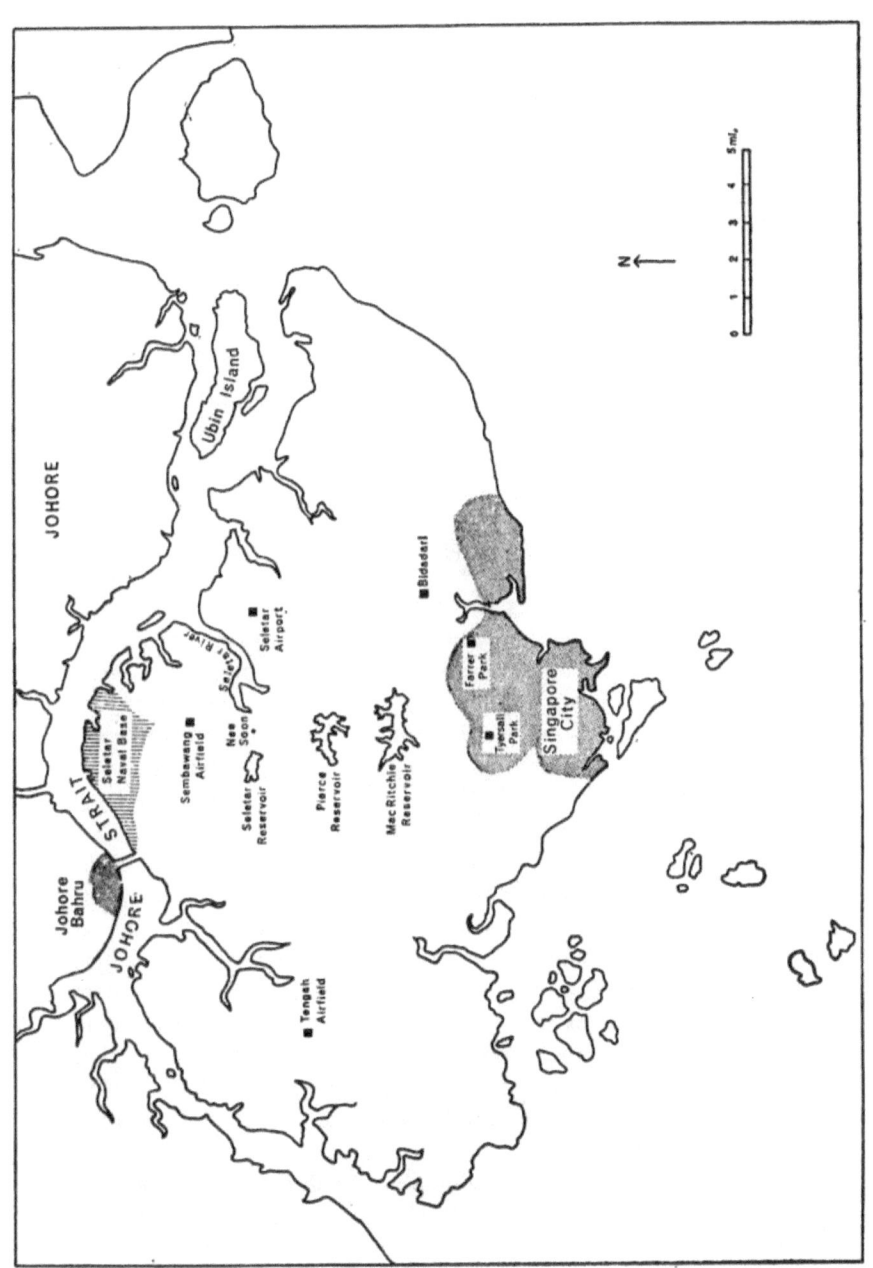
Singapore

CHAPTER THREE

Singapore Capitulates and the INA Blossoms

I BRITISH BASTION

IN 1824 Sir Stamford Raffles succeeded in effecting the transfer of the island of Singapore to the British East India Company. From that time on Singapore became the bastion of British domination of Asia. Fortification of the island had not been restricted by the Washington Naval Conference quotas of 1921-2, and Britain had subsequently spent many millions of pounds sterling making the defences "impregnable". Since the outbreak of fighting in China in 1937 Britain had completed the naval port and further consolidated its strength with Australian and Indian soldiers. As an island, Singapore had natural defences as well. Britain boasted the fortress could never be captured by sea. There was, however, an Achilles heel noted by Japanese intelligence: the rear defences near Johore Bahru across the strait to the north. The British discounted the possibility of the Japanese Army reaching Singapore overland through the jungles of Thailand to approach from the rear. British military intelligence reports failed even to mention the lack of fortifications for the defence of Singapore to the rear until 19 January 1941.[1] British strategy relied entirely on the defence of the sea-front, counting on Britain's traditional naval supremacy.

Prime Minister Churchill was dumbfounded to hear of the vulnerability of Singapore to the north. He telegraphed General Wavell, Supreme Commander of Allied Forces in the Southwest Pacific, on 20 January 1942, a month after the invasion of Malaya: "I want to make it absolutely clear that I expect every inch of ground to be defended, every scrap of material or defences to be blown to pieces to prevent capture by the enemy, and no question of surrender to be entertained until after protracted fighting among the ruins of Singapore City."[2] But for Churchill there was an even more critical objective than holding Singapore, as he indicated in a communiqué to General Ismay the same day: keeping open the Burma Road as the avenue to Chinese troops, who had been more effective than any others against the Japanese.[3] Despite Churchill's belated concern, however, little was done to strengthen the defences of Singapore to the north between 20 January and the night of 7 February when the first Japanese landing barges wove their way through dense mangrove swamps across the Johore Strait.

The pivotal point of the defences was the narrow causeway connecting Singapore with Johore Bahru to the rear. To the east of the causeway were the crucial Seletar 'naval port defences. Further east still was Ubin Island guarding the eastern entrance to the strait.

II JAPANESE ATTACK

Salient points of the Japanese strategy of attack were to destroy the enemy north of the strait in Johore, to make feints and block the sector east of the causeway, and then to mount the main attack from the west side of the causeway. Since the British had no inkling from which side of the causeway General Yamashita's main assault might come if from the rear, the strategy of feints from the opposite side was well calculated. The Japanese assault was to be a co-ordinated air force, naval, and artillery operation, and three divisions were deployed for the attack: the 5th, 18th, and the crack Konoe Imperial Guards Division. Small motor-boats and collapsible launches were prepared by the engineers for each division.

General Yamashita's command headquarters moved into the Johore Imperial Palace from which all preparations and movements in the strait could be closely watched. The palace on the promontory was so clearly visible from all sides that the British did not even suspect it was being used as the Japanese command post. It was a grand deception.

At midnight on 7 February a small force of twenty men had been readied under orders of Mohan Singh and Fujiwara to help decoy British attention to Ubin Island and the east of the causeway. The party was under command of Captain Allah Ditta and included three men from the *F Kikan*. This was the first crucial co-operative venture of the INA and *F Kikan*. It was a success. The Allah Ditta party manoeuvre was also co-ordinated with the action of the Konoe Division on the nights of 7 and 8 February.[4]

The feint by the Konoe Division on Ubin Island and the east end of the strait took the British by surprise on 8 February and diverted their attention, while the main Japanese attack was mounted from the west side. Columns of black smoke billowed up from the oil tanks at Seletar Naval Base as Japanese bombers weaved through the smoke trying to evade anti-aircraft fire and zero in on the airfields. The crossing of the strait was accomplished within twenty-four hours. Fujiwara led a party of thirty men into the midst of the action. The British Air Force lost control of the air and the island bastion was isolated. Japanese forces fought their way across the island to occupy airfields and other fortified areas, including the crucial reservoirs. On 15 February, Black Sunday for Britain, the British Army capitulated. Singapore, which the British boasted could only be captured after a six-month struggle, if at all, had surrendered after barely a week of bloody fighting.

III BURGEONING OF THE INA

F Kikan headquarters moved through groups of soldiers burying their comrades to a British police officers' residence near Raffles College. The surrender ceremony for the estimated fifty thousand Indian men was scheduled for the afternoon of 17 February in the Farrer Park race-course. Fujiwara wondered how his staff of fourteen would arrange barracks, provisions and health measures for the huge cadre of Indian troops with which the British had defended Singapore. He consulted with Mohan Singh and Pritam Singh, and they agreed that each would speak to the surrendered Indians following Fujiwara's speech accepting the surrender.

Fujiwara sat up most of the night drafting his speech. It was not an ordinary speech accepting surrender. The points he made were:

1) one of Japan's war aims was the liberation of Asian peoples from Western colonialism; 2) Japan would offer sincere aid to the Indian independence movement; 3) the fall of Singapore offered an excellent opportunity for Indian independence; 4) the Japanese Army had been helping Indians through the Indian Independence League and the nucleus of the Indian National Army; 5) the Japanese Army would treat Indian soldiers as equal friends; 6) those who joined the INA would not be treated as prisoners but would be assisted in the independence movement; 7) the Japanese Army would deal with the surrendered Indians through Captain Mohan Singh; and 8) the Japanese Army would do its best to raise their salaries.[5] Fujiwara showed his draft to Mohan Singh, Pritam Singh, and the chief of staff of the 25th Army for approval.

Next morning Fujiwara inspected preparations at Farrer Park as the race-course filled with units of Indian men. Lieutenant-Colonel Hunt for the British Army checked lists of Indian names as he received them from the unit commanders. Shortly after 2 p.m. the units had all poured into the race-course and Lieutenant-Colonel Hunt stepped to the microphone. The attention of forty-five thousand Indians was focused on him as he announced the transfer of the surrendered men to the authority of the Japanese Army.[6]

A hush fell over the race-course as Major Fujiwara next stepped to the microphone. He felt all ninety thousand eyes fixed on his face. His English interpreter. Lieutenant Kunizuka, stood on his right and next to him the ranking officer among the surrendered Indians, Lieutenant-Colonel N.S. Gill, who would translate into Hindi. Fujiwara gripped his draft in one hand and bowed to the whole assembly. Some of the kneeling Indian officers in the front rows returned the greeting. Fujiwara called: "Beloved Indian soldiers! On behalf of the Japanese Army I accept the surrender of Indian soldiers from British Army authorities! I am Major Fujiwara, head of the *F Kikan,* which will maintain ties of friendship between the Japanese Army, the Indian National Army, and the Japanese people." As Lieutenant Kunizuka translated into English the officers in the front rows nodded. When Lieutenant-Colonel Gill translated into Hindi several thousand Indian soldiers to the rear nodded in turn. Fujiwara explained the aim of associating liberated peoples of Asia in an Asian Co-Prosperity Sphere based on freedom, equality and friendship. When he announced Japan stood ready to aid Indian independence his audience went into a frenzy. The race-course reverberated with echoes of applause so that Fujiwara had to wait several minutes before continuing. "We hope you will join the INA. The Japanese Army will not treat you as prisoners but as friends. We will recognize your struggle for freedom and give you all-out assistance," Fujiwara concluded. As he finished the whole Indian audience stood and shouted enthusiastically. Thousands of caps were tossed into the air.[7]

Next Pritam Singh and Mohan Singh took their turns at the microphone. They spoke of the aims and activities of the IIL and INA to date. They spoke of India's tragic past of subjugation and urged their compatriots to seize the opportunity and rise for the motherland. Their words were accompanied by continuous applause, weeping and flying caps. When the speeches were over Fujiwara told Lieutenant-Colonel Gill and Mohan Singh he would meet with all officers.

Fujiwara was questioned closely by the Indian officers regarding Japan's real aim in helping the Indian independence movement, the substance of Japan's aid, relations between the INA and the Japanese Army, the organization of the INA, and equipment problems. Fujiwara conceded that some problems remained to be ironed out through subsequent co-operation but he reiterated assurances of Japan's sincerity. When the meeting was over the Indian officers made their way toward their allotted billets in four camps: Nee Soon, Bidadari, Tyersall Park and Seletar.

Mohan Singh was not surprised at the diffidence of many of the officers. He in fact expected vocal and even organized opposition by those whose loyalty to the British-Indian Army could not be easily shaken. Mohan Singh preached to these men that breaking the oath of loyalty to the British and taking a new oath to free India was a moral and even a religious act, that there could be no compromise with subjugation. But for many Indian officers and men the issue of co-operation posed a loyalty crisis; the personal dilemma was not easy to resolve. Mohan Singh appointed Lieutenant-Colonel Gill commandant of the POWs and asked him to establish his headquarters at the Nee Soon Camp and help in the administration of the INA. Mohan Singh's own headquarters was at Mount Pleasant near the headquarters of the *F Kikan*.[8]

Many thousands of officers and men volunteered for the INA, other thousands refused to volunteer.[9] Among those who refused to volunteer was Major Shah Nawaz Khan of the 1/14 Punjab Regiment, Mohan Singh's own regiment. Shah Nawaz felt Mohan Singh was a very average officer who would not be able to deal politically with the Japanese. Furthermore, Shah Nawaz was suspicious of the sincerity of the Japanese. In addition he came from a family with a long tradition of service in the British-Indian Army. He was not able to break with the past overnight. He decided he would not volunteer and warned other officers and men to refrain from joining. He organized a group of about twenty officers in Nee Soon Camp to resist the formation of the INA. "I felt all along that the Japanese were exploiting us and at heart I was an admirer of the British people," Shah Nawaz said later.[10] Long British training and conditioning and Indian suspicion of Japanese motives kept many officers out of the first INA. Habits of mind and heart could not be eradicated overnight.

IV INVITATION FROM TOKYO

Hostile feelings arose between volunteers and non-volunteers and led to violence and indiscipline. At length the non-volunteers were gathered together in a concentration camp and kept under guard. Under the circumstances it seemed to many non-volunteers that they were being coerced to volunteer. The volunteers were given INA rations, accommodations and pay, while the non-volunteers were given POW rations, pay and accommodations.[11] Major M.L. Bhagata was one who volunteered for the medical corps because "it was a question of saving one's skin in adverse circumstances". Lack of adequate sanitary measures in the camps flooded with troops aggravated health problems. There were also thousands of wounded soldiers. Medical services were organized under Lieutenant-Colonel A.C. Chatterji (later Major-General) and Colonel D.S. Raju.

After the Farrer Park speech and meeting with the surrendered Indian officers Pritam Singh introduced Fujiwara to two practising lawyers, S.C. Goho and K.P.K. Menon, both recognized leaders of the Indian community in Singapore. Indians in Malaya and Singapore were more politically conscious than in some other Southeast Asian nations. They had several organizations: the Indian Association of Malaya, the Central Indian Association of Malaya, the Indian Chamber of Commerce, the Ramakrishna Mission, and several other groups. Pritam Singh had already told the two lawyers about the *F Kikan* and its aid to the IIL and INA. The two men impressed Fujiwara as astute politicians determined to protect Indian lives and property in Southeast Asia against any threat. Pritam Singh had encouraged the organization of IIL branches throughout Malaya, and many of the existing organizations had joined forces with the IIL on the outbreak of war. Goho, who became head of the Singapore branch, discussed with Fujiwara plans to hold a meeting of Singapore Indians on 19 February. Fujiwara invited the two men and Lieutenant-Colonel Gill to dinner to celebrate their new friendship.[12]

On 18 February a large group of Indians of Singapore held a banquet for IIL members, INA officers, and members of the *F Kikan*. The following day several thousand Indians poured into Farrer Park again, and the gathering seethed with excitement and patriotic fervour. Goho shared the rostrum with Mohan Singh, Pritam Singh, and Fujiwara. Singapore was made headquarters for all IIL branches throughout Malaya.

Fujiwara was struck by the patriotism and unity of the Indian civilians. He began to consider ways to develop Japanese co-operation more effectively with the burgeoning IIL branches all over Southeast Asia and with various other Malayan groups. He visited the vice-chief of staff at Japanese military headquarters and asked for recognition and help for the Young Malay Association. Only after lengthy persuasion was Fujiwara able to move the narrow military attitude of the staff officer and get his consent to recognize the Malay youth organization and promise to help the organization's publication and other activities.[13] Fujiwara continually fretted at obstacles put in the way of co-operation with the Indian movement and other civilian organizations at all levels of command, from the 15th Army and the Southern Army to Tokyo.

Just as Fujiwara was consulting with Mohan Singh about the care of the forty-five thousand soldiers in Singapore and planning with his staff the expansion *of F Kikan* work in Malaya, Thailand, Burma and Sumatra, a telegram arrived from Tokyo Headquarters. It announced a meeting in Tokyo on 10 March of Indian representatives from all parts of Asia. The meeting was called by Rash Behari Bose, an Indian resident of Tokyo, and the invitation was forwarded through military channels.

About ten representatives of the IIL and INA in Thailand and Malaya were to be accompanied to Tokyo by Fujiwara and Colonel Iwakuro of the Konoe Imperial Guards Division. Fujiwara wondered if the arrangements had been made by Generals Tominaga and Tanaka, who had questioned him at Kuala Lumpur. Now surely he would have a chance to explain his views on Japan's India policy where it would do the most good: to Headquarters in Tokyo. Fujiwara was delighted too that a man of the political stature of Iwakuro had been chosen to accompany him. Perhaps this meant that Colonel Iwakuro would head an expanded *Kikan* such as Fujiwara had recommended.

Fujiwara showed the telegram to Mohan Singh and Pritam Singh, and the three decided to choose six IIL and three INA men as delegates to Tokyo. Fujiwara also told Pritam Singh he would like to add a leader from each of the two Indian organizations in Bangkok as an effort to conciliate them: the IIL and the *Thai-Bharat* Cultural Lodge, which had been organized in 1940 by Swami Satyananda Puri, a scholar and religious figure. The two Bangkok organizations represented an Indian community in Thailand of about forty thousand, mostly small shopkeepers.

After the outbreak of war the Indian National Council had been formed in Bangkok out of the membership of the *Thai-Bharat* Cultural Lodge. The Council remained suspicious of Pritam Singh's group, largely Sikhs, which it considered too much under Japanese influence. The Lodge-Council members were dubious of Japan's aims in Southeast Asia and were afraid of becoming Japanese puppets in their own homeland. They preferred to accept help when necessary from the Thai Government (such as broadcasting facilities) and to use the German Embassy for liaison with Subhas Chandra Bose in Berlin. Pritam Singh was accepting help from the Japanese, and though he might be a real patriot, he was under the thumb of the Japanese, perhaps even a spy, in the eyes of the Council. These suspicions of the Lodge-Council toward Pritam Singh and the Japanese were never allayed, and there was no real co-operation between the Council and the IIL until the arrival of Subhas Chandra Bose in Southeast Asia. "You could never become friends with the Japanese. They looked down on the Asiatics," said one member of the Indian National Council. When the invitation came to Satyananda Puri to attend a conference of Indians in Tokyo together with Pritam Singh, members of the Lodge-Council felt it was a great concession to allow Puri to go.[14]

Pritam Singh, at the suggestion of Goho, sent out invitations to the heads of all IIL branches in Malaya to a preliminary meeting in Singapore to discuss the delegation to Tokyo. About twenty chairmen assembled at Goho's residence on 3 March. N. Raghavan, a

Penang lawyer, presided. Fujiwara was invited as observer. The chief question at issue was the line of action the Indian delegates should follow in Tokyo. The delegates were not to make any decisions without first consulting the membership of the organizations they represented, which meant no decisions or commitments would be made in Tokyo. The primary aims of the delegates would be to promote goodwill and to get Japanese assurances of assistance.

Swami Satyananda Puri briefly addressed the Singapore meeting on the activities of the Indian National Council in Thailand. He reported a statement of Jawaharlal Nehru that Indians residing outside India could not interfere in Indian politics, or they would be considered traitors. He expressed the fear that unless all possibility of the stigma of being considered quislings in the pay of the Japanese were removed, nothing could be achieved outside India. Goho asked Pritam Singh to explain to the meeting the purpose of the delegation to Tokyo. Pritam Singh announced the conference was to discuss the problems of Indian representatives and to negotiate with Japanese authorities the terms of co-operation with Japan for achieving Indian independence. The meeting concluded with resolutions passed to try to secure the approval of the Indian National Congress, to work for the liberation of India with Japanese assistance, and to request Major Fujiwara to accord the Indian POWs in Singapore equal treatment with the INA. The members unanimously concluded that Subhas Chandra Bose should be requested to come to East Asia to accept the leadership of the independence movement. The meeting named IIL delegates to the Tokyo conference from Malaya and Thailand: N. Raghavan, K.A.N. Ayer, S.C. Goho, K.P.K. Menon, Pritam Singh, and Swami Satyananda Puri. INA delegates chosen were Mohan Singh, N.S. Gill, and Mohammed Akram. Fujiwara was pleased that Pritam Singh and Swami Satyananda Puri were selected to represent the two Indian organizations in Thailand. He kept his fingers crossed for the Tokyo talks.

CHAPTER FOUR

Tokyo Conference

I FLIGHT TO TOKYO

ON 10 March 1942 two planes left the Bangkok airport for Tokyo. Aboard one were Fujiwara, Colonel Iwakuro, Mohan Singh, Lieutenant-Colonel Gill, N. Raghavan, S.C. Goho, and K.P.K. Menon. Fujiwara felt Headquarters had singled out Colonel Iwakuro to succeed him in the expanded and reorganized *Kikan*. Iwakuro had taken part in the Washington peace talks between Hull and Nomura just prior to Pearl Harbour and was renowned in army circles for his political acumen. He was a powerful figure in the Army High Command, so powerful that some officers believed Tōjō had sent him to Malaya in command of an infantry regiment of the Konoe Imperial Guards Division to remove him from the scene in Tokyo. En route to Tokyo Fujiwara told Iwakuro of his hopes and plans for Japan's India policy and for co-operation with the Indian independence movement. Fujiwara was encouraged at the prospect of Iwakuro bringing his influence to bear on the military, the Government, and the Diet to impress on them the importance of India.[1]

Fujiwara's plane left Saigon on 11 March, was delayed two days on Hainan Island, and stopped in Shanghai en route to Haneda Airport in Tokyo. Headquarters had arranged for the delegates to be taken to the Sanno Hotel, where the meetings were to be held. Some Indian delegates had already arrived from Shanghai and Hong Kong.

It had been arranged that the second plane carrying the party of Pritam Singh, the Swami, Captain Akram and *F Kikan* member Otaguro would arrive in Tokyo on the evening of 19 March.

On the morning of 19 March a violent wind swept over Honshu and became increasingly fierce as the afternoon wore on. The sky over Tokyo grew black and toward evening a torrential rain began to fall. Fujiwara assumed the flight from Shanghai would have been cancelled because of the weather, but in the afternoon he received a report that the flight had left Shanghai for Tokyo. The logical course would be then to land in north Kyushu or Osaka and lay over until the weather cleared. Fujiwara had a call from Haneda Airport with word that the plane had reported over Ise Bay headed east. This was the last communication from the plane. By night the storm became a howling typhoon. Fujiwara sent word to all air bases in Honshu to launch a search for the plane. He tried to fight off a growing premonition but noticed the malaise on the faces of the Indian delegates waiting with him. Fujiwara was unable to sleep that night, and by morning there was still no news. By noon it was apparent that no plane had landed at any of the airports in central Honshu. Fujiwara felt he had to tell the waiting Indians and Mrs Otaguro that they had to expect the worst. He ordered all airports in the country to search for the plane, and his mood changed to despair.

At length reports reached Fujiwara explaining that a Japanese colonel had boarded the flight at Shanghai and demanded that the plane proceed to Tokyo where he was expected at a meeting. The pilot had no choice. About then the plane had landed at Tachiarai Airport to refuel. Airport authorities reported the storm was worsening and recommended the plane lay over until the weather improved. The irate colonel ordered the pilot to take off for Tokyo. Fujiwara was shattered to learn the cause of the death of Otaguro and the four Indian patriots who had become martyrs to the cause of Indo-Japanese co-operation. Mohan Singh told Fujiwara he had entrusted to Captain Akram aboard the plane a manuscript, now also lost. Mohan Singh had been keeping a daily record of his activities and co-operation with Fujiwara in inaugurating the Indian National Army, since the day of their first meeting near Alor Star. The manuscript, over one hundred pages, was titled, "The First Japanese Officer I Met". Fujiwara felt this secret record of the birth of the INA was also an irreplaceable loss to posterity.

II FUJIWARA REPORTS TO HEADQUARTERS

Fujiwara was disappointed that the guidance of his Indian friends was taken out of his hand by Headquarters. Instead, he got a chance to report directly to the chiefs of staff on the progress of the work of the *F Kikan*. He used the opportunity to press his views on India once again upon staff officers at IGHQ. He insisted on four points: 1) Japan should determine and publicly state her policy toward India, on the basis of Premier Tōjō's 20 January declaration on India in the Diet, 2) the Government and people should take steps to implement this policy impartially, 3) administration of the southern occupied areas must be a model for the New Order in East Asia, and 4) Japan must support to the limit the Indian freedom movement, with no hint of interference. He further suggested that the new *Iwakuro Kikan* replacing the *F Kikan* be given the status of a diplomatic mission or embassy rather than a proxy agency of Japanese policy. Colonel Iwakuro also sat in on the discussions. Fujiwara felt his report had made an impression on the men at Headquarters.²

Following this report, Fujiwara met with the 8th Section which was responsible for India and his own project. Fujiwara was shown the IGHQ plan for India, which he judged embodied the plan he had submitted earlier. He was disappointed, however, to see the title of the document, which read, "India Stratagem Plan". Fujiwara passionately pleaded for revision of the tone of the document and policy. After two days of discussion, he felt he had succeeded at least in part. The title of the draft was changed to "India Policy Project", and Fujiwara felt some of the Machiavellian tenor had been expunged from the contents of the document. His trip to Tokyo had been fruitful. Consultations in Headquarters had begun on an India plan based on his own suggestions. Now responsibility for execution of the plan was taken out of his hands.³

III   INDIANS IN TOKYO

Some of the delegates from Malaya, including Mohan Singh, were dissatisfied with the selection of some representatives from elsewhere in Southeast Asia. Those from Malaya regarded themselves as a goodwill mission not bound to accept any decision which might be reached by the Tokyo conference, even though they might personally agree with such decisions.

Furthermore, in Tokyo friction became immediately apparent between those who had come from Southeast Asia and the Indians resident in Tokyo. Mohan Singh and N.S. Gill felt that Rash Behari

Bose, leader of the Indian exiles in Japan, was manipulating the conference according to instructions from the Japanese Government. This feeling prompted the decision of the whole delegation from Southeast Asia that they would defer any final decision at the Tokyo meetings until a later and larger conference in Burma, Thailand, or Malaya. Mohan Singh's faction suggested the direction of the independence movement be assumed by a five-member Council of Action to be elected at the larger conference in Southeast Asia. This proposal was accepted, and the representatives decided the conference should be held in May or June in Rangoon or Bangkok.[4] The Indians in Tokyo, on the other hand, felt those from Southeast Asia had been too long loyal to British rule in India and had no experience as revolutionaries.

Fujiwara was embarrassed by the friction between the Indians from the south and those in Tokyo. He was well aware of the feeling of his IIL colleagues that the Tokyo exiles were under the thumb of the Japanese, had lost their Indian values and become Japanese puppets. Fujiwara was frustrated at not being able to conciliate the two factions, as he felt unity of the Indian movement was a prerequisite to close cooperation between Japanese and Indians in Southeast Asia.

The Indian community in Japan had its origins in the twenties. At that time there were some three hundred and fifty Indians in Japan, primarily merchants and students. There were several social organizations, including the India Club, the Indian Social Association, the *Bharat Mandir* in Kobe (a church), and the India Club in Yokohama. By Indian standards, the Indians enjoyed a high standard of living in Japan. There was also an Indian Chamber of Commerce recognized by the Japanese Government.

Among the Indians were also a few revolutionaries who were *personae non grata* to the British in India and who were living in exile in Japan. Among these were Rash Behari Bose, Devnath Das and A.M. Nair. Devnath Das had gone to Japan in 1932 as a political exile. He was close to Rash Behari Bose and a man named Sahay and became secretary of both the Japan branch of the Indian National Congress and the Indian National Committee of Japan.

By the pre-war decade, the Indian community in Japan had become sizeable. But not all the leading Indians appeared at the Sanno Hotel meeting, which was presided over by Rash Behari Bose.

One of the Indian leaders not present was A.M. Sahay, founder of the Indian National Association of Japan. Sahay had set out for the United States in 1923 to complete his studies as a medical student, but he encountered passport difficulties and did not get beyond Japan. He then determined to remain in Japan, and began to contribute articles on India to the Japanese Press. During a meeting of the Indian community in Kobe in 1929, Sahay announced the inauguration of the Japan branch of the Indian National Congress, with himself as representative. The following year he began publication of a journal called *Voice of India,* which became the organ of the Japan branch of the Congress. Sahay in 1931 helped to organize the India Lodge, a home for Indian students, and the Indo-Japanese Association. In 1936 the Japan branch of the Congress dropped the Congress name and was renamed the Indian National Committee of Japan. The change of name, however, did not alter the cause: promotion of the aims of the Indian National Congress. Sahay wrote a book, *India,* which was published in both English and Japanese in 1939. He was in correspondence with Congress in India and frequently issued pamphlets on the history of the Indian struggle for freedom.

Until the end of 1941 Sahay still cherished the hope that Indians would be able to work with the Japanese Government. He then lost hope of co-operation with Japan, broke with Bose, and refused to co-operate with Japanese military authorities. He made sporadic attempts thereafter to urge Bose not to condone Japanese interference with the independence movement.[5] Gill and other delegates from the south were disappointed not to find Sahay at the meetings at the San-no Hotel, and their suspicions of Japanese motives were heightened.[6]

Another notable Indian missing from the Tokyo meetings was Raja Mahendra Pratap. Gill and other delegates sought out Pratap and learned that he had been kept from the meetings. Pratap was an independent, sincere, even eccentric man in the eyes of the Indian delegates from the south. During his conversation with his compatriots he accused the Japanese of insincerity regarding the independence movement and of not keeping their promises to him. It came as no surprise to Indian delegates, therefore, that he had not been allowed to attend the meetings. He regarded Bose by this time as a Japanese puppet.

Pratap had had a bizarre career as a revolutionary. In the second decade of the twentieth century he had travelled in Afghanistan and Turkey. In 1918 he established a Provisional Government of Free India in Kabul. By 1934 he was in Japan, where he founded a World Federation Centre. He was a visionary convinced that peace and freedom would only come to the world when a federal world government was established.[7] Pratap tried to get Japanese support for organizing a World Federation Volunteer Corps for the freedom of Asia. He advocated the creation of a Pan-Asian province and an Asiatic Army within the Federation. He believed that with the cooperation of Iran, Afghanistan and Nepal, some Indian princes and Congress volunteers, Indian liberation would be achieved.[8]

Pratap often talked with Rash Behari Bose, Sahay and other leaders of the Indian movement in Japan, hoping to influence them to his way of thinking. When war broke out in the Pacific, however, he took an independent tack. Said Pratap, "Japan started its own Indian organisation. I could not agree with the Japanese plans and I was ordered to sit quiet at our Centre, on March 6, 1942. Then started my forced quiet life."[9]

IV AN INDIAN EXILE: RASH BEHARI BOSE

Rash Behari Bose was chosen president of the Indian conference at the Sanno Hotel in Tokyo. His name had been mentioned in the original communiqué Fujiwara received from Tokyo informing him that an Indian conference was to be held in March in Tokyo. Bose was one of the first Indian exiles to come to Tokyo during the inter-war period and was recognized as the leader of the Indian community in Japan. From the time of his arrival in Japan as a political exile he had been on friendly terms with many Japanese.

Bose as a boy of fifteen was a revolutionary, already disillusioned with Gandhi's non-violent stance and with Nehru's Congress leadership. He was more attracted to the militant Lajpat Rai, whose thinking affected many Bengali students.[10] Bose had escaped from Calcutta in May 1915 under the pseudonym P.S. Tagore, after being accused by the British of complicity in a plot against the life of Viceroy Hardinge. A bomb had been thrown at Lord Hardinge as he entered the new capital of Delhi in December 1912. Bose was wanted by the police for the attempt on Hardinge's life. For a while he went into the revolutionary underground in Lahore and Delhi. In Tokyo Bose almost immediately met other Indian and Chinese revolutionaries, including Sun Yat-sen and Lajpat Rai. In the decade following the Japanese victory over Russia in 1905 Tokyo was a Mecca for revolutionaries from all over Asia.

Japanese police were alerted to capture two Indian revolutionaries, Bose and a man named Sen Gupta. Pressure was being brought to bear on the Foreign Office by the British Embassy in Tokyo for extradition of Bose to India. Bose was desperately in need of help to elude the Japanese police. Luck was with him, for through Sun Yat-sen he met and came under the protection of Tōyama Mitsuru, leader of the Black Dragon Society and friend of revolutionaries from all parts of Asia. Bose also met Ōkawa Shūmei, ultra-nationalist, student of Indian philosophy, and later co-conspirator with the young officer movement against cabinet ministers. It was Tōyama's cloak-and-dagger power and influence with the Government, including prime ministers and the police, that kept Bose safely hidden from Japanese authorities. There were rumours that the police knew of Bose's whereabouts but did not dare to touch him so long as he was under Tōyama's protection. Articles about Bose in the Japanese Press only aroused popular sympathy for the young exile from British colonial rule.

One Japanese who became anxious about the fate of Bose was Sōma Aizo, proprietor of the Nakamura-ya, a famous restaurant in the Shinjuku district of Tokyo. Sōma learned from newspaper articles that Bose was in Tokyo and went to Tōyama. Sōma persuaded Tōyama to allow him to assume the care and protection of Bose. Four and a half months after Bose's arrival in Tokyo he was still being pursued by detectives from the British Embassy, although Japanese police had apparently been taken off the case. Tōyama was persuaded of Sōma's sincerity, and turned Bose over to him. Mrs Sōma was equally concerned about saving Bose from Japanese and British authorities.

Between the Sōmas and Tōyama, a plan was concocted to assure Bose's permanent safety in Japan. The Sōma daughter, Toshiko, would be given in marriage to Bose. In 1919 marriage between Japanese and foreigners was extremely rare, and this was indeed a radical departure for the Sōmas. The marriage took place, and Bose had a son and daughter by his Japanese wife before she died in 1925. It was a successful marriage, and Bose became a naturalized Japanese in July 1923. By this time Bose was proficient in speaking and writing Japanese. His son later served and was killed in the Japanese Army. It was not surprising that the Indians from Southeast Asia and POWs from the Indian Army regarded him as more Japanese than Indian.[11]

In 1926 Bose began organizing Asian and especially Indian revolutionaries in Japan. He was helped by Japanese friends, including

Ōkawa Shūmei, to organize an all-Asia meeting in Nagasaki in 1926, at which Bose spoke against Western exploitation of Asian peoples and of the great Eastern traditions. He organized a hostel for Indians in Tokyo and an Indian Association. He edited a journal. *The Voice of Asia,* in both English and Japanese. He also frequently wrote for journals of the *Kokūryūkai* (Black Dragon Society). Bose's connections with the Indian National Congress were not as close as Sahay's. In 1936 Bose organized an Indian Friendship Association to promote friendly relations between Japanese and Indians.[12] Several Japanese literary figures joined, including the poet Noguchi Yonejirō, who had visited India.

In October 1937, the Japan branch of the Indian Independence League was organized with Bose as president. During the Pacific War branches of the League mushroomed all over Asia, wherever ten Indians were able to gather. The Japan branch of the League maintained contact with the Japanese Government. Publicity about the Indian independence movement was the focus of the League endeavour in Japan.[13]

Bose decided sometime in early 1941 that it would not be possible to attain Indian independence without the help of the Japanese military. The only avenue he knew to leadership in Japan, whether military or civilian, was Tōyama. Accordingly, Bose went one day to visit his old friend and protector. Tōyama agreed to try to help negotiate with the military. The result was that Bose was several times called to General Staff Headquarters to explain his views on Indian independence. In the course of the conversations he requested the aid of the Japanese Army.[14]

In the fall of 1941 Army Chief of General Staff Sugiyama ordered Major-General Okamoto to have Lieutenant-Colonel Kadomatsu of the 8th Section devise an India policy. Before anything materialized, however, Japan was involved in the military thrust into French Indochina, and after 8 December into Malaya, Burma, and Java. There was no thought for India at the time, other than the dispatching of Fujiwara's mission. It was not possible to do anything about Bose's request at the time.

It was not until 1 January 1942 that Headquarters ordered Major Ozeki to visit Bangkok, Saigon and the front lines in Malaya and Burma to inspect the India project (the *F Kikan*) on the scene. He visited Colonel Tamura in Bangkok and went on to meet Fujiwara at Ipoh. It was here that Major Ozeki got his first glimpse of the India

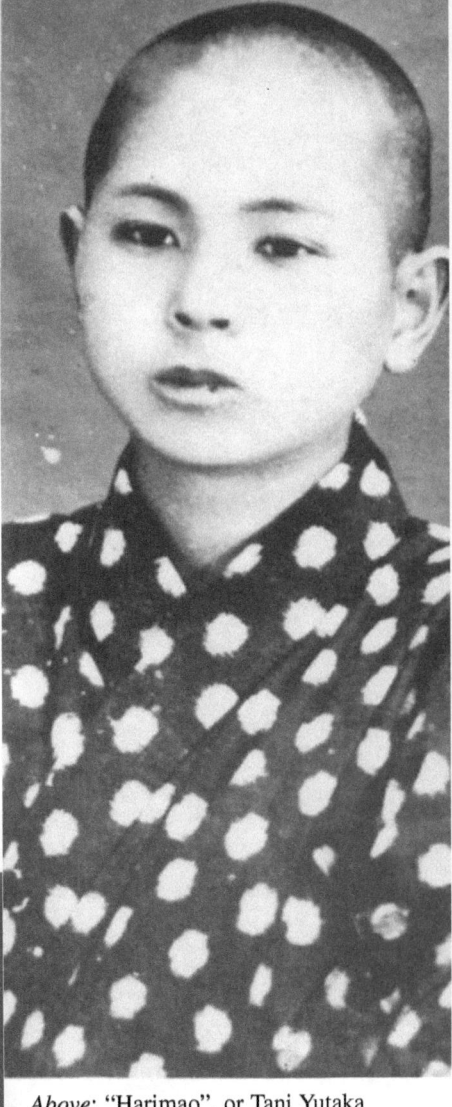

Above: "Harimao", or Tani Yutaka

Left: Isoda Saburō

Fujiwara Iwaichi

project in action. Fujiwara explained to him the problems involved in helping the Indian independence movement, including the initial stages of organizing the Indian National Army. When Ozeki returned to Tokyo it was arranged that he would work with Bose too, who was seeking Japanese help in Tokyo.[15]

Bose was again called to General Staff Headquarters and asked about his views on a concrete policy for developing the Indian independence movement. He proposed creation of a volunteer independence army with Indian POWs in Malaya as a nucleus. He also suggested calling a meeting of representatives of various independence organizations from all over Asia to organize a powerful political arm of the movement. This was apparently the origin of the telegram Fujiwara received from Tokyo inviting Indian representatives to a conference.[16]

V THE SANNO CONFERENCE

On 28 March the meetings began at the Sanno Hotel in an atmosphere of sorrow for the four martyred compatriots lost in the plane crash. On the first day Fujiwara and Iwakuro were invited to attend. Bose was chosen chairman of the meeting. Fujiwara thought it strange that Sahay and Pratap were not present. He apparently had no inkling of the nature of relations between authorities in Tokyo and Sahay and Pratap.[17]

Conference delegates determined that the Indian Independence League be recognized as the organization of all Indians in East Asia for achievement of Indian independence. Bose was recognized as head of the organization. It was further agreed that a meeting be held in Bangkok in mid-May of representatives of all IIL branches in East Asia. This meeting would consider the policy of the independence movement.

It was also resolved at the meeting in Tokyo that "military action against the British in India will be taken only by the INA and under Indian command, together with such military, naval and air cooperation and assistance as may be requested from the Japanese by the Council of Action" (which was the steering committee of the League), and further, "after the liberation of India, the framing of the future constitution of India will be left entirely to the representatives of the people of India."[18]

After the conclusion of the conference, some delegates from Malaya met with Premier Tōjō at the War Ministry. Tōjō gave the Indians assurances that the Japanese Government would assist the Indian independence movement. However brief the interview, "we returned quite satisfied with his lavish verbal promises of help", noted Mohan Singh.[19] N.S. Gill, however, was not quite as satisfied, and was left with the feeling that Tōjō's promises were perfunctory.[20]

The delegates felt the meeting in Tokyo had in general succeeded. There was a mood of elation over the determination to fight for Indian freedom and over the promises of help from the Japanese. Only the doubts about Japanese sincerity expressed by Gill, Pratap, and Sahay generated some suspicion in the minds of some delegates. And the feeling of tension between the Tokyo group and the representatives from Southeast Asia was never fully allayed, even after the Tokyo meetings.

One outcome of the hostility between the Tokyo leadership and the Southeast Asia group was the creation of the Council of Action as the steering committee of the IIL. This would have the advantage of reducing dissatisfaction with the leadership of one man. The responpse of the Indians from the south to Rash Behari Bose was from the beginning ambivalent. Mohan Singh put it this way:

> To us he appeared to be quite a weak person and we thought that the reigns [sic] of this movement should not be allowed to be entrusted to a single individual like him. We proposed that a Council of Action consisting of five members should be elected in a bigger conference to be held in Malaya ... and the Council of Action should take the joint responsibility of running this movement. It appeared to us that Shri Rash Behari Bose and his colleagues from Japan were not absolutely free in their actions.[21]

The main achievements of the Tokyo conference from the Indian standpoint were the affirmation of determination to fight for independence, the decision to hold an all-Asia meeting in Southeast Asia within two months, and the meeting of leaders of the Indian movement with Tōjō. The movement now had direct assurances from the Japanese Government of help in the struggle for independence.

The value of the conference from the standpoint of the Japanese Government was something quite different.

VI THE CULTURAL NEXUS

The history of Indo-Japanese relations was more a matter of ancient religious ties than of modern cultural exchange. Japan first attracted

Indian attention in modern times with the electrifying news of Japan's victory over Russian military might in the Russo-Japanese War of 1905. India was at the time under the unpopular administration of Viceroy Lord Curzon, a self-confident imperialist and the last of a type in India. It was only twenty years earlier that Indian nationalism had at last found political expression in the creation of the Indian National Congress. Indians were new at the game of politics British-style, but anti-colonial sentiments were an old story in India. Curzon had refused to recognize the strength of Indian nationalism and made two blunders that directly antagonized the articulate Bengalis. In 1904 he pushed through the Indian Universities Act which provided greater centralized control over colleges and universities. Bengali nationalists read this act as an attempt to keep them quiet. He followed this miscalculation with another, the partition of Bengal in 1905 into the Hindu West and Muslim East. This partition which so closely followed religious lines was interpreted as a divide-and-rule stratagem, and alienated Hindu and Muslim alike. Nationalists responded immediately by turning to acts of violence and boycotting British goods. Curzon's measures strengthened the radical wing of Congress and worried the moderates. It was four years before Congress sentiment swung back toward a more conciliatory and moderate attitude.

At the height of this anti-colonial mood in India came the startling news of the victory of Japan, a small Asian country, over the might of a Western power. The effect was instantaneous, not only in India but in all Asian nations under Western colonial régimes. The Japanese victory was a vindication of the prestige and honour of all Asian nations. It was the first time an Asian nation had successfully defied a Western power. Japan became suddenly a model of success for the aspirations of all Asia. Indians shared vicariously in the Japanese mood of elation. If Japan could succeed against the invincible colossus of Russia, there was hope for the subjugated people of India, and Indian patriots could take heart. Indian sympathy and sense of identification with Japan were reflected in the collection of funds in Bombay and Calcutta to aid wounded soldiers and Japanese widows and orphans. Enthusiastic literary paeans appeared in the Indian Press, recounting the exploits of the Japanese Army and Navy. The sacrifice and devotion to duty of the heroic Admiral Togo and General Nogi were hailed throughout India. Even Englishmen in India felt the Japanese victory had helped to transform Indian nationalism into a movement of revolutionary dimensions and ardour.[22]

It was not only nationalist and anti-colonial sentiment that had been stimulated. Japan's example engendered a strengthened sense of Asian unity and brotherhood, a consciousness of being Asian as opposed to being Western. Asian spirituality was a major ingredient of the new Indian Pan-Asianism. But Asia could now confront the West with more than traditional spiritual superiority. Japan had given proof that Asia was no longer helpless in the hands of European powers. Asian revolutionaries began to look to Japan as a source of inspiration. Political exiles sought sanctuary in Tokyo and were given help and protection by leaders of the patriotic societies in Japan and encouragement by government leaders. A pan-Asian political and cultural exchange was born of Japan's achievement. Tokyo became the Mecca for many Asian revolutionaries: Lala Lajpat Rai, Rash Behari Bose, Aguinaldo, Sun Yat-sen, and Kim Ok-kiun, among others. In Tokyo they met a warm welcome from double patriots like Tōyama Mitsuru and Uchida Ryōhei. The exiles received food, lodging and encouragement to continue their activities. In some cases they got financial support.

VII TAGORE IN JAPAN

Indian Pan-Asianism also had a cultural dimension, apart from revolutionary overtones. The Indian exponent of Asian cultural unity and idealism was Rabindranath Tagore, who visited East Asia and strengthened the sense of cultural identity. Tagore was eloquent in praise of Japan's achievement and its impact on the rest of Asia. He said:

> It was said of Asia that it could never move in the path of progress, its face was so inevitably turned backwards.... When things stood still like this, and we in Asia hypnotized ourselves into the belief ... that it could never by any possibility be otherwise, Japan rose from her dreams, and in giant strides left centuries of inaction behind.... One morning the whole world looked up in surprise when Japan broke through her walls of old habits in a night and came out triumphant. It was done in such an incredibly short time that it seemed like a change of dress and not like the building up of a new structure. She showed the confident strength of maturity, and the freshness and infinite potentiality of new life at the same moment. The fear was entertained that it was a mere freak of history, a child's game of Time, the blowing up of a soap bubble, perfect in its rondure and colouring, hollow in its heart and without substance. But Japan has proved conclusively that this sudden revealment of her power is not a short-lived wonder, a chance product of time and tide, thrown up from

the depth of obscurity to be swept away the next moment into the sea of oblivion. In a word, modern Japan has come out of the immemorial East like a lotus blossoming in easy grace, all the while keeping its firm hold upon the profound depth from which it has sprung.[23]

While he recognized Japan's achievement, Tagore still retained the great Indian dream of Asian spirituality and its ultimate superiority over Western material power. He prophesied the day when confrontation would make this apparent to all the world:

> The East with her ideals, in whose bosom are stored the ages of sunlight and silence of stars, can patiently wait till the West, hurrying after the expedient, loses breath and stops.... Therefore I ask you to have the strength of faith and clarity of mind to know for certain that the lumbering structure of modern progress, riveted by the iron bolts of efficiency, which runs upon the wheels of ambition, cannot hold together for long.... A day will come when it will fall in a heap of ruin and cause serious obstruction to the traffic of the world. Do we not see signs of this even now?[24]

Tagore opened his Calcutta home to Japanese and other Asian priests, poets, artists, and others interested in Asian culture. There was a fruitful cross-fertilization of ideas and inspiration. One Japanese visitor to Tagore's home was Okakura Tenshin (or Kakuzō), who published his famous *Book of Tea* in 1902, two years after his visit to India.[25] Another of Tagore's Japanese visitors was the poet Noguchi Yonejirō, who after his visit to India corresponded with Tagore. When Japan began to expand into China militarily while expounding the doctrine of Asia for the Asiatics, Tagore took Noguchi to task for his attempts to justify Japan's actions in China:

> You are building your conception of an Asia which would be raised on a tower of skulls. I have, as you rightly point out, believed in the message of Asia, but I never dreamt that this message could be identified with deeds which brought exaltation to the heart of Tamerlane at his terrible efficiency in manslaughter. ... I should have expected from you, who are a poet, at least that much of imagination to feel to what inhuman despair a people might be reduced to willingly burn their own handiwork of years....[26]

Japan's post-1937 interpretation of Pan-Asianism was unacceptable to Tagore, who expected his Japanese friends to share his repugnance at Japan's advance into China.

Earlier still, when Tagore visited Japan in May-June 1916, he felt Japan should be cautioned for adopting from Western civilization not its humane values but its lust for power and worship of the nation-state. In an address before an academic audience Tagore warned:

> True modernism is freedom of mind, not slavery of taste. It is independence of thought and action, not tutelage under European schoolmasters. It is science, but not its wrong application in life.... I do not for a moment suggest that Japan should be unmindful of acquiring modern weapons for self-protection. But this should never be allowed to go beyond her instinct for self-

preservation. She must know that the real power is not in the weapons themselves, but in the man who wields those weapons.... Japan must have a firm faith in the moral law of existence to be able to assert to herself, that the Western nations are following that path of suicide, where they are smothering their humanity under the unwise weight of organisations in order to keep themselves in power and hold others in subjugation. Therefore I cannot think that the imitation of the outward aspects of the West, which is becoming more and more evident in modern Japan, is essential to her strength or stability. It is burdening her true nature and causing weakness, which will be felt more deeply as time goes on.... What is still more dangerous for Japan is not this imitation of the outer features of the West, but the acceptance of the motive force of the Western civilization as her own.[27]

Tagore's words met a mixed response in Japan. While he had been welcomed as one from the land of the Buddha, there were some who felt his preaching to a free nation on the subject of freedom and modernism was gratuitous, coming from a man whose nation was neither free nor modern. But Tagore's many friends and admirers among the intellectuals respected him for his courage in saying what he did.

While Japan's military success over Russia stimulated Indian and Asian nationalism and anti-colonialism, academically India took virtually no cognizance of Japan, even following 1905. It was in Tagore's own school, Santiniketan, that Japanese and Chinese languages were first taught as academic subjects. India remained academically involved, first with India's own heritage, and secondly with Western Europe and particularly with England. There was not much academic energy to spare for the rest of Asia.

Prior to World War II Japan viewed India as the home of great spiritual traditions but also as a nation suffering under British colonial rule. India was the incubator of Hinduism, of the historial Buddha, and of the modern saint of nationalism, Gandhi. As birthplace of the Buddha and source of inspiration for centuries of artistic, literary and philosophical expression, India attracted (and still attracts) devout Japanese Buddhists on pilgrimage to the sacred places where the Buddha became enlightened and preached his first sermon.

VIII   JAPAN LOOKS TO INDIA

Asia's common spiritual heritage was recognized by Japanese counterparts of Rabindranath Tagore. Okakura Kakuzō in his book *The Ideals of the East* discussed the artistic expression of Asian spiritual ideals in Japanese art. Okakura traced the spiritual inspiration for Japanese art to India, though in methods and technique he felt Japanese art owed a debt to China. But the great epochs in Japanese art he attributed to waves of Indian spiritual influence. For Okakura it was this great spiritual heritage which made Asia distinctively Asian. As Okakura put it, "The task of Asia today, then, becomes that of protecting and restoring Asiatic modes. But to do this she must herself first recognize and develop consciousness of those modes."[28] Okakura travelled in Europe as an official of the Education Ministry in 1883. He was founder of the Japan Fine Arts Institute and for a time curator of Oriental Art for the Boston Museum. He later lectured on art history at Tokyo University.[29]

Another influential Japanese who looked to India as the source of Asian spiritual ideals was Ōkawa Shūmei, ultra-nationalist, politician, and philosopher. He studied Indian philosophy at Tokyo University and later published many articles and volumes in which he discussed Indian spiritual traditions and the growth of an Asian consciousness. Indian spiritual development and systems of logic and epistemology he felt gave India a unique position in world history.[30]

Out of these philosophic foundations grew a colourful career. On graduation from Tokyo University in 1911 Ōkawa was appointed director of the Research Bureau of the South Manchuria Railway Company, the arm which Japan thrust into Manchuria economically and later militarily. As his thinking became increasingly militant he founded the *Yūzonsha* (literally, Society of the Remaining) and the *Jimmukai* (a later successor of the *Yūzonsha*, taking its name from the legendary Emperor Jimmu), both ultra-nationalist political groups.[31] Through the *Yūzonsha* Ōkawa advocated national reconstruction along military lines in Japan and a messianic programme abroad. The foreign policy statement of the *Yūzonsha* in 1920 read:

> The Japanese people must become a vortex of a whirlwind which will liberate mankind. The Japanese nation is destined to revolutionize the world. The fulfilment of this ideal and the military reorganization of Japan are the work of the gods. We believe that our duty will not end with revolution and reformation of Japan alone, but we must be content to begin with the reform of our own nation because we have faith in the Japanese mission to free the universe.[32]

Out of these convictions Ōkawa became involved in the abortive March Affair (1931), the object of which was the establishment of a military régime, and he later plotted with young army and navy officers for the assassination of Premier Inukai Tsuyoshi in May 1932. Because of his implication in the assassination he was arrested and detained, but was later released in 1935. During the Mukden Incident of 1931 Ōkawa gave more than a hundred lectures throughout the country and worked for unification of patriotic groups.[33] After the war he was tried as a class A war criminal by the International Military Tribunal for the Far East. While on trial he became insane and his case was dropped.

Ōkawa's career and beliefs clearly emphasize the close connection between Pan-Asianism, ultra-nationalism, militarism, and expansionism. This was also apparent in Tōyama, though Tōyama was without Ōkawa's philosophic sophistication. The patriotic societies championed Japan's annexation of Korea in 1910 and later military expansion in Manchuria, as well as the cause of Asian revolutionaries against Western imperialism. Ōkawa's early respect for India's spiritual legacy to Asia thus took him on a circuitous course through schemes for Japan's revolutionary mission abroad and direct action at home aimed at destroying parliamentary institutions and creating a military state.

Tōyama, unlike Ōkawa, left no written evidence of his views. He was a man who worked entirely behind the scenes, the archetype of the *kuromaku* politician working through cloak-and-dagger methods. His place among the professional patriots was unique. Tōyama had connections with many strata of Japanese society. Though he eschewed public office and never made a public speech, he was entertained by prime ministers (he reportedly warned Inukai not to accept the premiership in 1931 since Tōyama could not guarantee to keep his followers in line), sought after by coal-mine owners, and followed with unquestioning loyalty by gangs of *sōshi,* the modern counterparts of the feudal masterless *samurai,* or *rōnin.* His charisma lay in his personification of the traditional personality ideal. His impeccable honesty, discipline, loyalty to nation, and Robin Hood activities made him a sharp contrast to the stereotype of the corrupt politician and venal capitalist of the twenties. He was adored by the common man, whether peasant or soldier.

Prior to the Pacific War India attracted little notice in Japan except among philosophers and super-patriots. Economically India did not have much to recommend it to Japan. Japan imported some Indian cotton, but there was little basis for bilateral trade of great volume.

Academically, modern India was a cipher in Japanese universities before World War II, just as India took no academic notice of Japan. Those who studied India were Buddhologists, Sanskrit scholars and philosophers or Indologists. Their perspectives were ancient, with little relation to contemporary developments in India. As an aspect of British colonial history there was some research on India by Professor Yanaihara Tadao of Tokyo Imperial University. Passing attention was also given to India in an article by Hani Gorō on the development of capitalism in Asia. During the Pacific War the Indian freedom movement was the subject of a study by political historian Katō Nagao. It was only after the war that works on Indian nationalism, the Indian Congress, Tagore, Gandhi and Nehru began to appear in Japanese. Translators for the Government and Army were trained in Hindustani and Urdu after 1911 at the Tokyo School of Foreign Languages, a government university.[34]

CHAPTER FIVE

Japanese Policy toward India

I POLICY-MAKERS IN TOKYO

JAPAN'S wartime aims in India were never as clearly defined as her aims in Southeast Asia. India was not embraced in the grand design for the Greater East Asia Co-Prosperity Sphere first conceived in 1940. Greater East Asia would sweep through Southeast Asia westward to the Indo-Burmese border. Everywhere in Asia Western colonial rule would be driven out and independence movements encouraged. Asia for Asians became the goal and shibboleth. The Greater East Asia Co-Prosperity Sphere would constitute an economically self-sufficient entity under Japanese tutelage. Both diplomatic and military means would be employed to realize the blueprint. But Japanese military administration would respect existing local organizations and customs.[1] By late 1941 control of resources necessary for the war effort became a focal point of the plan.

Still, India bordered the western perimeter of the Greater East Asia Co-Prosperity Sphere. And Japan was at war with the colonial power occupying India; Britain must be expelled from India. As Japan wished to see Britain purged from Asia so also Indian nationalists aspired to free India. Japan had to reckon with India for the mutual advantage of both Japan and India.

What agencies or individuals in Tokyo would do the reckoning? The Foreign Ministry was one obvious possibility. Japan had no ambassador in India under Britain, but there were consuls in the major Indian cities. In April 1941, Consul-General Okazaki in Calcutta, in a secret communiqué to Foreign Minister Matsuoka, described the independence movement of the Forward Bloc, a radical party in Bengal. Okazaki suggested establishing contact with this left-wing party in India and also with its leader, Subhas Chandra Bose, then in exile in Berlin. Going even further, he suggested, "We should secretly transport large quantities of weapons and substantially increase the actual strength of the Forward Bloc."[2] While Okazaki felt the movement would burgeon into a genuinely popular revolt, he felt Japan should do her part by establishing contact with Bose and aiding his party. This early Japanese notice of Bose preceded by several months Major Fujiwara's remarks about Bose to the 8th Section, Second Bureau, IGHQ.

From Ambassador General Ōshima Hiroshi in Berlin also came communiqués regarding the Indian revolutionary Bose and his desire to go to East Asia. In January 1941 Bose had already begun to visit Ambassador Ōshima and military attaché Yamamoto Bin in Berlin with plans for military co-operation with Japan against Britain in Asia. The *Gaimushō* (Foreign Ministry) then learned of the presence of Bose in Berlin and of his political significance from sources both in India and in Germany. The Foreign Ministry, however, refrained from any positive proposal regarding India or Bose during 1941. And when war erupted, the initiative obviously lay with the military rather than the *Gaimushō*.

From within the Cabinet Prime Minister Tōjō made several declarations of policy toward India in early 1942. These pronouncements were articulated in speeches before the Diet. They represented official policy aims toward India. The statements were made during the four-month interval from January to April, and the timing of the pronouncements suggested that by late March or early April the fundamental lines of Japan's India policy had already been drawn.[3] The policy aims had yet to be implemented, and measures were later adopted to implement some of the goals. Announcements made by Tōjō during 1943 and 1944 were designed to realize earlier decisions.

Major policy decisions on India also emanated from Liaison Conferences and Imperial Conferences. Liaison Conferences included important members of both the Cabinet and military high command, including the Prime Minister, Foreign Minister, and Army and Navy chiefs of staff and vice-chiefs of staff. The Liaison Conferences were inaugurated by imperial order in late 1937 to provide liaison between the Cabinet and military on crucial policy questions. For a time Conferences lapsed, but they were resumed in November

1940 and continued until 1944.⁴ A major decision reached at a Liaison Conference was not final until ratified at an Imperial Conference, that is, the Liaison Conference plus the Emperor and President of the Privy Council. This imperial ratification in effect made a decision irrevocable.

Still another government agency directly under the Prime Minister's office was involved in Japanese policy in Asia. This was the Total War Research Institute, created in 1940 to do research on total warfare and to train officials for it. This agency was the brainchild of two officers, Colonel (later Lieutenant-General) Tatsumi Eiichi, section chief in the European and American Section, IGHQ, and Lieutenant-General Iemura Minoru, chief of staff of the Kwantung Army in Manchuria. General Iemura was appointed director of the Institute in January 1941 and remained in that post until October of the same year. Colonel Tatsumi, former military attaché in London, envisaged an agency on the same pattern as the Royal National War Institute in England. Topics for study by the Institute were selected at the discretion of General Iemura, though the choice reflected the concerns of the military which he represented. Iemura reported directly to the Prime Minister, at that time Konoe. During August 1941 (following discussion by the Army and Navy), the Institute held a map manoeuvre on the problem of what would happen should Japan advance in the south in search of oil. The study postulated Soviet entry into the war; the conclusion was that Japan's material strength would be deficient, and the Cabinet and Planning Board would be impelled to resign. Bureau chiefs of several cabinet ministries participated, and many top-ranking military officers observed the manoeuvre, including War Minister General Tōjō.⁵ The Institute autonomously devised plans for the independence of Asian nations from Western colonial rule and their incorporation into the Greater East Asia Co-Prosperity Sphere. Policies recommended by the Institute were later implemented by military administration in Southeast Asia, though testimony at the Tokyo War Crimes Tribunal maintained the military had no special interest in the Institute.⁶ There was, however, no separate focus on India in the studies and manoeuvres of the Total War Research Institute during 1941.

Besides these agencies the military high command of course had a direct concern with India policy during the Pacific War. Army Chief of General Staff Sugiyama Gen took a special interest in India, derived from his service in India as military attaché. Sugiyama, like

Tōjō and Shigemitsu, developed a special sympathy for Subhas Chandra Bose. Under the Second Bureau (Intelligence) of IGHQ, headed by Major-General Okamoto (later in the war by Lieutenant-General Arisue), was the 8th Section, whose purview included India. From among staff officers in the 8th Section Major Fujiwara had been selected to establish liaison with and encourage the Indian independence movement in Southeast Asia. Fujiwara had been dismayed at the lack of information on India available in IGHQ at the time of his assignment in October 1941. Within the 8th Section Major Ozeki was assigned to deal with the *Fujiwara Kikan* and its successor organizations, the *Iwakuro Kikan* and *Hikari Kikan,* in the field. 8th Section chiefs, for example Colonel Nagai Yatsuji, were at times called on to deal with the Indian National Army or with Bose. Civilian specialists on India, few though they were, were also consulted by the 8th Section during the war.

These were the major official sources from which policy decisions on India emanated during the war. There were others who influenced India policy in a private capacity. These included Tōyama Mitsuru and other patriotic society members, and their military counterparts such as Ishiwara Kanji and Hashimoto Kingorō. These officers advocated Pan-Asianism of a somewhat different version from Tōyama's. Tōyama, in particular, went beyond the ideology of Pan-Asianism to actively protect revolutionaries from all parts of Asia.

Another constant factor affecting Japan's India policy was the traditional orientation of Japanese Army ideology. The Army traditionally looked northward, toward Soviet Russia and north China, rather than southward. The north was the major legitimate concern of the Army, the direction from which Japan had to be on guard. Assignment of the best officers in the thirties to Manchuria and north China, especially to the Kwantung Army, reflected this orientation. This was true through most of 1941. "In Manchuria there were many superior officers, but in the South Fujiwara was a single player," observed Ishikawa Yoshiaki, interpreter for the *Kikan* throughout the war.[7]

II ISSUES AND POLICIES

The first hypothesis to emerge regarding Japanese policy toward India is that Japan at no time planned a major invasion of India or the incorporation of India into the Greater East Asia Co-Prosperity Sphere (contrary to the suspicions of Indians in the independence movement). There did emerge, however, several indications of more limited concern with India in late 1941 and early 1942. Decisions reached in Liaison Conferences and Prime Minister Tōjō's speeches revealed this concern.

On 15 November 1941, an Imperial Conference decision, the "Plan for Acceleration of the End of the War with America", called among other things for 1) separation of Australia and India from Britain, and 2) stimulation of the Indian independence movement.[8]

One problem concerning policy toward India was the calculation of the *Gaimushō* that the Indian National Congress was anti-Japanese. A corollary of this was the postulate that, even if the Indian independence movement should succeed, it would be difficult for Indian revolutionaries to establish a stable orderly state. Nor would it be possible for Japan to control a nation of four hundred million in addition to her other commitments in Southeast Asia.[9] On the other hand, it lay within the realm of feasibility for Japan to launch a vast propaganda effort to encourage Indian disaffection to Britain. Accordingly, a Liaison Conference decision reached on 10 January called for 1) intercepting India's sea communications, and 2) stimulating anti-British sentiment within India.[10]

Tōjō declared in the Diet early in 1942, "Without the liberation of India there can be no real mutual prosperity in Greater East Asia," and further, in April, "It has been decided to strike a decisive blow against British power and military establishment in India."[11] This was a general policy statement rather than a directive to the Operations Bureau of IGHQ; Tōjō gave no suggestion of its tactical or even strategic implementation. Tōjō mentioned India in Diet speeches on 17 January, 12 February, 14 February, 11-12 March and 4 April. Repeatedly he called on Indians to take advantage of the war to rise against British power and establish an India for Indians. Tōjō also stated he hoped India would co-operate in the "establishment of the Greater East Asia Co-Prosperity Sphere". This too was a general pronouncement not alluded to again, either generally or in further explication.

There was no plan for an invasion of India in 1941. At several points it was conceivable that a Japanese invasion of India might have succeeded had it been planned. The best time would have been in the spring and summer of 1942, following Japanese successes in

Malaya and Burma, when Japanese air, sea and land power could not have been checked by the British. But Japan passed up the opportunity. Japan made no concerted attempt to establish a base in Ceylon or Calcutta, though Ceylon had been mentioned in Tokyo as a desirable base. Two years later, when Japan mounted a military offensive into the borders of India, it was with the limited objective of "securing strategic areas near Imphal and in north-east India for the defence of Burma".[12] An auxiliary objective was to disrupt the air routes between Chungking and India. This was clearly not envisioned as a full-scale invasion of India. India remained a peripheral interest for Japan in terms of 1) the Greater East Asia Co-Prosperity Sphere and 2) the major action of the war. Nevertheless, the attention of Tokyo had been drawn to India at the close of 1941 at the time of the outbreak of the war. One of the reasons Tōjō took notice was the policy recommendation of the young Major Fujiwara, who had been sent to Bangkok on an intelligence mission late in 1941.

Another major aspect of Japanese policy, this toward the INA, was that Japan desired to use and support the INA chiefly for propaganda purposes, particularly to foster anti-British sentiment. All major Japanese policy decisions regarding the INA pointed toward this goal. Beginning with the Fujiwara mission in 1941 (and a brief assignment for Fujiwara in late 1940), and continuing with the expanded propaganda functions of the *Kikan* under Colonel Iwakuro, the major Japanese thrust was to encourage the proliferation of Indian intelligence activities throughout Southeast Asia. Under Fujiwara and still more under Iwakuro, training centres and liaison facilities were developed to expand propaganda and sabotage missions behind enemy lines.

Yet another aspect of Japanese policy was a corollary to the above, namely: even during the Imphal campaign and the actions in Burma, the Japanese Army was reluctant to see the INA evolve into a large fighting force, partly because of the problems of equipping such an army, partly out of questions about possible actions of such an army once the Indian border was crossed, and partly because of doubts about whether an Indian army would constitute a military asset to Japan. During the Imphal campaign Japan conceived of the INA as a series of guerrilla fighting units and special forces which would perform intelligence functions. Shah Nawaz Khan alleges that General Terauchi, commander of the Southern Army, told Bose unequivocally that Japan did not want large formations of the INA at the front. Shah Nawaz was particularly sceptical of Japan's motives, and charged not only Japanese inability to supply arms and provisions during the Burma campaign, but also reluctance.[13]

Support for the hypothesis that Japan was primarily interested in using the INA for propaganda purposes is found in several steps taken by Japan. These include the Japanese recognition of the Free India Provisional Government, the transfer of the Andaman and Nicobar Islands to the FIPG, and the sending of a diplomatic representative to the FIPG. In all these measures Japan conceded the form but not the substance of Bose's demands. These steps were designed to create the impression abroad, and with Bose, that Japan was dealing with a large, independent government and army.

Another problem which beset Japan's India policy throughout the war was a time disjunction between three factors: 1) military intelligence in the field and its evaluation and response in Tokyo, 2) policy planning by IGHQ, and 3) tactical implementation of policy at the operational level. Part of the delay was attributable to normal processing of proposals and policies through a bureaucratic establishment, even during wartime. For example, the decision to invite Bose from Berlin to Tokyo to evaluate his utility from the standpoint of Japanese policy was reached on 17 April 1942, jointly by the War, Navy and Foreign Ministries.[14] Bose did not actually reach Tokyo until the end of May 1943. Apart from normal bureaucratic delays, part of the time lag was occasioned by the German Foreign Ministry's reluctance to release a potentially valuable bargaining instrument in dealing with the British. Part of the delay was also caused by the presence in Tokyo of another Indian revolutionary, Rash Behari Bose, who many felt was the logical leader to work through.

Another case in point was the planning of the offensive into north-east India and its execution. In the fall of 1942, and even earlier, Tōjō and IGHQ contemplated a military thrust into north-east India, Operation 21 as it was then called. But in 1942-3 there were too many obstacles to the idea—inadequate supply lines, British deterrent strength in the Akyab sector through early 1943, a shortage of trained Indian troops for a joint campaign, not to mention events in the Pacific. Consequently the plan for an India offensive was postponed to early 1944. In 1944, however, despite the rationale for the campaign, the above obstacles were even more acute and it was not possible for Japan to succeed.

Regarding this disjunction of time factors, it may be noted that

Indian Independence League members at the Sanno Conference in Tokyo, April 1942—Fujiwara and Mohan Singh shaking hands, Goho in the centre and N. Raghavan on the right.

From left to right: N.S. Gill, Mohan Singh, and M. Akram

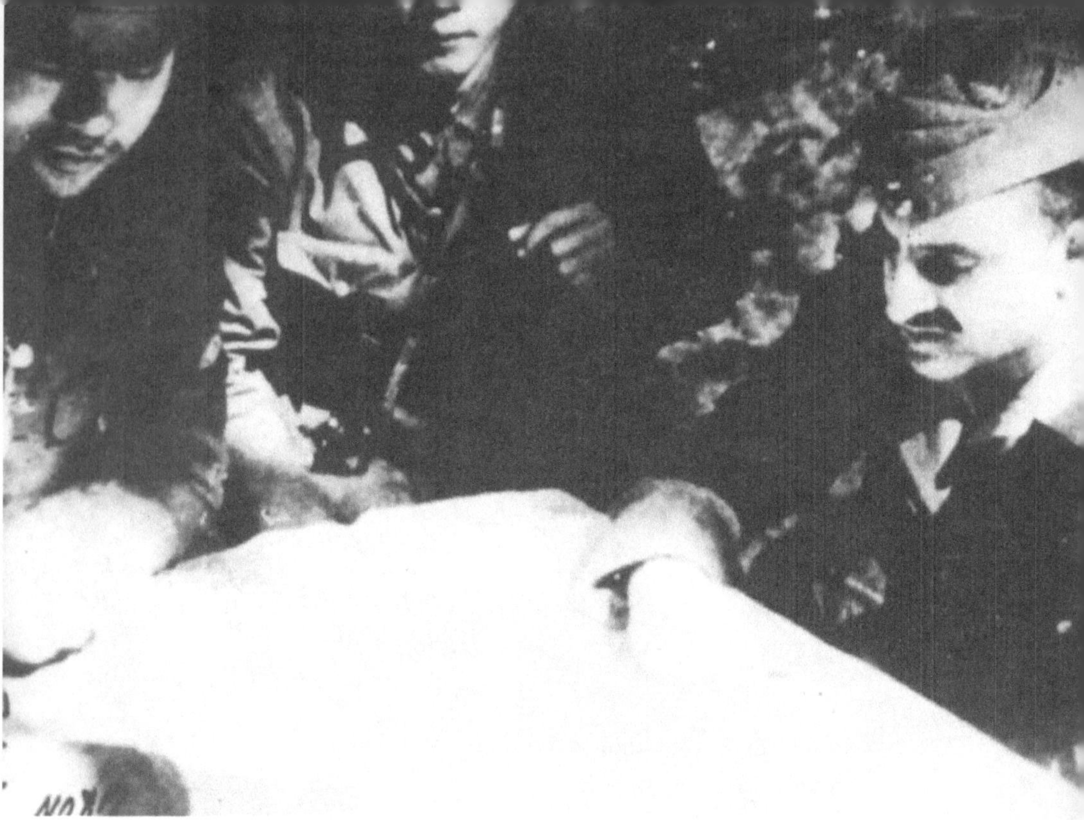

Above: Shah Nawaz Khan and Staff Officer Okamoto discuss strategy during Imphal campaign.

Right: Kawabe Masakazu

Bose's role in the timing of most aspects of the Japan-INA cooperation was minimal. The timing of his arrival in East Asia was not of his own choice. For over a year before he arrived in Asia he had been pressing the Japanese ambassador and military attaché in Berlin to arrange his transportation to East Asia. Bose was similarly unhappy about the timing of the Imphal campaign, but again his expressions of urgency carried little weight in Tokyo. Bose would have had Japan push across the border soon after his arrival in the summer of 1943. But because of the above reasons and because India remained for Japan a peripheral concern in the deployment of her resources for a total war, other considerations overrode the logic of not postponing the campaign. In other respects, however, Bose did make an impact on Tokyo, particularly with Tōjō, Foreign Minister Shigemitsu, and Chief of General Staff Sugiyama.

To summarize, then, Japan had several objectives in cooperating with the INA: to encourage anti-British sentiment in Southeast Asia, within the British-Indian Army and within India; to develop an intelligence network to implement this aim; to defend Burma and the western border of the Greater East Asia Co-Prosperity Sphere, and to support and assist the FIPG and INA, within certain limitations, to achieve these aims. These were both political and military objectives. There was a distinction made between the political aims, which fell within the purview of the Second Bureau, Intelligence, and the military issues, which fell within the scope of the First Bureau, Operations, in IGHQ. The First Bureau was the more powerful of the two.

III   POLICY IMPLEMENTATION AND TRANSFORMATION IN THE FIELD; COLONEL IWAKURO

From the agencies of Headquarters in Tokyo directives to implement these general policies filtered down through channels to the agencies which implemented them in the field. Once the war began, orders were passed through the Headquarters of the Southern Army, then through the 25th Army staff, before they reached the *F Kikan*. During 1944 the 25th Army was replaced by 15th Army Headquarters as the military channel through which the *Kikan* had to pass. Fujiwara felt the channels were cumbersome and bureaucratic, often diluting the urgency of his proposals regarding India. Further, he felt impatient with the lack of concern for India in Tokyo in late 1941. But Fujiwara's instructions were broad and general, leaving him much room to use his own initiative. He did, proving his resourcefulness, efficiency and vision. Only as Fujiwara's proposals were discussed in Tokyo did the limits of Japan's India policy begin to emerge. Fujiwara seized every opportunity to present his case to officers from IGHQ or, better yet, in Tokyo in person. He was gratified when his proposals to expand the whole India project were accepted in Tokyo, even though this meant the end of his own assignment and his replacement by the enlarged operation under Colonel Iwakuro, the *Iwakuro Kikan*.

Reorganization of the *Kikan* under Iwakuro under command of Southern Army Headquarters occurred soon after he arrived in Saigon in late March, following the Sanno Conference. In May Headquarters moved to Bangkok, and branches were then operating in Rangoon, Saigon, Singapore, Penang, and Hong Kong. Under the reorganized *Kikan* were some two hundred and fifty members, a far cry from the handful of men with which Fujiwara began the operation five months earlier. A few months later the number of members had risen to five hundred. Fujiwara took this as a hopeful sign that IGHQ was paying more attention to his proposals for the India project. There were six departments in the *Iwakuro Kikan:* 1) the Administrative Section under Lieutenant-Colonel Maki Tatsuo; 2) the Political Section—most important of all—under Diet member Takaoka Taisuke, who was known as an India specialist, and including several interpreters, whose business was liaison with the IIL; 3) the Intelligence Section, like the Administrative Section under Maki Tatsuo, whose task was to co-ordinate all intelligence regarding India; 4) the Special Mission Section under another Diet member, Koyama Ryo, whose responsibility it was to send agents into India by submarine and parachute; 5) the Military Section under Major Ōgawa Saburō, who was in charge of Indian POWs, liaison with the INA, creation of intelligence units and special mission units which would infiltrate behind enemy lines; and 6) the Propaganda Section under Colonel Saitō Jirō, who was to take charge of the distribution of propaganda leaflets and of radio broadcasts from Singapore, Saigon, and Rangoon.[15]

Iwakuro was clearly emphasizing the political and intelligence functions of the *Kikan* rather than solely the military function. He had under him an imposing array of men, military and civilian leaders alike. Iwakuro's experience had been in intelligence and special mission projects. He had founded the Army Intelligence School, the *Rikugun Nakano Gakkō*. But his work in Southeast Asia was not easy, despite the legacy of goodwill among Indian patriots left by Fujiwara. There were several knotty problems confronting Iwakuro almost as soon as he arrived in Singapore.

He tried to create an initial impression of goodwill by meeting with Indian leaders in every city where there was a *Kikan* branch. On 21 May he met with IIL representatives in Singapore and assured them that the Japanese Government had recognized the IIL as the only political organization of Indians in Malaya. The same evening he entertained IIL representatives and certain officers of the INA at the Raffles Hotel and again sought to reassure them that he would continue Fujiwara's policy of cooperation. He reiterated Japan's desire to see a free and independent India and disavowed any Japanese territorial or political designs on India. He referred to Japan's determination to give any assistance or cooperation necessary to free India from the yoke of British imperialism. He alluded to the century-old cultural bond between Japan and India and to Japan's cultural debt to India. Japan would spare no effort to help in the liberation of four hundred million Indians. In other Southeast Asian cities too he reiterated these assurances.[16]

One problem affecting *Iwakuro Kikan* relations with the Indian independence movement was the problem of Burmese independence. Operations of the *Kikan* in Burma had begun at the time of the Singapore campaign when Captain Tsuchimochi was ordered back from Johore Bahru through Thailand to Rangoon. He took with him an INA unit under Second Lieutenant Ram Swarup and Ishikawa Yoshiaki as interpreter. Tsuchimochi encouraged the organization of the IIL and expansion of the INA unit in Rangoon.[17] In early July Lieutenant-Colonel Kitabe Kunio was ordered to Burma to take over from Tsuchimochi. Kitabe spread the network of the *Kikan* north from Rangoon through the whole of Burma.

Part of Japan's initial ideological appeal in Southeast Asia was the slogan "Asia for Asiatics" and the assurance that Japan would liberate Southeast Asian nations from Western imperialist rule. Burma, however, was still chafing under Japanese military administration, despite early promises of independence. Aung San and other Burmese leaders were becoming impatient. How could a Rangoon branch of the *Iwakuro Kikan* promise to help the Indian independence movement when Burma had not yet been made independent? Kitabe visited 15th Army Headquarters and asked Commander Lieutenant-General Iida to declare Burma independent as soon as possible. General Iida pointed out that this was a problem not for the 15th Army but for the Southern Army under whose command the 15th Army operated. After receiving this report from Kitabe, Iwakuro himself visited Southern Army Headquarters and asked staff officer Colonel Ishii to see what he could do about accelerating Burmese independence. Ishii was concerned with the timing of Burmese independence and its possible implications for India. But he opposed early independence. At the same time he assured Iwakuro of material support for the INA. Not until August 1943 did Burma gain independence. This followed closely the arrival of Subhas Chandra Bose in Southeast Asia and the consequent need for a redefinition of Japanese policy. In the interim this problem continued to plague Iwakuro and his relations with IIL-INA.[18]

Another problem for Iwakuro was the matter of Rash Behari Bose's leadership. This had created difficulties in IIL-INA liaison and in relations between the Tokyo Indians and those in Southeast Asia ever since the Sanno Conference. Fujiwara had not been able to resolve it, and Iwakuro was equally helpless. The feeling that Bose was a Japanese puppet and would do nothing to oppose Japanese wishes grew among Indians in Malaya. INA commander Mohan Singh grew increasingly impatient with Bose's role as go-between and representative of Indian aims *vis-à-vis* the *Iwakuro Kikan*. This animosity was to fester until it caused a rupture at the end of the year.

The most serious problem of all, and one that underlay the others, was the ambiguity of Iwakuro's role and uncertainty in Tokyo itself about how far Japan should go in support of Indian independence. Fujiwara had urged full and sincere support of the independence movement, but IGHQ had many reservations, some of them based on practical difficulties such as material support. For Iwakuro the limits of Tokyo's support of the INA-IIL were not clear. His instructions left him latitude for interpretation and the use of his own political acumen. Iwakuro was working from an IGHQ attitude of grudging and limited support, but this still left the problem of determining the limits. The one point that was clear, about which Tokyo would not quibble, was that the India project was part of a secret war in which the weapons of intelligence and espionage were to play a key role. Political propaganda and secret diplomacy were an old story to Iwakuro. These were areas where he had proven his versatile talents, and these he made good use of in the *Iwakuro Kikan*. But the IIL, INA, and especially Mohan Singh continually pushed Iwakuro with specific requests to the limit of Japan's willingness or capacity to commit herself. This fundamental problem of defining Japan's policy limits persisted for Iwakuro and ultimately led to dissolution of the first INA. Not until the arrival of Subhas Chandra Bose was Tokyo forced to re-evaluate and redefine its policy toward the Indian independence movement.

IV PENANG ISLAND PROJECTS

Captain Kaneko Noboru was assigned head of the Penang Island branch of the *Kikan,* Actually, the Penang branch was under the Special Mission Section of the *Iwakuro Kikan*. Several *Kikan* staff members, including graduates of the *Nakano Gakkō* and civilian interpreters were assigned under Kaneko, who was himself a graduate in intelligence and sabotage techniques. They were to infiltrate into India, Ceylon, and Nepal.

One of the most important tasks of the Penang *Kikan* was liaison and supervision of the *Swaraj* Institute (Freedom Institute) under the directorship of N. Raghavan, a distinguished lawyer from Madras and leader of the Indian community in Penang in peacetime. Part of the curriculum of the Institute consisted of political and cultural training prescribed by Raghavan. The rest of the curriculum prepared the Indian trainees for infiltration. Kaneko referred to the *Swaraj* Institute as "actually a *Nakano Gakkō* to train Indians for espionage, propaganda, counter-intelligence, etc."[19]

The training course supervised by *Nakano Gakkō* graduates included instruction in opening letters, tapping telephones, monitoring wireless, coding and decoding, developing secret ink, forging documents, making explosives, countering guerrilla warfare, and camouflaging. Propaganda training was given in broadcasting, printing leaflets, and producing films. Field training included techniques of infiltration, secret communication, disguise, following, ambush, and escape. The Indian trainees at the *Swaraj* Institute developed considerable ingenuity for their missions into India.[20]

Another small unit of trainees in Penang, the Osman group, was composed exclusively of Sikhs from the Punjab, most of them with some revolutionary experience. Leader of the group, the tall, handsome Osman, had become involved in the Mexican revolution, and, escaping from Mexican officials, had made his way to Shanghai where he became leader of the independence movement there. There he came into contact with Japanese naval officers who were impressed with his talents. The independent, martial spirit of the Sikhs had been well represented in the nationalist movement in India since early in the century, and there were Sikh exiles scattered throughout the world. Osman seemed to his Japanese colleagues a giant, and stories of his prowess in felling trees with his bare hands and breaking rocks with his fist became legendary. But he had a soft heart, a fondness for children, and was loved by his followers.

A third Indian group under Lieutenant-Colonel Gilani was composed entirely of Muslims. Gilani was from an aristocratic family and seemed to *Kikan* members a British gentleman with pro-British sentiments. Gilani was watched closely and his whole group was later arrested as spies for the British Army. Lieutenant-Colonel Mahmood Khan Durrani, after the war awarded the Victoria Cross for his counter-espionage work in the independence movement, recalls he was asked by the *Iwakuro Kikan* to submit a plan for the Gilani unit project. Durrani prepared a list of sixty officers and men he knew to be hostile to the INA. He gave lectures and cooperated in this and similar projects in the hope that large numbers of Muslims would be sent into India and thereby spared suffering and charges of desertion. At the same time the purpose of the *Iwakuro Kikan* would be subverted, and the British-Indian Army would get first-hand information about INA activities.[21] The Japanese supervisor of the Gilani unit had spent several years in the Middle East, and, assuming personal responsibility for the conduct of the group, he committed *harakiri* when they were arrested in April 1943.[22]

Still another group was organized for operations in Nepal, composed appropriately of Gurkhas. For liaison with this tough unit Kamimoto, the ex-*F Kikan* member who had promoted the famous *Harimao* operation in Malaya, was selected. Kamimoto had trouble "educating" the Gurkhas, who were noted for their unwavering loyalty to the British. Even for the wiry Gurkha mountaineers the hill country between Nepal and the Assam-Burma border was virtually impassable. Those who attempted to cross the border were either arrested or stopped by malaria. Kamimoto took a party of Gurkhas north from Rangoon for reconnaissance. The group made its way to the upper reaches of the Chindwin River and contacted Japanese units of the 15th Army in the midst of the disastrous Imphal campaign. The unit made its way on foot through impossible jungle and mountain paths all the way to Kohima before the Imphal defeat halted its advance. A handful of Gurkhas managed to break through into Nepal, ending their epic six-thousand-mile march.[23]

Another group was organized on Penang to infiltrate into Ceylon and was actually sent there by submarine. The *Kikan* officers felt a special affinity with this group of Buddhists. An Indian sent with the unit to Ceylon later reported that they rendezvoused at the port of Trincomalee and, contacting a group of priests, successfully carried out sabotage activities.[24]

Another group was trained as wireless technicians for infiltration by parachute behind enemy lines. One of the problems of all the intelligence units was that, though collecting information on the spot posed no special difficulties, it was often impossible to communicate the information to headquarters where it was needed. This communications unit was designed to overcome the difficulty. The unit had especially high morale, and in the evening after long fatiguing hours of training, the strains of *"Bande Mataram"* ("Hail, Mother") —a nationalistic Bengali song) could be heard coming from the barracks of the wireless technicians. After completing a six-month training programme in an accelerated two-month period, they were sent to Burma, where they were parachuted into the jungles of Bihar and Orissa by the 5th Airborne Division. They communicated valuable information on east India back to the *Kikan*.

The Penang *Kikan* also set up a laboratory for training in the manufacture of incendiaries, explosives and poisons—the weapons of chemical warfare. In this laboratory trainees turned out secret ink, time bombs, hand grenades, carbide bombs, tear gas, bottled incendiary bombs, and sulphur bombs. A specialty was concealing lethal materials in whisky bottles, telephones, alarm-clocks, shaving cream and other innocuous-appearing objects.[25] Most expensive and least successful of all the projects of the Penang *Kikan* was the attempt to devise and break codes.

The time came in the Penang *Kikan* timetable to send the first party of Indians home by submarine to carry out propaganda, sabotage, and terrorist activities within India. It would be the test of their training. Without the knowledge of N. Raghavan, Indian director of the *Swaraj* Institute, two parties of ten Indian trainees each left the Penang naval base by Japanese submarine under cover of the night. When Raghavan learned the next morning that the first graduates had been spirited away without his consent, he was outraged. He resigned as principal of the institute, and no Indian could be found in Penang or Malaya to take his place. This was a serious breakdown in co-operation for the Penang branch of the *Kikan*. Other training centres on the island, however, continued to operate through 1944 and into 1945. From the standpoint of intelligence the missions sent to India were not a success, since they did not return from India or communicate with the *Kikan*. Once they reached India they either defected or were arrested.

CHAPTER SIX

The Crisis of the First INA

I BANGKOK CONFERENCE

ON 15 June 1942 over a hundred delegates of the Indian Independence League all over Asia assembled in Bangkok, as had been agreed at the Sanno Conference in Tokyo. Representatives of the two million Indians in East Asia came from Malaya, Burma, Thailand, Java, Sumatra, Borneo, the Philippines, Japan, Manchukuo, Nanking, Shanghai, Canton and Hong Kong. For nine days they discussed plans for organizing the independence movement on an Asia-wide scale and for co-operating with the Japanese. Thai Premier Marshal Phibun Songgram opened the conference with a welcome in which he referred to the close cultural ties which bound India and Thailand. He paid his respects especially to Swami Satyananda Puri, who had worked in Bangkok for closer cultural and spiritual relations between the two nations.[1]

Rash Behari Bose from Tokyo was elected presiding chairman by the delegates. Despite the feelings of antipathy and mutual suspicion between Indians in Southeast Asia and those in Tokyo that had come to light during the Sanno Conference, Bose had after all instigated the Tokyo meeting. Mohan Singh, who proposed Bose's name as chairman, felt Bose would be most influential with the Japanese. Mohan Singh's judgement was shared by most Indian delegates. No other candidate for president of the League was proposed, since there was unanimous recognition of Bose's long record as a revolutionary and his working relationship with many Japanese leaders. Furthermore, he seemed lacking in personal ambition.[2] From this point on, however, it seemed to some Bangkok Indians that the meeting was in the hands of a small group including Mohan Singh and N. Raghavan but headed by Bose. As one Bangkok businessman put it, "There were two groups, one pro-Japanese and the other not. We didn't participate, as we knew everything was being done as they wanted; we only attended."[3]

Bose in his presidential address portrayed Japan as liberator of all Asia from Western imperialism:

> We have been working in Japan for decades so that we can see Japan in a position to stand by the oppressed Asiatics and to liberate Asia. We were anxiously awaiting the day when Japan would fully realise the great significance of creating a free and united Asia and would feel convinced that it was in the interest of Japan herself, as also for the rest of Asia if not for the world as a whole, that the octopus grip of the Anglo-Saxon imperialism in the East must be destroyed root and branch. We all were fully convinced that Japan alone was in the position to take the honour.[4]

Japanese Ambassador Tsubokami and the German and Italian ambassadors were also at the opening session of the conference and read congratulatory messages on behalf of their Governments. Their messages supported the image of Japan Bose meant to conjure. Japanese Foreign Minister Togo Shigenori sent the following message, which was read to the Indian assembly:

> Japan has no desire whatever toward India except to see her realize the restoration of freedom and has the firm determination to destroy Britain and America as has been announced previously by Japan. The Indian peoples who are now faced with the golden opportunity should ... devote themselves to greater moral principles. They should endeavour internally to unify the general public opinion and externally co-operate with Japan, Germany and Italy to destroy British Imperialism to bring about the realization of the aspiration of Indians.[5]

Ambassador Tsubokami's address, like Togo's message, reiterated Japan's desire to see India attain freedom and realize "India for Indians". Both Togo and Tsubokami were repeating assurances already made by Prime Minister Tōjō in the Diet several times between January and March.

A message from Subhas Chandra Bose in Berlin was also read in which he referred to his eighteen months of activity abroad in anti-British countries and exhorted all Indians to take up arms, saying, "Indian independence must be attained by the hands of we Indians."[6]

Following the opening greetings Mohan Singh made a lengthy address, recounting his campaign experiences in Malaya, his early contact with Japanese authorities, and the creation of the Indian National Army. "The first day was entirely taken up by me; I spoke for seven and a half hours continuously, keeping the delegates spellbound for the whole day," Mohan Singh recalls.[7]

S.C. Goho, in a secret statement to the INA History Committee after the war, accounted for Mohan Singh's power at the time of the Bangkok Conference:

> Among the delegates of the Bangkok Conference there were about thirty Indian military men who followed a system of bloc voting and were prepared to obey the wishes of Captain Mohan Singh. He had thirty military votes to control in any case. Most of the non-military people were men of straw. Captain Mohan Singh was prepared to pass all kinds of resolutions, realizing that Mr. Raghavan with his party was standing in his way; he joined forces with those men of straw.... The Malayan delegates, at one stage, threatened to withdraw from the movement on account of this bloc voting of the military.[8]

Thus, even as early as the Bangkok Conference, there was evidence of a military/civilian split apart from the Tokyo/Southeast Asia schism which had developed earlier. Goho also felt all Indians in Tokyo were spies or informers for the Japanese military.

II THE BANGKOK RESOLUTION

Several days of general discussion by delegates followed. By the close of the nine-day conference the delegates had accomplished several things. A thirty-four-article resolution was unanimously adopted setting forth the policies of the Indian independence movement in East Asia. The Indian Independence League was formally proclaimed the organization in East Asia to work for the goal of independence. The Indian National Army was declared the military arm of the movement, with Mohan Singh as commander-in-chief. Ultimate authority in the event of war, however, was to be a Council of Action of the IIL, which would be a steering committee. INA members would therefore owe allegiance to the League.[9] The League was to make arrangements for the supply of men, money, and material for the INA and was to request the Japanese Government to supply arms and equipment. The Council of Action was also to ascertain that any action contemplated was in accord with the wishes of the Indian National Congress.

Rash Behari Bose was elected president of the Council of Action. The other four members elected to the Council were: Mohan Singh, army commander; K.P.K. Menon, publicity and propaganda; N. Raghavan, organization; and Lieutenant-Colonel G.Q. Gilani, military training.[10] For organizational purposes the IIL divided Asia into several regions; a network of regional and branch organs was created under League headquarters in Bangkok. Determination was expressed to carry out a vigorous propaganda programme through broadcasts, leaflets, lectures and any other means available.

More important from the standpoint of cooperation with Japan, the Bangkok Resolution included several requests of the Japanese Government. These requests included the following items: all Indian soldiers in territories under Japanese occupation should be placed under Indian control; the Indian National Army should be accorded the status of allied army on an equal footing with the Japanese Army, and the INA should be used only in the struggle for Indian independence; the Council of Action would from time to time request financial aid of Japan with the understanding that it would be treated as a loan repayable to the Government of Japan; the Government of Japan should provide all facilities for propaganda, travel, transport, and communication in areas under its control as requested by the Council of Action; in matters of local administration affecting Indians the local Japanese authorities should consult with the nearest branch of the IIL.[11]

The Resolution further requested of the Japanese Government a declaration to the following effect:

> a) That immediately on the severance of India from the British Empire, the Imperial Government of Japan shall respect the territorial integrity and recognise the full sovereignty of India, free of any foreign influence, control or interference of a political, military, or economic nature, b) That the Imperial Government of Japan will exercise its influence with other Powers and induce them to recognize the national independence and absolute sovereignty of India..., c) That the Imperial Government of Japan may be pleased to arrange with the authorities in the territories now freed from the domination of the Anglo-Saxons and their Allies by the Imperial forces of Japan to hand over properties owned by Indians (including those owned by Indian companies, firms, or partnerships) and left behind by them owing to the exigencies of War to the Council of Action of this movement, in trust for their rightful owners, to manage and control the said properties and advance the income thereof for the use of this movement to be repaid as and when claimed by the said owners ... the Imperial Government of Japan may be pleased to make a declaration to the effect a) that the Indians residing in the territories occupied by the Imperial forces of Japan shall not be considered enemy nationals so long as they do not indulge in any action injurious to this movement or b) that the properties both movable and immovable of those Indians who are now residing in India or elsewhere ... be not treated by Japan as enemy properties. ... the Japanese Government use its good offices to enable Subhas Chandra Bose to come to East Asia.[12]

The Resolution reflects the meticulous drafting of two lawyers, N. Raghavan and K.P.K. Menon, both members of the newly created Council of Action. Both men were anxious that a free Indian government be assured the attributes of a government legally constituted in international law. This far-sighted concern of Raghavan and Menon was vindicated during the post-war trial of INA officers in Delhi. The numerous specific requests in the Resolution were made in the expectation that Japan would answer each one individually. Some of the items bore witness to conflicts which had already arisen in the confrontation between Japan as a military occupying power and Indian civilian residents in Southeast Asia. This concern for the protection of Indian residents and property became a decisive factor in pushing some Indian POWs toward volunteering for the INA. If the IIL-INA and Japan were to be allies in the struggle against the Western imperialist powers, then it followed that Indian property should not be confiscated as alien property.

Finally, Bangkok delegates expressed thanks in the Resolution to the Japanese Government for past assistance and the hope that amicable relations would continue. The Resolution was passed unanimously by the delegates. Toward the close of the conference receptions and informal gatherings were held for delegates at the invitation of Thai and Japanese officials. Thai hospitality closed the conference with a colourful public reception in Lumbini Park, with Thai and Indian dancers performing on a rotating platform emblazoned with the Indian National Tricolour along with the flags of Burma, Thailand, and Japan.

III IWAKURO AND THE RESOLUTION

Following the close of the Bangkok Conference, the Council of Action handed over the Resolution to Colonel Iwakuro, chief of the *Iwakuro Kikan*. The Council sought a formal reply from the Japanese Government to the specific requests for support and clarification of policy. "We were told that by the 30th June, the Japanese Government would make a formal announcement accepting our resolutions and we will also receive a written communication from the Government," recalls General Mohan Singh.[13] Iwakuro forwarded the Bangkok Resolution to Tokyo by telegram.

Upper echelons in IGHQ were plunged into a quandary. Tōjō had basic policy aims regarding India and sympathized with the Indian desire for freedom. But there were limits to how far Japan could go in aiding the independence movement. Further, there was a feeling in Tokyo that the men in the field, especially Fujiwara, had on their own initiative been pampering the Indians.[14] The politically astute Iwakuro read the Tokyo mood well. His communiqué to IGHQ reflected his grasp of the dual aspects of Tokyo's dilemma. His telegram read:

> From here the contents of the resolution appear from the Japanese standpoint to be counting their chickens before they are hatched.... Judging from present circumstances we must spur these people on for the broad objective of the anti-British independence movement. So, rather than worry about each individual item, I believe we should show an attitude of generally accepting their ideas.[15]

Though the ultimate decision on the reply to the Resolution was Tokyo's, Iwakuro's recommendation from the field was also an accurate reflection of the IGHQ position; Iwakuro's recommendation went no further than he judged Tokyo was willing to go. When Iwakuro said the responsibility was Tōjō's[16] he was technically correct, but Iwakuro may have had other reasons for saying so.

There was a long-standing animosity between Tōjō and Iwakuro based on the relative power of the two men within the Army. Iwakuro's political acumen was obvious to Tōjō at the time of the 1941 peace talks in Washington. Iwakuro, as Army representative in Washington, was in some respects more powerful than either Ambassador Nomura, who was after all a Navy man, or Kurusu, who represented the Foreign Ministry.

Thus, when Iwakuro returned from America in late 1941, Tōjō arranged to have Iwakuro sent off to Malaya as 5th Regimental Commander in the Konoe Imperial Guards Division. After Iwakuro recovered from a wound received in the Malaya campaign, Tōjō, anxious that Iwakuro remain in Southeast Asia, engineered his appointment as Fujiwara's successor in March 1942. In view of the political and propaganda significance of the India project, Iwakuro's appointment was easy to justify, since he had helped articulate the phrase "Greater East Asia Co-Prosperity Sphere"[17] and since he had also founded the *Rikugun Nakano Gakkō* (Army Intelligence School) in 1939. He was well equipped by temperament and experience to execute a *bōryaku* operation.[18]

By temperament, inclination and experience Fujiwara and Iwakuro were obviously very different men. Fujiwara was picked directly from the 8th Section of IGHQ to initiate the India project. He was imbued with a sense of mission in his new assignment and concerned about the relative lack of information on India within IGHQ. He came to see himself as midwife of the INA and a catalyst in Mohan Singh's transformation into a real revolutionary. He became a kind of "Lawrence of the Indian National Army",[19] a Japanese with a genuine and deep commitment to the Indian independence movement. Fujiwara's sincerity led him at times to take a jaundiced view of Tokyo's policies toward the INA. The friendships Fujiwara formed with Mohan Singh and other officers of the INA have endured. Fujiwara is a man who measures his own conduct by the demanding standard of the feudal *bushi* ideal.

Iwakuro, on the other hand, was the military politician, a man shrewd and uncommunicative, always playing the political game. It was no surprise that a man of such brilliant talents and power as Iwakuro demonstrated should eventually reach a confrontation with Tōjō. Iwakuro was a man of broad-ranging ideas in a great many areas.[20] He demonstrated a creative approach to Japan's wartime problems and a professional dedication to the job certainly equal to Fujiwara's. He had more experience in more areas than Fujiwara. But he had no personal commitment to the men in the INA and formed no close personal relationship with individual Indians. The men and especially the officers of the INA felt the difference. But the situation as well as the men spelled the difference.

IV IMPENDING CRISIS

During late 1942 IGHQ Tokyo had no more intention than Iwakuro of replying point by point to the Bangkok requests. The military situation was already showing signs of deteriorating for Japan. Japanese forces had been shattered at Guadalcanal. The "Hump" route air lift had reopened the supply line to Chiang Kai-shek from India via Assam to Kunming. Allied bombings in Burma were intensifying daily and made it obvious that a counter-attack in Burma was in the offing. The confidence of IGHQ was not shaken, but the attention of Tokyo was at least diverted from the INA. In July Southern Army Headquarters was transferred from Saigon to Singapore, and the name of Singapore was changed to *Shōnan* (Brilliant South), reflecting Japanese expectations in Southeast Asia.

Iwakuro was thus unable and also disinclined to meet the requests of Bose and the Council of Action. Iwakuro realized too that the

Council was divided against itself. Represented on the Council were both the Indians from Southeast Asia and the Tokyo faction—the latter represented in Bose. Further, the IIL as civilian wing vied with the INA as military wing of the independence movement. Mohan Singh had had doubts about the IIL under the leadership of Pritam Singh, whom he regarded as too weak and amenable to the Japanese. Certainly the civilian-military schism would continue under Rash Behari Bose. Iwakuro did the only thing feasible: he temporized.

Ten days after Iwakuro sent the telegram to Tokyo a reply arrived. It read: "Understand your idea. Endeavour to realize the requests of the Indian Independence League." Iwakuro, after learning of the dissatisfaction of the IIL-INA over this failure to respond to the individual items of the Bangkok Resolution, went personally to Tokyo. He found neither IGHQ nor Tōjō in particular willing to go beyond the reply already cabled from Tokyo. Tōjō meanwhile sent a message to Lieutenant-General Kuroda, chief of staff of the Southern Army, expressing his pique at Iwakuro. Tōjō cabled Kuroda, "Iwakuro's handling of the Indians is haphazard."[21] Iwakuro reports he felt Tōjō did a *volte-face* when the following year, after the arrival of Subhas Chandra Bose, Tōjō agreed to recognize Bose's Government and to hand over to it the Andaman Islands.

On 10 July 1942, Iwakuro conveyed to Bose by letter Tokyo's assurances of general support:

> I have the honour to inform you that the Imperial Japanese Government is determined to extend whole-hearted and unstinted support, as evidenced in the repeated statements made by Premier Tōjō and also in his recent message of felicitation to the Bangkok Conference in regard to the request dated on June the 22nd, 1942, from the Indian Independence League to the Imperial Japanese Government with the objective of attaining complete independence for India by supporting the Independence Movement in India and removing Anglo-American influence. The Imperial Japanese Government agrees with your view to keep the resolutions of the Bangkok Conference secret, and it is also the wish of the Imperial Japanese Government that this reply will be kept under strict secrecy.[22]

There was no mention in the reply of any of the specific requests embodied in the Bangkok Resolution. This was as far as the *Iwakuro Kikan* and Tokyo would go. It did not satisfy the members of the Council of Action or allay the suspicions of Mohan Singh and other INA officers regarding Japanese motives.

Other problems heightened the already tense atmosphere. Indians in Southeast Asia all knew of the "Quit India" resolution of Congress of August 1942. They grew impatient. Mohan Singh was eager to expand the INA to full strength of about thirty thousand armed troops from among the forty-five thousand volunteers but could get no satisfactory Japanese response. He had to be content with the *Kikan* suggestion of one rather than two divisions. Mohan Singh could see no sense in the *Kikan* timetable of four months to organize the single division. He insisted he could have the division ready within one week. Major Ōgawa of the *Kikan* agreed that Mohan Singh should have a chance to prove it; he did.[23]

By 1 September the organization of the division was formally proclaimed. It contained three guerrilla brigades, the Gandhi, Nehru, and *Azad* Brigades. Special groups for sabotage, intelligence, propaganda, medical services, reinforcements, a base hospital, and an Officers' Training School under Lieutenant-Colonel Shah Nawaz Khan were also created. About seventeen thousand troops were under arms, the arms surrendered by British troops a few months earlier.[24]

The Bangkok Resolution had also demanded Japanese recognition of equal status of the INA as an allied army. This relationship Tokyo never conceded. There was no political or military prospect that it would. As Devnath Das, Indian revolutionary in exile in Japan since 1932, put it: "This was like saying to the vice-chancellor of a university, 'Promise me a degree first; then I'll read.'"[25]

More serious still was the issue of Indian POWs who had not volunteered for the INA at Singapore. By most estimates these numbered close to twenty-five thousand of the forty-five thousand Indian POWs taken at Singapore. They were, according to Fujiwara, to be organized into labour units under Mohan Singh's command and used in co-operation with the Japanese Army. But the Indian understanding was that they were to be regarded as reserve units of the INA to be trained by the INA, and in no case were they to be placed under Japanese command.[26] These POWs were kept in separate camps from the INA volunteers and their status remained unclear. Many complaints about conditions in these camps came to light during the trial of INA officers in Delhi after the war. Mohan Singh was anxious to train these men as reserves rather than use them as labour units. The *Iwakuro Kikan*, however, needed labour units to use in projects for the Japanese Army. Distrust and suspicion of Japanese motives spread among INA officers from Mohan Singh downward.

When Fujiwara was *Kikan* chief there was direct and friendly communication between him and Mohan Singh. Now Rash Behari Bose was the intermediary between the *Iwakuro Kikan* and the INA.

Iwakuro relied on Bose to persuade Mohan Singh of Japan's sincerity in replying to the Bangkok Resolution. But since Japan had not replied to any of the specific requests, INA officers were not to be persuaded, least of all by Bose. Mohan Singh and N.S. Gill came increasingly to look on Bose as a Japanese puppet. The gulf between Iwakuro and Mohan Singh and between Rash Behari Bose and Mohan Singh deepened. Mohan Singh increasingly became convinced that Japan and the *Iwakuro Kikan* regarded the INA not as a revolutionary army but as a unit for propaganda and espionage projects for the Japanese Army.

Another problem which contributed to the atmosphere of crisis was the leadership of Mohan Singh. Mohan Singh had been a logical choice as commander when he first encountered Fujiwara near Alor Star. He was ranking Indian officer of the first Indian unit Fujiwara encountered and became a committed revolutionary. He and Fujiwara worked exeptionally well together. But after the surrender at Singapore there were several other Indian officers who had outranked Captain Mohan Singh in the British-Indian Army. These men, for example Shah Nawaz Khan, felt restless under Mohan Singh's command. Doubt about Mohan Singh's political ability to deal with the Japanese was one concern which led Shah Nawaz to refuse to volunteer at first. A revolutionary army needed absolute commitment to the cause and complete confidence of all Indian officers. Many objected that he demanded an oath of personal loyalty to himself rather than to the INA.

Mohan Singh himself recalls that some officers were "secretly carrying on anti-INA propaganda and it was about this time that such elements should be separated. Consequently a Separation Camp was started."[27] Mohan Singh listened to complaints daily about conditions in the camp and took special pains to see that quarters and rations in the camp were adequate. Iwakuro was aware of the dissatisfaction with Mohan Singh's leadership among some high-ranking Indian officers. Both the INA and the *Iwakuro Kikan* had grown in size and complexity since the days of the early *F Kikan* and the nucleus of the INA. And Japan's overall military position in late 1942 was not what it had been in the optimistic days of early 1942.

Apart from the doubts about Mohan Singh among some of the officers, civilian members of the League and Council of Action felt that Mohan Singh was dealing with the Japanese in cavalier disregard for the Council and League.

S.C. Goho and his lawyer friend N. Raghavan were especially apprehensive. Goho recalled their anger at Mohan Singh's actions:

> Unknown to other members of the Council of Action, Mr. Mohan Singh had removed to Burma four hundred men of the Intelligence Department of the Army under his command. He gave an explanation that they were sent for some reconstruction work. But my own view is that members of the Intelligence Service are not generally experts in hut building.... Again, unknown to other members of the Council of Action, he had arranged to send a battalion of about eight hundred soldiers to Burma. He was definitely dealing secretly with the Japanese military. All these informations [sic] came to the ears of Mr. Raghavan who severely reprimanded him.[28]

The plan for the advance of the INA to the Indo-Burmese border in November or December was thus contributing to the impending crisis. This plan had been suggested by Southern Army Headquarters and was discussed by Mohan Singh and Iwakuro. Advance parties of INA intelligence units had already been sent into Burma at Mohan Singh's behest and with the cooperation of the *Iwakuro Kikan* without reference to the Council, as Raghavan and Goho pointed out.

In Rangoon relations were strained too. An organization parallel to the *Iwakuro Kikan* had been established there for liaison with the Indian independence movement, the *Minami Kikan* under Lieutenant-Colonel Kitabe. There was also an IIL branch in Rangoon which was engaged in lecturing to and organizing local Indians. The first intelligence unit to go to Burma at Mohan Singh's command was a unit of about fifty men, including four or five civilians, under the leadership of Ram Swarup. This party reached Rangoon in early March. Ram Swarup was to contact Indians still in the British-Indian Army within India. He eventually made his way beyond the border into India, but was unable to return. The agreement to send this advance party to Burma was made without reference to the Council.[29]

V N.S. GILL'S ARREST

A second unit was sent to Burma following the Bangkok Conference under the leadership of Colonel Gill. Gill had been commissioned at Sandhurst and had experience in intelligence for the British Army in Bangkok before the outbreak of hostilities in the Pacific. Gill's assignment was to send specially trained men into India for intelligence and propaganda. Once Japanese-INA forces prepared to enter India, Gill's team was to foment anti-British sentiment among Indian troops. Gill's party split into two groups, one operating in the Chin

Hills near Imphal, the other in the Akyab sector. Gill sent the first party to the border through Kalewa under Major Mahabir Singh Dhillon, who was to report back on the political situation in India and the attitude of Indian leaders toward the INA. The INA had to know what Gandhi and Nehru were thinking about INA-IIL plans and actions. The Dhillon party left Rangoon by train, then pushed to north Burma by elephant. Colonel Gill returned to Singapore in early December and immediately reported to Mohan Singh that Dhillon had been seen beyond his post in Kalewa from which he was to have reported. Gill was afraid Dhillon, a man commissioned from Sandhurst like himself, would defect to the British. He did, and was arrested by the Japanese.[30]

The second party sent by Gill went by steamer to Akyab, then upriver by boat and finally on foot. As they were about to leave for India they were surrounded and captured by British-Indian forces who had apparently been tipped off by M.S. Dhillon.[31]

Now Gill was in an extremely vulnerable position from the Japanese viewpoint. One of the parties under his command had been caught deserting to India; the other was also caught en route to India, also presumed by the Japanese to be defecting. Gill was suspected of complicity in both cases. When he returned to Singapore in early December he was invited to attend the meetings of the Council of Action, which was already embroiled in the crisis with the *Iwakuro Kikan.*

At this critical juncture Colonel Iwakuro called in Gill and asked him to co-operate, hinting at Dhillon's action and offering Gill any post in free India. Iwakuro asked Gill to go to Tokyo for discussions with Headquarters. Gill, however, was uncertain of the purpose of the invitation and refused, since the Council still had no reply from Tokyo to the major Bangkok requests. On 8 December Gill was arrested. He was kept in solitary confinement until the end of the war, first in *Kempeitai* (military police) prisons, then in Pearl's Hill Prison, Singapore. On Dhillon's person were discovered several letters written by Gill to persons in India. These the Japanese claimed were evidence of espionage. Gill points out that they were personal letters to his family and his banker, and that the Japanese themselves later realized these letters were flimsy evidence.[32] Nevertheless, Gill's conflict of loyalties was clearly indicated in his statement to the INA History Committee:

> I was attracted by the movement and wanted to act. But something in my conservative past held me back. Nor could I adjust myself to the Japs, nor did I think they could win. Furthermore, bad as the British were I thought they

were better than the Japs. I knew that Indian National Congress and her leaders were anti-fascists and pro-allies if anything yet I wanted to remain with my colleagues in the INA due to these conflicting ideas. It would be true to say I drifted into the movement. My trip to Tokyo made me more suspicious of the Japs and no wonder they sent me to Bangkok... against my will. I carried on working, never liking the Japs, and yet knowing, however big the INA, it would be subordinate to the Japs. So when the Japs asked me to take up "finding information' work for them, I accepted, not having the least intention of working for the Japs. But I wanted to contact India, to find out what they really wanted us to do, because I was rather doubtful if leaders in India were happy over our co-operation with Japs, however well intentioned. But when I found the Japs method of doing things, I revolted and eventually returned to Singapore to take part in the crisis.... I feel I was a pawn in the hands of the unseen power, who by my drifting attitude made me play the required part. It may be true to say if I had not gone into the INA it would have had an adverse effect. Again had I believed the Japanese, the crisis may not have taken place. Yet destiny wanted these actions to make the picture one whole.... In August Mohan Singh and I had signed a secret oath at the Gurdwara [Sikh temple] Singapore whereby I was to help him in spite of my doubts and he was to stand up to the Japs if our doubts about Japanese sincerity proved true. This came about in December.[33]

Meanwhile the *Iwakuro Kikan* was exerting pressure on the Council of Action for co-operation in sending the INA to the Indo-Burmese border. But Mohan Singh and the Council made a reply to the Bangkok requests a pre-condition of this approval. Mohan Singh's initial eagerness to promote an INA advance westward had been cooled by mounting suspicions. Gill's arrest coming at this time enraged Mohan Singh.

VI STALEMATE

Fujiwara was informed of the deteriorating situation between the Council and the *Iwakuro Kikan* by three former members of the *F Kikan* who were still with the *Iwakuro Kikan*—Yamaguchi, Kunizuka and Ito Keisuke. They visited Fujiwara secretly at night and grieved with him over the impasse. Fujiwara in turn visited Mohan Singh's quarters secretly before dawn more than once. Despite Mohan Singh's predicament he still greeted Fujiwara with a smile and begged him to help. Fujiwara was saddened that he could only ask Mohan Singh to be patient since an operation as big as the INA inevitably meant suffering and distress. Fujiwara was sleepless at night, turning over in his mind the birth of the INA a year previously and the possibility of destruction of the INA or even bloodshed between the INA and the Japanese Army. "Secretly I was determined I would give up my life to prevent this from happening, standing between Japan and the INA. I told this to Lieutenant Yamaguchi, putting everything in order and entrusting my heirs and my will to him," Fujiwara recalled.[34]

Meanwhile, apart from the stalemate over the Bangkok Resolution, other issues also approached a crisis. Mohan Singh discovered in his talks with Iwakuro during September that the Japanese had no enthusiasm for expanding the INA. "They wanted the army and the organization just as a show-piece and as convenient puppet of theirs but not a strong and powerful reality which may become a problem for them later on in thwarting their secret designs on India .... Quiet submission and unconditional surrender of soul was demanded," Mohan Singh recalled.[35]

In October the problem of handling Indian evacuee property in Burma exacerbated relations further. In early October a plan for the management of ownerless Indian property in Burma was handed to Mohan Singh by *Kikan* representatives. Council of Action members found it unacceptable and wished to propose some amendments. On 10 October League members went to the *Kikan* office in Burma and informed Captain Tsuchimochi that certain amendments were necessary. Tsuchimochi asked for a copy of the amendments they proposed. On 12 October League members returned to the *Kikan* office where Lieutenant-Colonel Kitabe, Tsuchimochi and others were assembled. Kitabe addressed the League members:

> It was all right for the Bangkok Conference to pass those resolutions, but you will be mistaken to think that those resolutions are binding on the Japanese Government. The Japanese Government have never announced that they have accepted all the resolutions passed at Bangkok by the Indian Independence Conference. What the Japanese Government have up to now said about the resolutions amounts to that they would help the Indian Independence Movement to the best of their capacity. Moreover, the Japanese Government have never accepted the Council of the Indian Independence League as a Government body with whom they could enter into any treaty or pact. Therefore, what I would like to say is, that, although you may look up to the Council of Action for orders or instructions, it is not necessary for us, who represent the Japanese Government, to always respect those orders and instructions which the Council of Action may issue for you. The Council of Action being a body without any territory to rule over and without any financial status, it cannot be looked upon as a Government, but is only an organization having come into existence to fight for India's independence and deriving its power from the Japanese Government. Any decision of the Council of Action, in order to be worked upon, must be such as to be found acceptable to the Japanese Government.[36]

One of the Indian representatives objected to Kitabe's statement, suggesting it would be wise for the *Kikan* to take a more conciliatory attitude in order to dispel apprehensions of the League about Japanese motives. Kitabe retorted, "Since the IIL and its activities are solely dependent on the help and assistance given by the Japanese Government, why not the public be told straitway [*sic*] that the IIL works under the leadership of the Japanese Government. In my opinion it would be better to do so in order to avoid a lot of misunderstanding in the future." This insult to the pride of the Indians was followed by another from Mr Yutani, who added, "Indians here are labouring under the wrong impression that the ownerless Indian properties belong to Indians. Absentee Indian property according to International Law is enemy property and belongs to the Japanese Government, and the Japanese have never intended to make a secret of this fact.... You can only manage it under the control and discretion of the C-in-C, who is the sole owner of the properties."[37] It seemed now to Mohan Singh and other Council members that they were coming under increasing control of the *Kikan* and that they were rendered powerless to influence the course of events. Even the status of the IIL itself was questioned by the Japanese.

VII THE COUNCIL OF ACTION *v* IWAKURO

K.P.K. Menon of the Council was also having difficulties in broadcasting from Singapore. Menon understood when he took over this department that he was to be in charge of appointment and supervision of staff and programming of news and commentaries. The Japanese military authorities might censor and remove any item objectionable from their point of view but not alter or modify it in any way. The Japanese censor, however, soon began interfering with news broadcasts, redrafting items in broadcasts to India. Some staff appointments were also made without reference to Menon.[38]

By this time Mohan Singh had grown so suspicious that he was using his own intelligence sources to get information about Japanese plans. He learned, for example, that propaganda leaflets which had been drafted by the IIL-INA for use in India had been altered and some had already been flown to Burma. He also got information about Indians being trained by the Japanese independently in Burma and the Andamans for intelligence in India. And the issue of expanding the INA persisted. Differences between the INA and Japan were mounting up. Mohan Singh now wanted to bring Indian volunteers from Hong Kong and Shanghai to Singapore. The *Iwakuro Kikan* prevaricated, neither accepting nor rejecting Mohan Singh's requests. It became increasingly clear to Mohan Singh that the Japanese wanted to use the INA as a political weapon rather than allow it to grow into a strong military force.[39]

Mohan Singh felt the time had come to clarify Japan's position toward the INA before making any further commitments. "It was quite clear to us now that they wanted to conquer India through Indians and by extending help and also material aid to us they were simply helping themselves," Mohan Singh felt.[40]

The Council of Action met several times during October and November. After evaluating the whole imbroglio the Council on 29 November addressed a letter to Iwakuro to be forwarded to Tokyo, asking for clarification of the following points: 1) the attitude of the Japanese Government on the Bangkok resolutions; 2) recognition of the Council of Action as executive body of the Indian independence movement in East Asia, and acceptance of its status; 3) formal recognition of the INA and provision of facilities for its expansion into a strong army; 4) a declaration binding on any Japanese Government recognizing the absolute independence and sovereignty of India.[41] It was quite apparent to Mohan Singh, Raghavan, and others on the Council that Rash Behari Bose was reluctant to send the letter to Iwakuro. Mohan Singh felt that by this time Bose had simply become a liaison man between the Japanese and the IIL rather than a forceful president.[42] But Bose could not directly antagonize the other four Council members.

The position of the *Iwakuro Kikan* was that, since all arrangements had been made for the transport of INA troops to Rangoon, the move should take place as planned. The Council of Action, on the other hand, was standing firm on the demand that the four points in the letter should first be clarified. A showdown seemed inevitable.

On the evening of 30 November the Council was asked to meet with Iwakuro on the following morning. With Iwakuro in the meeting room were Mr Senda, Kunizuka and several other members of the *Kikan*.

Iwakuro stated the position of the Japanese Government on the Council's requests. Japan had already announced she had no ambitions in India and would aid the independence movement. Iwakuro had studied the Bangkok resolutions carefully and found eighty per cent of the items had already been put into effect. And the reason for not announcing the existence of the INA was that there would be political repercussions. If the INA was to engage in military action in India it would be wiser to keep it secret until the time for action arrived. This was the reason for secrecy, not lack of recognition by the Imperial Government. Iwakuro was an astute politician, but his replies did not convince the Council.[43] Regarding the Council itself, Iwakuro pointed out it was technically impossible to make a treaty with the Council since it was not a state. POWs, Iwakuro said, were under Japanese control and intended to be used for work detail. They were not available to Mohan Singh without consultation with the Japanese.[44]

Old Mr Senda then had his turn. Actually, there were only two points to be settled. First, the Government's declaration on the Bangkok Conference, and second, a definition of the Co-Prosperity Sphere. The latter point was indeed a basic problem in Japanese policy, but it was overshadowed by more immediate demands of the Council, which failed to press the point. Raghavan pushed for the first point, a reply to the Bangkok Resolution. A response had to be made for three reasons. First, the Bangkok Conference had been given much publicity, but most Indians were still in the dark about Japan's attitude. Second, some Japanese had no understanding of the independence movement. Third, Tōjō's declarations applied to all of Asia, but there should be a more binding declaration. If Japan's policy were the same as toward Burma, the Council would not be satisfied.[45]

Senda then argued that creation of the *Iwakuro Kikan* was evidence of Japanese recognition of the independence movement. "In times like these when a treaty is a mere scrap of paper the main thing is not any document but good will on both sides," he protested.[46]

Raghavan persisted in a legalistic line of questioning. How could the Japanese Government communicate to the Council through the *Iwakuro Kikan* without recognizing the Council as a juristic person? The Council was not seeking a treaty or pact but a formula for surmounting this difficulty. These were questions Mr Koyama, a Diet member, could answer. He replied, "The Council of Action is not a real Government. It is only a political body. The Government therefore cannot make any formal promise to the Council." The case of the Nanking Government was different, since it had territory, people, and sovereignty. Furthermore, there was no unity among Indians even in East Asia. Menon answered Koyama's objections: "There is complete unity among Indians regarding this movement. ... The

Council of Action is united on this issue. There is no use evading the main issue by talking about unity."[47]

Iwakuro offered his opinion that there were two basic requests the Council should ask of Japan: 1) that the Council not be made a puppet, and 2) that Japan should ask for nothing in return for assistance to the movement. These were the basic guarantees for the movement.[48] Iwakuro concluded that he could not forward the Council's letter to Tokyo, but that he would try to resolve all issues between Japan and the INA on a day-to-day basis. This was not acceptable to the Council. Mohan Singh's attitude hardened.[49]

Iwakuro sent Kunizuka to Mohan Singh on 2 December to sound him out further and try to soften his resistance by appealing to his sense of accomplishment in the past record of the INA. Kunizuka asked Mohan Singh why he had suddenly lost confidence after first agreeing to the move to Burma. Mohan Singh replied it was his duty to take all precautions to safeguard the interests of India.[50]

Major Ōgawa, who was with Kunizuka, then took over the arguments. Ōgawa suggested again that, since all arrangements had been made, the INA troops should go to Burma on schedule. Mohan Singh replied that the move was of secondary importance; the main issue was the clarification of Japan's stand. Ōgawa appealed, "If you miss this opportunity, you will be losing a golden chance for gaining the independence of the whole of India. If you cannot see your way through the Council of Action as regards this move, you better resign." Mohan Singh rejoined, "This is why we are very serious about it. We understand this is the question of the freedom of the Indian people. That's why we have stopped a further move till the fundamental questions are decided." Ogawa pressed, "The contents of your letter are very serious. You should have verbally talked instead of writing it." Mohan Singh answered again, "Yes, they were very serious. That's why I put them in black and white." Ogawa tried to cajole Mohan Singh by citing the example of Manchurian "independence". Mohan Singh's reply was, "This is exactly what we do not want. Who says there is any independence in Manchuria? India is already more independent than your so-called free and independent Manchuria. Your object in our country is to fight the British and our object is to achieve complete independence."[51] The meeting ended inconclusively.

Iwakuro met Mohan Singh later the same day. Iwakuro announced the movement could not continue in the current atmosphere and that, if Mohan Singh and others had doubts about continuing further, they could revert to their former status of POW. Iwakuro assured Mohan Singh that he had tried to get a satisfactory reply from Tokyo to the Bangkok Resolution, but that there were constitutional obstacles. At the same time he reiterated the Government had already given practical shape to several of the requests.[52]

Iwakuro told Mohan Singh he had prepared a communiqué for his Government which included the following suggestions: 1) Japan should fully help in satisfying the desire of patriotic Indians for complete independence; 2) Japan should bring about friendly relations between Indians and Japanese in a spirit of goodwill; 3) Japan should not force Indians to join any sphere politically, economically, militarily, or culturally; 4) Japan must respect the territorial integrity and full sovereignty of India; 5) all treatment should be on an equal basis and on mutual understanding; 6) Japan should not aspire for new interests in India beyond those already existing before the war; 7) all Indian property should be handed over to the Indian Government soon after the occupation; 8) on the request of the Indian people Japan should give all technical advice and assistance; 9) Japan should not interfere in any Indian internal affairs and all occupied territories should be immediately handed over to the Congress or Indian Independence League; 10) in case of external invasion, on India's request, Japan should give all possible help: defence of India should be left entirely in the hands of the INA, but while the British are still there, the Japanese will fight the British.[53]

Mohan Singh in reply expressed dissatisfaction with Japanese measures in Malaya and Burma and the hope that Japan would adopt a different policy in India. "We cannot tolerate these types of government in our country,"[54] he said. Iwakuro's proposed communiqué had not actually conceded any of the points requested in the Council's letter or promised anything beyond current agreements.

On 3 December Fujiwara was called in to meet with Mohan Singh. Fujiwara expressed his regret at the atmosphere between the INA and the *Kikan* and begged Mohan Singh for his final approval to the shipment of troops, saying he, Fujiwara, was personally responsible for the transportation arrangements. If Mohan Singh did not agree, Fujiwara continued, he might have to commit *harakiri*. Mohan Singh stood fast. The only honourable course for the INA was to see where they stood before any further commitment was made. The basic issue had to be settled first. "It is strange that you think it to be a minor incident, but for us it is the pivot of the whole organization, and the whole show might be suddenly stopped if it is not talked out satisfactorily and immediately," Mohan Singh concluded. Fujiwara was no more successful than members of the *Kikan* had been.[55]

On 4 December Council member N. Raghavan outlined the Council's dilemma as he saw it in a letter to Rash Behari Bose:

> The first mistake the Army Command committed was to have agreed to organise the Army ... without sanction from or discussion with the Council of Action, by direct negotiation with the *Iwakuro Kikan,* and before any reply to the Bankgok Resolutions was received from the Japanese Government. The second mistake that the Army committed was to have arranged and agreed to the transport of troops into Burma without the prior sanction or knowledge of the Council of Action and again, before a reply to the Bangkok Resolutions was obtained.... The request for and obtaining transport has placed us in a very awkward and serious position—in fact between two sharp horns of a dilemma. If we agree to the transport we are doing so before vital and outstanding questions have been solved and therefore placing ourselves in a much worse position. If we do not agree to the transport there will be (a) going behind the GOC's word, and the Japanese side will consider it as *our* word, (b) serious estrangement between Japanese side and our side which will be a vital injury to Indo-Nippon relations of the future ... and (c) wrecking of the present movement....[56]

Raghavan was airing his grievances not only against the Japanese, but also against Mohan Singh and his disregard of the Council of Action. The position of the INA commander with respect to the Council was thus a serious outstanding issue.

VIII   MOHAN SINGH *v* RASH BEHARI BOSE

On 4 December the Council of Action met. Mohan Singh and Gilani presented several items for immediate consideration by the *Iwakuro Kikan.* If agreement were not forthcoming, Gilani and Mohan Singh announced they would be compelled to resign. Their ultimatum was: 1) assurance from Iwakuro that he would forward the Council's letter to Tokyo for clarification; 2) assurance that a reply would be forthcoming by 1 January at the latest; 3) pending the reply no action would be taken by the INA; 4) the INA should take action to a) place all surplus volunteers and POWs under control of the GOC, INA, b) make no movement inside or outside Malaya of the INA or POWs, c) bring all guards and detachments under the Japanese under control of the GOC, INA, d) inform the advance party already in Burma that no further action should be taken until further orders from the GOC.[57] Rash Behari Bose was visibly upset at the ultimatum. Reluctantly he agreed to see what he could do in getting Iwakuro's agreement, but it would take time. He must have known the likelihood was nil.

The Council again convened on the following day for its last full meeting. Bose had met with Iwakuro before the meeting, but without results. Raghavan arrived late at the meeting and announced that he had already resigned, since no reply had been made to the Bangkok Resolution. Gilani, Menon, and Mohan Singh added that they had also prepared a letter of resignation and that it would be advisable to resign jointly. By now the animosity between the civilian and military members of the Council was in the open.

In the early hours on 8 December Japanese officers appeared at Mohan Singh's quarters and arrested Colonel Gill who was also staying there. There seemed no way out of the crisis now. Bose was unable to make any headway with the 5 December ultimatum. The *Iwakuro Kikan* played its last card now. A meeting was arranged between Fujiwara and Mohan Singh at the residence of old Mr Senda. Fujiwara had already been informed of Gill's arrest and pleaded with Iwakuro to avoid a direct clash between the Indian and Japanese armies and also to avoid dissolving the INA.

Mohan Singh demanded an explanation. Fujiwara related that Gill had been watched, and the Japanese were sure he had a network of spies within the INA. "In Tokyo I was warned not to trust Colonel Gill by some of the Indians there to whom Colonel Gill had told what he thought of the Japanese. In Saigon Colonel Gill telephoned to someone that this movement was nothing and that he was definitely pro-British.... At Bangkok Gill tried to do as much harm as possible to the Japanese and the INA." Fujiwara continued to recount Japanese reports of Gill's activities, at the same time disavowing his own belief in them. Six parachutists had reportedly landed at Pegu and confessed under questioning that they were to contact Gill and Dhillon. Mohan Singh asked if he could meet the parachutists or officers allegedly sent to contact Gill, but Fujiwara said it was impossible. Mohan Singh was also denied permission to see Gill.[58] By now there was nothing Fujiwara could do to placate Mohan Singh, despite tearful and sincere entreaty.

In the evening Gilani, Menon and Mohan Singh submitted their resignations to Rash Behari Bose. It was clear with Gill's arrest that there was no further possibility of compromise. The following day these Council members had a reply from Bose, referring to his efforts to get clarification from Tokyo even if it meant going to Tokyo. Bose accepted the resignation of the three Council members regretfully.[59]

Mohan Singh had so far resigned only from the Council of Action. There was still the matter of the status of the INA with respect to the Council chairman to be resolved. On 10 December Bose issued a statement about the resignation of the Council members together with a letter circulated to all branches of the IIL and officers of the INA. Mohan Singh comments, "The statement and this letter were both full of half truths, misstatements and twisted perversion of facts. A vicious campaign of propaganda had been let loose against us."[60]

The denouement developed immediately. Bose on 11 December sent Mohan Singh a letter stating that he wished to meet certain INA officers the following morning at the Sea View Hotel. Mohan Singh shot back an immediate reply asking to know the purpose of the meeting. Bose in turn warned that if the officers did not appear he would take further action. Mohan Singh wrote asking Bose under what authority he was acting, since there was no longer a Council of Action. Bose replied, "As President and sole surviving member, all powers and duties of the Council of Action are vested in me."[61]

Mohan Singh wrote Bose a lengthy letter on 13 December, challenging him to appear in a public debate and questioning his authority in the Council of Action since all but he had resigned. Mohan Singh related the history of the Council of Action since its creation, and stated the powers of the president were limited to giving effect to the Council's decisions. Until vacancies on the Council were filled in the prescribed manner, Bose had no authority.[62]

The leaders of the civilian and military wings of the independence movement in all East Asia had locked horns. On 29 December Bose, with the knowledge and support of the *Iwakuro Kikan,* had the last word in the struggle with Mohan Singh. Bose's letter to Mohan Singh accused him of insubordination in ignoring his letter of 11 December and of attempting to create a personal army. Bose announced that Mohan Singh was therefore dismissed as commander of the INA.[63]

Bose evaluated Mohan Singh's role in the crisis in the following terms:

> Mr. Mohan Singh, from the very beginning, wanted to carry on his work despotically. He wanted to have a free hand in his undertakings, and as such, he would not bear the idea of being interfered with by others in his work, but

constitutionally he had to work under the Council of Action.... Moreover, in the last meeting of the Council of Action Mr. Mohan Singh tried to blot out the Council of Action pressing upon the Council to get an immediate clarification of a few questions from the Japanese authorities which ... was impossible because there was none in Malaya who could answer on the spot.[64]

On 29 December Iwakuro called Mohan Singh to his quarters and asked whether he was willing to work with the Japanese. Mohan Singh refused, noting as he did Bose's discomfiture and dejection. Mohan Singh was then arrested on orders of the *Iwakuro Kikan* with the concurrence of Bose. Later Mohan Singh was confined on a small island in the Johore Strait north-east of Singapore, and he spent the duration of the war under house arrest. Iwakuro states he handled both Mohan Singh and Gill according to Bose's demands.[65] Before Mohan Singh was sent to his place of exile Fujiwara was able to meet him once again for a two-hour conversation. Mohan Singh told Fujiwara the final condition of his co-operation was that the Japanese bring Subhas Chandra Bose from Germany, as had been repeatedly requested. Fujiwara promised to do what he could. He then begged Mohan Singh to persuade the other officers of the INA, through Fujiwara, to carry on the struggle for Indian independence in the INA. Fujiwara promised to work for the return of Mohan Singh to the INA. The two parted with emotion, and did not meet again until after the war. Fujiwara went to Iwakuro for permission to visit the INA officers' quarters at Seletar, then hurried to meet them. He asked them to remain calm and to save the movement for Indian freedom.[66] The whole crisis revolving around Mohan Singh was referred to in Tokyo as "Mohan Singh's anti-Japanese sabotage of the INA".[67]

IX COLLAPSE OF THE FIRST INA

Before Mohan Singh was actually arrested he took several steps in anticipation of his arrest. He held a secret meeting with the officers to discuss the dissolution of the INA in case of his arrest; the officers agreed. He also left sealed instructions for the burning of all INA records at the time of dissolution. Fujiwara was aware of the sentiment among the officers for dissolution and had tried to head it off. After Mohan Singh's arrest the ranking officers of the INA announced to the *Kikan* that they were ready to revert to their former status as POWs. The *Kikan* argued that as India was not at war with Japan, INA officers could not be taken as POWs.[68]

Rash Behari Bose now worked desperately to salvage the IIL and some semblance of the INA. Raghavan had severed his connections with the movement and returned to Penang. Menon had announced he would not have anything further to do with the movement while the Japanese had a hand in it. Both men carried a good deal of weight among Indians in Malaya.[69]

In January Bose Sent questionnaires to all INA officers asking whether they wished to remain in the INA, and if not, to state their reasons. When the replies came in, he announced that, while nearly all wanted to continue the fight, some were still reluctant to fight the British for various reasons. Bose held several meetings with the officers, exhorting them to protect Indian lives and property in East Asia and to liberate the motherland. He pointed out that India could not be freed without Japanese co-operation. He assured the officers he was one hundred per cent Indian and that his son in the Japanese Army would one day join the INA. Other officers also spoke for continuing the struggle, regardless of what individual happened to be leader.[70]

X   HALTING REVIVAL OF THE INA

On 15 February 1943, the INA was reorganized and former ranks and badges revived. The Director of the Military Bureau, Lieutenant-Colonel Bhonsle, was clearly placed under the authority of the IIL, to avoid any repetition of IIL-INA rivalry. Under Bhonsle were Lieutenant-Colonel Shah Nawaz Khan as chief of general staff; Major P.K. Sahgal as military secretary; Major Habibur Rehman as commandant of the Officers' Training School; and Lieutenant-Colonel A.C. Chatterji, and later Major A.D. Jahangir, as head of enlightenment and culture. Apart from this policy-forming body was the Army itself under the command of Lieutenant-Colonel M.Z. Kiani. This was the organization which held the INA together until the arrival of Subhas Chandra Bose from Berlin six months later.[71] Because of opposition to the reorganization, only eight thousand officers and men rejoined the INA as opposed to nearly forty-five thousand who volunteered for the first INA.

In Pearl's Hill Prison Mohan Singh heard news of Indian casualties in New Guinea. Thousands of Indians who refused to rejoin the reorganized INA were sent to New Guinea, Java and Sumatra. He bitterly regretted that they had been sent to fight in the East Indies, and felt they should have been fighting on the Indo-Burmese front; "then the story of the INA would have been different".[72]

Raghavan, on his return to Penang, called a meeting of branch presidents of the IIL in his capacity as president of the Malaya IIL. There was a unanimous decision to carry on the movement, but Rash Behari Bose was to be requested to secure from Tokyo a clarification of all matters at issue. A lengthy memorandum was drafted and presented to Bose. It included the following thirteen points: 1) a formal declaration should be made by the Japanese Government clarifying its policy toward India; 2) there should be full co-operation and co-ordination of the civilian and military sides of the movement; 3) civilian members of the IIL should be consulted in the matter of recognition and expansion of the INA; 4) the development of information and publicity work should be left entirely in the hands of the Malaya IIL with advice from the *Iwakuro Kikan;* 5) no parties other than accredited leaders of the League should receive the confidence of the Japanese and be used for work in connection with India and Indians; 6) vacancies in the Council of Action should be filled at the earliest opportunity; 7) generous assistance should be given to the Malaya IIL by the Japanese in solving local problems involving education and economic development; 8) the *Kikan* should take no direct action in matters connected with the Indian community except when asked by the League, the attempt to organize an Indian Youth Movement by the *Kikan* should be stopped; 9) stringent action should be taken against Indians who are guilty or reasonably suspected of activities that are bound to injure Indian unity or Indo-Japanese friendship, and assistance should be given by Japanese authorities in pursuit of this policy; 10) similar assistance should be given by the Japanese to the League regarding collection of donations from the Indian community; 11) steps should be taken to engender mutual confidence and understanding between Japanese and Indians; 12) no further forward move should be made until the above conditions are fulfilled; and 13) unless satisfactory solution of all above problems is made, all members of the Territorial Committee and presidents of branches would resign.[73]

Bose decided Raghavan and others were trying to destroy the movement. He used his power to force Raghavan's resignation and proceeded to reorganize the League himself.

There were rumours that Iwakuro was trying to organize an Indian group of his own, the Indian Youth Movement, as a counter to the faltering IIL. The new group was reportedly under the IIL rather than the INA. Meetings were held in which full support was pledged to the Japanese. Many local branches of the League were in fact losing leadership and support during early 1943. In Burma Colonel Kitabe pushed Karim Gani as leader over Burma IIL chairman Baleshwar Prasad, who became *persona non grata* with the Japanese.

Bose meanwhile worked to reorganize the IIL with headquarters in Singapore. He established five departments: General Affairs and Finance under Lieutenant-Colonel A.C. Chatterji, Social and Welfare under D.M. Khan, Intelligence under Deshpande, and Housing and Transport and Stores under various assistants. Bose was trying to hold the IIL together with those leaders who were left and to create at the same time an inter-locking leadership with the INA.

To re-establish the IIL and INA as viable bodies of the independence movement, Bose called a successor to the Bangkok Conference in Singapore in April 1943. There was little of the excitement and enthusiasm of the Bangkok meeting. During the two-day conference questions were asked about the president and his possible dereliction of duty. Bose replied that in this event the president could be shot. Delegates again requested the Japanese to bring Subhas Chandra Bose from Berlin; Rash Behari Bose announced the Japanese had just consented to do this. The conference made other decisions also, empowering the president of the IIL to nominate his successor, to make laws or regulations as he deemed necessary for the independence movement, and forbidding Army members from participating in political activities. These were sweeping powers, with no checks except Bose's own assurances of benevolence.

Bose also made new arrangements with the Japanese for expanding publicity and propaganda under S.A. Ayer, and for publishing several newspapers under the editorship of M. Sivaram. Broadcasting and publishing activities under IIL auspices were stepped up. Bose's dictum for broadcasts was: "the Independence League must be the voice of the Indian National Congress". With this no Indian would quarrel.

Bose left for Tokyo in early June for discussions with Japanese officials on plans for continued co-operation. When he returned next to Singapore he would have with him Subhas Chandra Bose, the revolutionary so long awaited in Southeast Asia.

Through these efforts Bose succeeded in holding together a somewhat dispirited IIL and INA. The crisis had made it obvious to Tokyo that, even if all other conditions were favourable for an invasion of India, the co-operation of the INA was not assured, and the INA itself might not be a military asset. And within India the "Quit India" resolution of Congress and Gandhi's fast had created an unstable political atmosphere. There was no certainty about possible reaction within India to Japanese military penetration of the Indo-Burmese border.

CHAPTER SEVEN
Subhas Chandra Bose, Hitler, and Tōjō

I THE MAKING OF A REVOLUTIONARY

ON 23 January 1897 at Cuttack, Orissa, was born Subhas Chandra Bose, ninth child of Janakinath and Prabhavati Bose. Janakinath was a lawyer of a Kayastha family, and was wealthy enough to educate all his children well. By Indian standards this family of Bengali origin was well-to-do. Janakinath was raised in the atmosphere of the nineteenth century reform movements of Bengal through which English social reformist thought filtered into India. He had resigned posts within the bureaucracy of the British Raj in protest against its repressive policies. Bengal was at the same time the funnel for new ideas from the West and the province which felt most keenly the oppressive hand of the British. It was natural that Bengal nurtured leaders of the stature of Rammohan Roy, Keshab Chandra Sen, Rabindranath and Debendranath Tagore, and Bankim Chandra Chatterji.

At the age of five Subhas was enrolled in a school for European and Anglo-Indian boys run by the Baptist Mission. Subhas and his brothers and sisters were all admitted as part of a small quota for Indians. For a Bengali child of the late nineteenth century learning English was one of the first requisites of life. The curriculum also included Latin and the Bible. The school might almost have been in London rather than Cuttack, for the teachers were also British. Sanskrit, India's classical language, and Bengali, the language of Bose's family, were neglected. Subhas spent seven years of his life in this English public school.

In 1909 Subhas entered a public school in Cuttack, Ravenshaw Collegiate School. Here he recalls being laughed at by his fellow students because he knew so little Bengali. At the age of fifteen Subhas first read the works of Vivekananda and found a goal for his life —spiritual salvation for oneself and service to humanity. Subhas began to practise yoga. From Vivekananda Subhas's quest took him to Ramakrishna and the ideal of renunciation. He continued his meditations. Subhas felt his religious life was more important than his studies.[1]

At the age of sixteen Subhas was sent off to the Presidency College in Calcutta and began to make decisions apart from his family. He joined a group of students who wanted to bring about a fusion between religion and nationalism. It was more moderate than some of the terrorist student groups in Bengal. Bose's group talked with the political visionary Aurobindo Ghosh and with Surendra Nath Bannerji, one of the founders of the Indian National Congress. Bose never forgot the words of Aurobindo: "I should like to see some of you becoming great; great not for your own sake, but to make India great, so that she may stand up with head erect amongst the free nations of the world."[2] Though Bose the college student was more interested in religion and social work than politics, Aurobindo's words were to return to him later with stunning impact.

Two things began to make Subhas politically aware. One was the behaviour of Britishers in Calcutta, whose insults to Indians in public places were galling and offensive. This was the psychological basis of the revolutionary movement in Bengal. The outbreak of World War I wrought another change in Bose's thinking. Political emancipation was a desirable goal for India, but without military power India could not hope for independence. It was for Bose a significant conclusion.

In 1916 an incident occurred at the College which changed Bose's life. There were rumours that one of the teachers, an Englishman, had manhandled some students. The teacher was attacked by a student in reprisal. Bose was held responsible, and though he had only witnessed the attack, his appeals were ignored and he was expelled. His family called him home.

For a while Bose studied then at Scottish Church College in Calcutta. Then he matriculated at Cambridge and prepared for the Civil Service examinations in London. At Cambridge there were again cases of social discrimination against Indian students. There was also discrimination in the University Officers' Training Corps which carried over into the British Army. This was more serious and was to have repercussions for the British in India.

In the summer of 1920 Bose took the Civil Service examinations and passed fourth. The next seven months he spent in self-examination, after which he renounced the security of a comfortable life in the Civil Service and resigned his appointment. He was elated at his own decision, knowing he was the first Indian to voluntarily relinquish a Civil Service post out of patriotic motives. The rest of his life he would dedicate to the cause of Indian freedom. For Bose it was a moral decision, and the sacrifice would be far outweighed by the satisfaction of service to the motherland. The best way to end a government was to withdraw from it. Subhas had taken his first conscious step as a revolutionary.

From this point on Subhas entered the vortex of the nationalist movement, first in Calcutta, then in the National Congress. The atmosphere surrounding Bose's decision was full of public hostility to the introduction of the repressive Rowlatt Bill of 1919. There was also shock and anger over the Amritsar massacre, in which four hundred Indian demonstrators were killed at the order of a British officer in charge of law and order in that city. Bose wrote for the newspaper *Swaraj* and was in charge of publicity for the Bengal Provincial Congress Committee. Bose's political mentor was C.R. Das, principal of the Congress National College and a spokesman for the aggressive nationalism of Bengal.[3]

One of Bose's first political acts was participation in the civil disobedience of December 1921 against the visit of the Prince of Wales. As Bose had hoped, he was arrested and given his first jail sentence, at the same time gaining the confidence of C.R. Das, who was also jailed. Bose followed Das into the Swaraj Party within the Congress. When Das became mayor of Calcutta, Bose was elected chief executive officer at the age of twenty-seven. It was a far more responsible position than he could have hoped for in 1924 had he remained in the Civil Service. In a round-up of terrorists in 1925 Bose was arrested again and this time sent to jail in Mandalay, where he remained for two years.

When Bose returned to India in 1927, his mentor, C.R. Das, was dead and Bose had become a leader in his own right, with confidence and determination gained through his jail experience. He was also ill, having contracted tuberculosis in prison. He became general secretary of the Congress, and, with Nehru, worked to form the Indian Independence League opposing any qualification of independence.

Again in 1930 Bose was arrested and jailed for participation in a civil disobedience campaign against Dominion status. This time he emerged from prison mayor of Calcutta. Jail sentence had become an almost indispensable qualification for political success in India.[4]

During 1932 and 1933 Bose visited Berlin, Rome, and many of the capitals of Eastern Europe several times, where he met with Indian students and sponsored formation of a students' association to help Indians in Europe. He met politicians whenever possible, including Hitler in 1936. He observed party organization, and saw communism and fascism in action. In April he returned to India, was arrested on landing at Bombay and again imprisoned.

Bose had become a leader of national stature. In 1938 he agreed to accept nomination as Congress president. He meant to take his stand on unqualified *swaraj*, to confront the British Raj with force if necessary. This would also mean a confrontation with Gandhi, but Bose was not prepared to compromise with freedom. He believed Gandhi had failed to meet India's political needs. Bose opposed any hint of compromise with freedom, any co-operation with the Government under the 1935 Government of India Act.

For Bose 1938 marked the beginning of the political stagnation of the Gandhian movement. Prior to 1938 Gandhi had maintained his political viability and leadership by absorbing elements in the programme of the political left. In 1938, however, Gandhi lost the support of part of the left, just as Bose became Congress president. This was the first overt sign of a break between Gandhi and Bose. In Bose's presidential address to the Congress at Haripura he still paid deference to the Mahatma but insisted that Congress should continue in power after independence was won. It would have to be a strong government to achieve the reconstruction of India. But unity within the Congress was destroyed, as the followers of Bose and Gandhi chose sides.

The differences between Bose and Gandhi were sharpened by correspondence between the two men during 1939, while illness kept Bose in bed. For Bose the danger was not violence and corruption, which he felt were decreasing in India in the thirties, but submission to the British. On 2 April 1939, Gandhi finally wrote Bose that their views were so diametrically opposed that there did not appear to be any possibility of accommodation. Gandhi wrote, "I smell violence in the air I breathe."[5] He was also apprehensive of the widening gulf between Hindu and Muslim. Gandhi advised Bose accordingly to form his cabinet, draft his own programme, and submit it to the All-India Congress Committee. Bose demurred, maintaining their common aims were greater than their differences. There was, however, little political meeting ground between the two men.

Differences with Gandhi also led naturally to a schism between Bose and Nehru. Writing to Nehru in 1939 Bose accused Nehru of disliking him, of encouraging his opponents at every opportunity, and of talking like a doctrinaire politician.[6] Many think this rift between Bose and Nehru would have been of signal political importance in post-war India had Bose lived.

Bose approached the final break with more reluctance than Gandhi. The stalemate between Gandhi and Bose was still unresolved when the Congress met at Tripuri in late April 1939. Bose's proposal on the struggle for *swaraj* was voted down. Bose appeared at the meeting on a stretcher, still suffering from illness. He consequently delayed the appointment of the Congress Working Committee as he was unable to meet with Gandhi to discuss the appointments or the differences between the two men. Some accused Bose of temporizing and of dictatorial tactics. In fact, there was little room for compromise in Bose. "I am an extremist," he once said, and his career gave witness to his statement. In late May Bose presented his resignation as Congress president to the meeting of the AICC in Calcutta.

Shortly thereafter Bose organized the Forward Bloc with the object of consolidating the political left. The Congress Socialist Party and National Front had so far failed to achieve an amalgamation of the left. Nor could Bose get the support of the Congress Socialist Party.[7] This despite Bose's programme for a modern, industrialized, socialist free India. Bose's principal support for the Forward Bloc remained in his home state, Bengal.

Bose envisioned a strong government to reconstruct India after independence. "You cannot have a so-called democratic system, if that system has to put through economic reforms on a socialistic basis. Therefore, we must have a political system—a State—of an authoritarian character.[8]... with a democratic system we cannot solve the problem of Free India." The new Indian state would embody a synthesis of fascism, or national socialism, and communism. Through such a synthesis radical reform would be possible and India's pressing problems would be solved. To lead the government, Bose believed in a "strong party bound together and preventing chaos, when Indians are free and are thrown entirely on their own resources".[9] Because of Bose's programme for a synthesis of fascism and communism, many of his contemporaries were unable to decide whether he should be considered politically right or left.[10] Some argued that when Bose appeared in Southeast Asia in 1943 in a uniform resembling Mussolini's and with the name *Netaji* (Leader or Fuehrer), he had moved close to his Axis mentors. But for Bose the synthesis between fascism and communism would achieve viability because there were traits common to both systems. "Both Communism and Fascism believe in the supremacy of the state over the individual. Both denounce parliamentarian democracy. Both believe in party rule. Both believe in dictatorship in the party and in the ruthless suppression of all dissenting minorities. Both believe in a planned industrial reorganization of the country. These common traits will form the basis of the new synthesis,"[11] Bose believed.

When war erupted in Europe the Government found a pretext for Bose's arrest. He organized a popular demonstration in Calcutta for the removal of the memorial to the Black Hole of Calcutta victims, which offended nationalist sentiment. For this and for charges of sedition, he was arrested on 2 July 1940.[12] While in prison he decided the only path to independence lay through Axis assistance against Britain. He had faith in German victory. But Bose could do nothing in jail. He announced that on 29 November he would begin a fast for freedom until death. He began his fast, refused food, and six days later was allowed to go home. His trial for sedition was to begin on 26 January 1941. On that day Bose could not be found

Bose had for several days been "meditating", refusing to see even his mother. She had no idea of his whereabouts. Those who had seen him two weeks earlier had remarked that he had grown a beard.

Before dawn on 17 January a car had pulled away from Bose's home in Calcutta. In the car were a Muslim religious teacher and Bose's nephew, Sisir Kumar Bose. In Muslim disguise Bose made his way by car to a town some two hundred miles west of Calcutta, where he caught a train to Peshawar. At Peshawar Bose became a deaf-mute Pathan, since he could not speak the Pashto language. A prearranged contact accompanied Bose from Peshawar to Kabul,

Afghanistan, first by car, then, when the car broke down, on foot, with two armed Pathan guides. They travelled several nights on foot, through the rugged country of the Khyber Pass and past frontier guards until they were well inside Afghanistan. At length they found a truck to take them up the frozen valley approach to Kabul.

In Kabul there was the danger of attracting British attention. Any Indian might be a British agent. Bose tried unsuccessfully to get help at the Soviet and Japanese embassies. In early February he found refuge with another Indian, Uttam Chand. With Uttam Chand Bose hid until 18 March, when his passage from Kabul was finally arranged. It was the Italian ambassador who finally agreed to help Bose. Bose was given an Italian passport and transport to the Russian border by car. Bose passed the ancient cities of Bokhara and Samarkand, reached Moscow by train, and on 28 March flew to Berlin.[13] This escape began the legend of Subhas Chandra Bose, the revolutionary who could not be caught.

II AN INDIAN IN BERLIN

Bose was sure he would be welcome in Berlin. His enemy was the Axis enemy. Hitler had already decided to invade Russia and to liberate the Italians in Libya. There were Indian forces fighting in the Middle East; some of them had already been taken prisoner. Hitler would be interested in Indian opinion. So might Mussolini.

Bose's hopes were deflated. His first request was for an Axis declaration in favour of Indian independence. Bose visited Ciano in Rome in June 1941, but Ciano refused a declaration. Ciano noted in his diary that both Berlin and Rome had received Bose with reserve, "especially since the value of this upstart is not clear".[14] Ciano held Bose under virtual house arrest in a hotel in Rome, not knowing what to do with him.[15] Returning to Berlin, Bose encountered similar resistance among the Nazi High Command. The Nazis were reluctant to announce India's liberation as one of their war aims. Hitler did not wish to make declarations which would not be followed by direct action, as Ribbentrop told Bose in late November.[16] The following May, Ciano was still unwilling to agree to Bose's request for a declaration.

With a propaganda offensive from Berlin Bose had better luck. He was allowed the use of broadcasting facilities in Berlin and inaugurated the *Azad Hind* (Free India) Radio. By early March, Goebbels was willing to take some credit for influencing Bose's activities in Berlin. Goebbels wrote in his diary of March 1, "We have succeeded in prevailing upon the Indian nationalist leader, Bose, to issue an imposing declaration of war against England. It will be published most prominently in the German press and commented upon. In that way we shall now begin our official fight on behalf of India, even though we don't as yet admit it openly."[17] This way Germany, so Goebbels reasoned, would reap the benefits of the support of Indian opinion without the disadvantages of an open declaration in favour of Indian independence. Goebbels believed this decision was justified by the effect Bose's broadcasts were already having in both India and England, where Bose's exact whereabouts were still unknown. By 12 March, Goebbels remarked of Bose, "He is an excellent worker."[18] In May, Goebbels wrote that Mussolini wanted Bose to establish a government-in-exile, but the idea had not been approved in Berlin. Hitler was still reluctant. "Also," wrote Goebbels, "the Japanese are very eager for some such step."[19]

While Bose continued his radio broadcasts and also the publication of a monthly magazine, *Azad Hind,* he decided something more was needed to fire the imagination of Indian patriots around the world. An army equipped, armed, and trained to fight against the English for Indian freedom would strike an even bigger propaganda blow at the British. The Nazi High Command agreed, and the Indian Legion was born. Made up of POWs from units which had fought in Africa, the Indian Legion grew to approximately three thousand troops, trained and drilled by German advisers, using German commands. It was never as Indian as its successor in Southeast Asia, the Indian National Army. But the plan was for the Indian Legion to march with the Germans across central Asia and into north-west India, following the victory which Hitler was confident of at Stalingrad. All Indian POWs were concentrated at Annaburg Camp near Dresden where Bose talked with the officers and men about Indian freedom. Some of the officers wanted to bargain, but Bose recruited only unconditional volunteers. There were many who volunteered without trying to bargain, swayed by Bose's eloquent appeal for Indian independence. One Indian in Berlin, watching Bose with the soldiers, was struck by Bose as a natural leader of men. "I became convinced that Bose had an indefinable influence over them which they could not resist. It was almost a kind of magic and indeed there was magic in the words he used."[20] Though Bose was without any previous military experience, he got his training and discipline German-style, along with the soldiers of the Indian Legion. Bose had no real hopes that it would become a large army but was anxious that a corps of Indian POWs receive German military training and discipline. He wanted to see whether the same training which worked so well in the German Army would also work with Indians.

But Berlin was not the answer to all Bose's hopes. Though Bose was eventually received by Hitler, the meeting was a disappointment to Bose, and "he did not like very much to speak about it".[21] An even greater source of disillusion for Bose was the German fiasco at Stalingrad. Bose began to turn elsewhere for help for the cause of Indian independence. The logical place, since Italy and Germany were both proving disappointing, was Japan. Tōjō had issued statements in the Japanese Diet about Indian freedom in early 1942, and by March there was a Japanese proposal for a tripartite declaration on India.

III BOSE TURNS TOWARD TOKYO

A direct avenue for Bose was the Japanese Embassy in Berlin. Sometime in October 1941, Colonel Yamamoto Bin, military attaché in Berlin, got a telegram from IGHQ in Tokyo. Yamamoto was ordered to "make a direct observation of a man named Bose and report". Yamamoto first of all needed permission from the German Foreign Ministry to meet Bose, who was under the personal "protection" of the German Vice-Minister. The reply from the Foreign Ministry was discouraging. Yamamoto's next appeal to meet the Indian exile was made in the name of the Japanese ambassador, Lieutenant-General Ōshima Hiroshi. This time there came a favourable reply. Bose himself had been attempting to contact the Japanese Embassy. Toward the end of October Bose met Ōshima and Yamamoto and talked to them for an hour of India's desire for independence and his hopes for Japanese aid. Bose had read Okakura Tenshin and it was Okakura's writings which first turned his thoughts toward Japan. Both Ōshima and Yamamoto were impressed by the passion of Bose's appeal. This was the first of Bose's frequent visits to the Japanese Embassy.[22]

When the Pacific War exploded and Japan overran Malaya and Singapore, Bose expressed his elation to Ōshima and Yamamoto. Japan would soon be in Burma, pressing on the Indian border. India's hour was imminent. Bose wanted to go immediately to East Asia and fight beside Japan for Indian liberation. Would Ōshima use his good offices to secure Bose's passage to Asia?

Ōshima had received no instruction from Tokyo regarding India since the outbreak of hostilities in the Pacific. He and Yamamoto had a feeling that the German Foreign Ministry would not let Bose go in any case. They were guarding Bose like a tiger cub.[23] Germany would not want to let Japan lead India to independence. And Bose would serve several purposes for Germany. He was already a useful ally as an Indian patriot, and his propaganda broadcasts to India were affecting both India and Britain. Furthermore, in the event of a German defeat, Bose would be valuable for bargaining purposes, since Britain would be itching to get her hands on Bose. Bose himself mentioned this prospect to Ōshima and to other Indians in Berlin.[24]

Apart from German reluctance to share Bose with Japan, there was no guarantee of Tokyo's willingness to have Bose in Asia. Three telegrams went from the Embassy in Berlin to Tokyo before a reply came from IGHQ, and then it was couched in noncommittal bureaucratese: "Under consideration." In Tokyo too there was doubt about whether Germany would release Bose. Meanwhile, Bose was asking Ōshima and Yamamoto at regular intervals, "Not yet? Not yet?"[25] Ōshima asked Bose to be patient a bit longer.

Ōshima, unlike Yamamoto, was under direct orders from the *Gaimushō*. Ōshima was advised that Bose would be welcome if he arrived in Tokyo, but Ōshima should avoid making a direct commitment to Bose. There was more interest in Bose for the moment in IGHQ than in the *Gaimushō*, and the two had not yet coordinated their views on the possible value of Bose to Japan.[26] For the *Gaimushō* the broader problem of a tripartite policy declaration on India took precedence over the immediate question of Bose.

Aside from the questions of German and Japanese willingness, there was the problem of possible routes from Germany to Japan should agreement be reached. British power was spread athwart all routes. Germany and Japan could not risk Bose's capture by Britain. Bose suggested a polar route, but Japan was too unsure of the Soviet attitude and wanted to wait for a Moscow-Tokyo pact.

Tōjō refused this route. Yamamoto had a feeling Tokyo was prevaricating and promised to bend all efforts for Bose's passage to East Asia when the former returned to Tokyo in early 1942. After Yamamoto left Berlin Bose continued to press Ōshima to expedite arrangements.

There was another reason for Tokyo's reluctance to make commitments regarding Bose. There was already an Indian revolutionary named Bose working with Japan in Tokyo—Rash Behari Bose. Why go to the trouble of bringing another Indian all the way from Berlin to Tokyo through the hazards of British-controlled routes? General Arisue in the Second Bureau feared bringing Bose to Asia might lead to a rift in the Indian independence movement, with the two Boses heading two factions. These fears were allayed when Arisue asked Rash Behari Bose what would happen if Subhas were brought to Asia. "I would step down," Rash Behari replied without hesitating. [27] It was not until the crisis of the first INA at the close of 1942, however, that Tokyo was finally convinced of the need for a stronger leader than Rash Behari Bose. This was what the Indians in Southeast Asia had been urging all along. Now at last the requests of these Indians were beginning to make sense to IGHQ. And for Bose the German fiasco at Stalingrad made it more urgent than ever that he leave for East Asia.

A cabinet-level discussion on the matter of Subhas Chandra Bose yielded a decision, "Treatment of Subhas Chandra Bose", 17 April 1942. Present were Army, Navy, and Foreign Ministries representatives. There were two parts to the decision. The first read, "We shall use Subhas Chandra Bose according to present policy and concomitant with the development of the situation of the 10 January 1942 decision."[28] It was, nevertheless, several months after this basic decision was reached regarding Bose that arrangements for his transport to East Asia were completed with the German Foreign Ministry.

It was not until January 1943 that Ōshima felt Tokyo had come around and he could approach German Foreign Minister Ribbentrop. Ōshima told Ribbentrop of Bose's desire to leave. There was no immediate approval from the Foreign Ministry. Bose suggested he might be able to iron out problems in liaison between Berlin and Tokyo. After December 1942 the German High Command was more anxious for liaison with IGHQ in Tokyo, but now Tokyo was cool.[29] The Axis alliance never yielded any Berlin-Tokyo strategy planning, and it was unlikely that Berlin would take Bose's offer seriously. There was no real joint Berlin-Tokyo consideration of India policy, apart from Tokyo's suggestion of a tripartite policy declaration on India. And Bose was under the purview of the Foreign Ministry in any case. The only Tokyo-Berlin military agreement was an accord between the German and Japanese navies which fixed the borderline of Japanese and German spheres in the Indian Ocean at 70° E. longitude and determined that German submarines could use the facilities at Penang harbour.[30] Ōshima then made a direct appeal to Hitler, and Hitler's response was to agree immediately to Bose's departure.[31]

One fascinating sidelight of Bose's stay in Germany was his mysterious and controversial marriage. Bose had vowed in Calcutta not to marry until India became independent. Bose's slightly Mongoloid features and impressive physique, added to his magnetic personality and passion for independence, had always made him extremely attractive to Indian women. Though there were women among his friends of student days and later, he had refrained from any serious alliance or thought of marriage. During his trip to Europe in the mid-thirties, he had hired as his secretary a Viennese woman, Emilie Schenkl. Now in Berlin Schenkl was again at Bose's side. This time there was a deeper emotional involvement, a marriage performed in secret, and a daughter, Anita. Bose made no public announcement of his marriage to his Austrian secretary. Neither did he discuss or even mention his wife to any of his Indian co-revolutionaries, either in Berlin or in Southeast Asia. There were none among the officers or men of the INA who would or could acknowledge Bose's marriage. Why would a patriot completely devoted to Indian independence have forsaken his vow and married, and then not even an Indian but a European? Bose had always been more Indian than Nehru and extremely bitter about European exploitation of Asia. It was beyond the realm of logic, beyond all probability. It must have been because Bose accurately gauged the probable impact of news of his marriage on his Indian followers that he kept the whole thing secret. Even his family went uninformed until Bose's arrival in Asia and the involvement of the INA in the Imphal campaign. When Japan's defeat appeared imminent Bose sent a letter to his family, telling them he had married and asking that they accept his Austrian wife as a member of the family. It was only this letter that convinced Bose's brothers and the post-independence

Indian Government that Mrs Bose should be honoured as the widow of Subhas Chandra Bose.[32]

Now that both Berlin and Tokyo had agreed on Bose's departure from Germany, there still remained the problem of what route and carrier Bose should take. Tokyo had already refused the polar route, and in any case Germany had no planes to spare. Italy was also short of planes now. Sea lanes were unsafe. The only alternative, and the means finally selected, was for Bose to go secretly by German and Japanese submarines. This possibility had been considered earlier but had been abandoned in view of the long distance involved. Now there was no alternative, and Ōshima communicated with both Tokyo and the German Foreign Ministry, making final arrangements. In February 1943 Bose and his Indian secretary Hassan slipped away aboard a German submarine, as stealthily as Bose had left Calcutta two years earlier in his escape from India. On 20 April by prearrangement, a Japanese submarine left Penang Island for the tip of Africa, under strict orders not to attack or risk detection. It was to rendezvous south-east of Madagascar with the German submarine. On 26 April the two submarines sighted each other and confirmed identity. After waiting a day for the sea to calm, the transfer was made on a rubber raft, and a drenched Bose was welcomed aboard the Japanese submarine. The submarine avoided Penang, taking a circuitous route to Sabang Island off the north coast of Sumatra, where Bose was met by Colonel Yamamoto. From Sabang Bose and Yamamoto left for Tokyo by plane, stopping en route at Penang, Saigon, Manila, and Taiwan. On the morning of 16 May the plane landed in Tokyo, where Bose was escorted immediately to the Imperial Hotel.[33]

IV BOSE IN TOKYO

After several weeks on a submarine Bose was exhausted and in need of rest. But he had one aim in Tokyo, an obsession. He had to meet Premier Tōjō. Yamamoto after a few days arranged meetings with Army Chief of Staff Sugiyama, Foreign Minister Shigemitsu, Navy Minister Yonai, and various section chiefs of the Army, Navy and Foreign Ministries. Bose's opening words to Sugiyama took the chief of staff by surprise. "The war will end in victory for Japan!" Bose boomed. Japan was in the midst of adverse circumstances in Guadalcanal and the campaign was obviously not going well for

Japan. Perhaps Bose's statement was a reflection of his faith in Japan's human and material resources. Bose continued, without waiting for a response from the bemused chief of staff, "Will Japan send soldiers to India or not? We are going to fight our way to India step by step. If we don't push on with determination we won't be able to achieve independence."[34]

The immediate reaction of Sugiyama was that Bose had none of the humility or reserve a Japanese would have shown in such an interview. But there was no doubting his sincerity or his aims. He was a known quantity, whatever the Operations Bureau of IGHQ thought of his value to Japan. Sugiyama, despite his interest and sympathy derived from two years' experience in India, could only respond to Bose with a briefing about Japan's current military position. Bose, dissatisfied with Sugiyama's general discussion, explained with great fervour his hope of first taking Chittagong, then pushing on into Bengal. Sugiyama assured Bose of his sympathy with Bose's aspirations, and Bose's first interview in Tokyo ended more calmly than it had begun. But Bose was dissatisfied. He had to meet Tōjō and get a Japanese commitment.

Yamamoto, meanwhile acting as guide for Bose, for ten days escorted him through factories, schools, and hospitals, trying to distract his attention from Tōjō and keep him occupied. Bose was impressed with what he saw but not deterred from his object.

Why was Tōjō putting Bose off? In the first place, there were many more pressing military problems than India, and Tōjō's pleas that he was too busy were not simply excuses. Secondly, there was a group in the Operations Bureau of IGHQ which took a dim view of India and the INA. The INA had no direct relevance to military strategy and operations in the Pacific or even in Southeast Asia. And there was no proof of Bose's propaganda impact within India in any case. But the main reason for Tōjō's reluctance to meet Bose was Tōjō's own attitude. Tōjō was a man of strong prejudices and often formed an opinion of a man before meeting him. The INA had been only a headache so far as Tōjō was concerned. The trouble between Mohan Singh and Rash Behari Bose had disposed Tōjō unfavourably toward the INA. And the demands in the Bangkok Resolution Tōjō regarded as presumptuous.[35] How could a small revolutionary group which did not even represent a government presume to make demands on the Imperial Government of Japan? There was no need for Tōjō to meet another Indian, even if he had just come from Berlin.

It was persuasion by Sugiyama and Shigemitsu which at length prevailed on Tōjō to meet Bose. On 10 June the first of two meetings took place. The magic of Bose enchanted Tōjō immediately. It had been the same with Sugiyama, Shigemitsu, and nearly everyone Bose met, whether Japanese or Indian.[36] Apart from the impact of Bose's words and passionate devotion to Indian independence, there was something about his face, his voice, and his eyes that captured the minds and hearts of men. Tōjō was enthralled. The meeting was brief but Bose had succeeded, and Tōjō promised another interview four days later. This time Shigemitsu and other officials also were present, and there was a brief but fruitful exchange of views between Bose and Tōjō. Tōjō explained Japan's ideas on the Greater East Asia Co-Prosperity Sphere. Bose, with his customary frankness, asked Tōjō, "Can Japan give unconditional help to the Indian independence movement? I would like to confirm that there are no strings attached to Japanese aid." Tōjō immediately gave Bose an affirmative reply. Bose continued, "Can the Japanese Army push its operations into India proper?" This time there were complex military matters involved, and Tōjō was unable to answer as decisively. But Bose had been favourably impressed and was grateful he had made a friend in Tōjō.[37] If Bose was to secure meaningful help from Japan for the INA Tōjō's sympathy and co-operation was the crucial point. In this Bose had succeeded admirably, and Tōjō was ready to make public his official support of Bose and the INA.

On 16 June Bose visited the House of Peers in the 82nd extraordinary session of the Diet. Tōjō made an historic address on the Greater East Asia Co-Prosperity Sphere which attracted attention outside Japan. Bose listened intently in the audience to interpreters as Tōjō said, "India has been for centuries under England's cruel rule. We wish to express righteous indignation at their agony and sympathy for their aspirations for complete independence. We firmly resolve that Japan will do everything possible to help Indian independence. I am convinced the day of Indian freedom and prosperity is not far off...." Tōjō spoke too of the emancipation of all of East Asia and of the welfare of the people of Greater East Asia.[38] This was not Tōjō's first mention of India in the Diet. Early in 1942 he had spoken of the Pacific War as an opportunity for India to rise against British rule. But this time when Tōjō promised aid and co-operation for Indian independence Bose was listening in the audience and felt Tōjō was making him a personal promise which he would follow through.

Bose was also ready to make public his willingness to co-operate with Japan in the struggle against Britain. On 19 June he held his first Japanese Press conference, attended by some sixty reporters. He expressed gratitude at Tōjō's Diet speech and referred to the two-thousand-year-old cultural bond between Japan and India. Bose expressed his faith in Axis victory and in the armed struggle for Indian independence. Tokyo radio on the same day quoted Bose as saying, "General Tōjō is not only taking personal interest in India but he is leaving no stone unturned in order to give all the assistance that lies within the power of the Japanese Government to help India in her struggle against British Imperialism.... I can say with utmost confidence that apart from any assistance we may receive from the Japanese Government, Prime Minister Tōjō is personally anxious to see India free from the British yoke at an early date."[39] Bose referred also to Japan's victory over Russia in 1905 as "the first harbinger of Asian resurgence. That victory was hailed with great joy not only by the Japanese but also by the Indians. Therefore, Indians feel that the existence of a strong Japan is essential for the reconstruction of Asia."[40]

Bose two days later went on the air in his first broadcast to India from radio NHK Tokyo. He appealed, as he had from Berlin, for armed revolt by the Indian masses.[41] Now Tōjō and Bose were both on record to cooperate against the common enemy for Indian liberation.

While in Tokyo Bose visited his older compatriot and fellow revolutionary, Rash Behari Bose. Though the two men had communicated, it was their first meeting. The reputations of the two men had already engendered a mutual respect, and there was none of the antagonism some Japanese officials feared. The older Bose told Subhas the IIL had already voted to make him commanding general of the INA. The two men paid a visit to the first Japanese patron of Rash Behari, Toyama Mitsuru. Toyama welcomed the young revolutionary warmly.[42] Though Subhas had little time to see people outside the Government, he enjoyed this visit with the old patriotic society leader who had protected so many Asian revolutionaries.

On 27 June after a successful month in Tokyo marked by many official banquets and public statements, Bose was on his way to Southeast Asia. Colonel Iwakuro was replaced as head of the *Kikan* by Colonel Yamamoto, Bose's old friend of Berlin days. IGHQ wanted to get the co-operation with Bose off to an auspicious start, and Yamamoto was known to be sympathetic to Bose. The name of the *Iwakuro Kikan* was changed to *Hikari Kikan*.[43]

V BOSE AND THE INA, IN SINGAPORE

Indians gave Bose a tumultuous welcome when he arrived at the Singapore airport from Tokyo on 2 July. Everywhere he went Indians garlanded him with flowers and shouted greetings. Those who saw him recalled his stormy career as president of the Indian National Congress, as mayor of Calcutta, and as a revolutionary serving jail terms. The magic of his legend enveloped him and infected his audiences. He seemed electrified at the sight of INA soldiers and unable to take his eyes off them. Rash Behari introduced Subhas to leaders of the IIL and officers of the INA. The contrast between the two men was apparent to everyone. Rash Behari was by this time old and ill, fatigue showing in his face and his drooping posture. The younger Bose by contrast was full of energy and self-confidence, a towering, imposing figure.[44] His exhilaration at being in Singapore, "graveyard of the British Empire", was irrepressible.[45]

Both Boses tried to allay the doubts of some of their fellow revolutionaries regarding Japanese motives toward India. Rash Behari recalled his recent visit to Tokyo when Prime Minister Tōjō had reaffirmed Japan's pledge of all-out aid to India in the fight against Britain. Rash Behari had been impressed by the sympathy for India's cause among Japanese of all walks of life. He spoke of Japan's production of wartime needs in weapons, machinery and food in his attempt to impress his cohorts with the advantages of cooperation and assistance from Japan.[46]

Subhas Bose also dealt with Indian fears and suspicions about Japan. He himself had been sympathetic to China when in 1937 Japan swept through the country. He had been instrumental in sending an Indian medical mission to Chungking. Now he reminded all Indians in the independence movement that his loyalty was to India alone. Bose felt Tōjō had proven his sincerity by repeated assurances of all-out aid from Japan to the Indian independence movement. Bose spoke of Japan's "Asian consciousness", of her desire to help other Asiatic nations achieve liberation. "This is a unique development which affords a golden opportunity to all enslaved nations in Asia to emancipate themselves and set up a new order based on freedom, justice, and morality," he remarked. He also noted that Japan's attitude toward Burma and the Philippines would be the most convincing proof of her good faith. "If cunning British politicians could neither cajole nor deceive me, no one else can hope to do so,"[47] Bose remarked. At the same time, he cautioned, "We shall have to be awake and alive, on our guard, not only against the enemy British imperialism, against imperialistically inclined Japanese bureaucrats, but against Indians in our own ranks."[48] There were individuals even among the Indian community in Southeast Asia who disappointed Bose in their lack of dedication to Indian independence. There were many dangers in the path of Indian liberation but they would be overcome. This Bose did not doubt.

For the next two weeks there were public meetings, military parades, women's rallies, and inspection tours. Bose was busy through the early hours every morning, planning the future of the INA with leaders of the independence movement. At a public meeting in the Cathay hall on 4 July, Rash Behari Bose formally handed over to Subhas Chandra Bose leadership of the IIL and command of the INA. The hall was jammed to capacity with representatives from all of Asia. In his last speech as leader of the movement Rash Behari Bose said, "Friends! This is one of the happiest moments in my life. I have brought you one of the most outstanding personalities of our great Motherland to participate in our campaign. In your presence today, I resign my office as President of the Indian Independence League in East Asia. From now on, Subhas Chandra Bose is your President, your leader in the fight for India's independence, and I am confident that, under his leadership, you will march on to battle and to victory."[49]

Subhas Bose spoke at length in response. He reviewed the political crisis in India and the war situation in Europe and Asia, expressing again his confidence in Axis victory. He accepted command of the newly named *Azad Hind Fauj* (Free India Army), acknowledging the honour and exhorting his audience "to do or die in the cause of India's freedom". He announced too his plan to organize a Provisional Government of Free India. "It will be the task of this Provisional Government to lead the Indian Revolution to its successful conclusion.... the Provisional Government will have to prepare the Indian people, inside and outside India, for an armed struggle which will be the culmination of all our national efforts since 1883."

Bose ended his lengthy speech with a flourish of Bengali oratory: "We have a grim fight ahead of us.... In this final march to freedom, you will have to face danger, thirst, privation, forced marches—and death. Only when you pass this test will freedom be yours."[50] The audience response was deafening.

On 5 July Premier Tōjō, on a visit from Manila, arrived in Singapore in time for a review of INA troops. Bose addressed the soldiers on parade, saying, "Comrades, my soldiers! Let your battle cry be—Chalo Delhi! To Delhi—To Delhi! How many of us will individually win this war of freedom, I do not know. But I do know this: that we shall ultimately win and our task will not end until our surviving heroes hold the victory parade at the Red Fortress of Ancient Delhi."[51] He continued, "If you will always follow me in life as well as in death, then I will lead you on the road to victory and freedom. It does not matter who among us will live to see India free. It is enough that India shall be free and that we shall give our all to make her free."[52] Bose called on INA troops not only to fight for freedom, but to form the nucleus of the permanent army of free India. They would be charged with national defence after Indian freedom became a reality.[53]

Tōjō watched the march-past and listened to Bose's call to revolution. His presence at Bose's side seemed proof again of Japan's good faith. Tōjō then addressed the gathering, repeating the assurances that Japan had no territorial, military, or economic ambitions in India, that India would achieve independence from foreign domination, and that Japan would extend all-out aid for Indian liberation.[54] Newspapers all over East Asia announced the existence of the *Azad Hind Fauj,* with pictures of Bose and Tōjō standing together in uniform.

On 9 July there was another mass rally in Singapore, attended by Indians together with some Malays and Chinese. Bose recounted his earlier actions on behalf of India's freedom. After many jail terms he became convinced he would have to leave India and carry on the struggle from abroad to supplement the struggle going on at home. "It will not be possible to win the freedom of India without external aid," Bose explained. The struggle within India would require both moral and military aid. Once the INA attacked the British Army in India, "A revolution will break out, not only among the civil population at home, but also among the Indian Army which is now standing under the British flag. When the British Government is thus attacked from both sides—from inside India and from outside—it will collapse, and the Indian people will then regain their liberty. According to my plan, therefore, it is not necessary to bother about the Axis Powers' intentions toward India."[55] Bose's faith that the INA would spark a revolution within India came to be shared alike by officers and men of the INA. Bose spoke for two hours in a drenching monsoon rain, but neither the audience nor the rain abated.

Bose called for total mobilization of Indian manpower and financial resources in East Asia. He wanted three hundred thousand men under arms. He asked too for a unit of Indian women, to be called the Rani of Jhansi Regiment after the heroine of the 1857 Mutiny who led her troops against the British. Women volunteered immediately and a women's training camp was opened under the command of Captain Lakshmi Swaminadhan, a capable woman doctor from Madras who had been practising in Singapore. The women were given uniforms and military training and took special pride in being trained to fight for Indian freedom.

So far as the Japanese were concerned, the Rani of Jhansi Regiment was a headache. Bose tried to overcome their opposition to the idea of a women's regiment, opposition based on the traditional position of women in Japan. Women had no place in the Japanese military tradition, and Japanese authorities at first refused Bose a site for a camp for women. Moreover, the Japanese did not want to expend precious resources on women soldiers. Bose persisted until he won his point.[56]

There was a large-scale reshuffling and expansion of departments of IIL Headquarters, preparatory to organizing the Provisional Government. New departments were created: a Reconstruction Department to administer freed territory, an Intelligence Department, Planning Department, and Department of Women's Organizations. The Publicity Department under S.A. Ayer was renamed the Department of Publicity, Press and Propaganda. Lieutenant-Colonel A.C. Chatterji was appointed first secretary-general of League Headquarters. Bose discussed the functions of the various departments in informal personal conversations with the new department heads and members. In these chats with the leaders of the nascent Provisional Government Bose suggested that neither Gandhi nor Nehru would fight the British, that both were working for some sort of compromise.[57]

Bose's new German-inspired title, *Netaji*, was brought into use by his private secretary Hassan, who had come from Berlin by submarine with Bose. Hassan suggested *Netaji* was the name by which Bose wished to be known in free India. When members of the Publicity Department objected that the title might be interpreted as Fuehrer, Hassan agreed, saying, "The role of India's Fuehrer is just what Subhas Chandra Bose will fill." From this time on the League's four newspapers—in English, Hindustani, Tamil, and Malayalam—referred to Bose as *Netaji, Netaji* rapidly became Bose's popular name in Asia.[58]

A new greeting was also coined for Indians in the independence movement. *"Jai Hind"* was a salutation which caught on among all Indians in Asia, and after the war even within India. It was not associated with any single communal group but was a symbol of a new all-Indian nationalism which the INA helped to foster.

Both Mohan Singh and Subhas Bose were very conscious of the need to appeal to all the religious groups among Indians, to cut across communal and other divisive segments of Indian society. In great measure they both succeeded. Sikhs and Muslims, together with Hindus, were prominent among the officers and men of the INA.

Soon after his arrival in Singapore *Netaji* was invited to Rangoon to participate in the celebration of the establishment of the new Independent Government of Burma under Dr Ba Maw. Ba Maw and the Burmese Government promised help in the struggle for Indian liberation, for Indian and Burmese independence were linked. While in Rangoon Bose reviewed a parade of INA troops and spoke before a large gathering of Indians. He also visited the tomb of Emperor Bahadur Shah, last of the Mogul emperors.[59]

In August when Bose assumed command of the renamed *Azad Hind Fauj* he reorganized it. Though he became commander he refrained from assuming any personal military rank. This he did on advice from INA officers. Lieutenant-Colonel J.K. Bhonsle, who had maintained continuity of command after the resignation of Mohan Singh, became chief of staff. The organization of Headquarters was as follows: 'G' Branch under Lieutenant-Colonel Shah Nawaz Khan, for planning, operations, training and intelligence; 'A' Branch under Lieutenant-Colonel N.S. Bhagat, for administration and the issuing of general orders; 'Q' Branch under Lieutenant-Colonel K.P. Thimmayya, for supply and equipment; the Medical Branch under Lieutenant-Colonel A.D. Loganadhan as director of medical service; and the Department of Education and Culture under Lieutenant-Colonel Jahangir for education and propaganda.[60]

Bose and his staff officers discussed with Colonel Yamamoto and other Japanese officers the role of the INA in the pending campaign on the India border. It was decided that, in view of the small size of the INA, the troops should be trained and used in guerrilla warfare. They would be lightly equipped for mobility and for penetrating enemy lines, and would have to live off the country in which they were operating.

Japanese officers gave the INA units guerrilla training, including musketry, bayonet practice, and camouflage work. The Officers' Training School turned out men who were also able to instruct new trainees. Camps for training civilian volunteers were established under the IIL in Kuala Lumpur and at Seletar in Singapore. Volunteers took an oath of loyalty to India and to the INA, and a pledge to *Netaji* as well. Bose frequently inspected the troops in their quarters and on manoeuvres. The training of volunteers was also carried on in Shanghai among Sikh policemen at the local Sikh *Gurdwara*.[61]

When the reorganization of the INA was complete in August *Netaji* met with Field-Marshal Count Terauchi, commander of the Southern Army. Terauchi explained to Bose that Japanese forces were preparing a campaign into India. The burden of the battle would be borne by the Japanese Army, Terauchi continued. India would be freed of British domination, then handed over to the Indians as an independent territory. What the Japanese wanted of Bose was personal co-operation. Terauchi was less impressed by Bose's charisma and stature than any other Japanese commander who met him. His conversation with Bose clearly pointed to propaganda as the primary purpose of Japan's co-operation with the INA.

Terauchi's explanation of the INA role was unacceptable to Bose, both at this first meeting and later when the strategy of the Imphal campaign was being planned. Bose made it clear to Terauchi that the only role acceptable to the INA in an Indian campaign would be spearhead of the advance. Indian freedom had to be won by Indians. Freedom secured through Japanese sacrifices would be worse than slavery. "The first drop of blood shed on Indian soil must be that of a soldier of the INA," Bose asserted. Terauchi agreed to consider Bose's suggestions, and the first interview between the INA commander and the Japanese commander of the Southern Army ended.[62] But Terauchi continued to disagree with Tokyo over the handling of Bose. Terauchi felt Tōjō was pampering Bose, giving him too much free rein. Terauchi was noticeably missing from the review of INA troops held on Bose's arrival in Singapore.

Another delicate issue which confronted Bose soon after he arrived in Singapore was the matter of Mohan Singh, who was still under house arrest and Japanese guard. The question of what to do about Mohan Singh had been mentioned to *Netaji* by several officers, including Dr Raju, Bose's personal physician, and Shah Nawaz Khan.[63] Now a delegation of Sikhs came to request that Bose secure Mohan Singh's release so that he might rejoin the struggle. "I was ill with malnutrition and malaria, in serious condition," Mohan Singh recalls. Dr Raju took Mohan Singh milk and medicine. He told Mohan Singh there were some who were talking against him to *Netaji*. Next Dr Raju visited Mohan Singh with an eleven-point note from *Netaji*, asking for Mohan Singh's agreement prior to their meeting. Among the eleven points was the question of whether Mohan Singh would agree to accept Bose's leadership, not only within the INA but also within India. Mohan Singh balked at the second part of the question. The two revolutionaries finally met in December 1943. *Netaji* expressed his gratitude for Mohan Singh's efforts and appreciated the problems he encountered in dealing with the Japanese. Mohan Singh in reply to Bose's written questions told him that Nehru was Mohan Singh's hero and he could not change his ideals overnight. In the course of the four-hour conversation Bose said to Mohan Singh, "There is a group outside who is discontent with your leadership. The moment you come out there will be trouble. It is in the interest of the movement that you remain here longer."[64]

The two men also discussed Japan's military prospects. Mohan Singh questioned *Netaji* about his faith in Japanese military victory and a successful campaign into India's border." I said it would be a misadventure," Mohan Singh recalls. "I asked how he was so certain of Japanese victory." Bose replied, "My name carries enough weight. When I land in Bengal everyone will revolt. Wavell's whole army will join me." Mohan Singh demurred, reminding Bose that at least ten thousand POWs at Singapore had failed to volunteer, even though they were dependent on Mohan Singh for water, food, even their lives. "How then can you expect Wavell's army commanded mostly by British officers to desert?" Mohan Singh inquired. Bose paused in thought, his head in his hand. "There is some truth in what you say," he responded at length. He left Mohan Singh in a somewhat altered mood.[65]

Though Bose was unwilling to press the Japanese for Mohan Singh's release after their prison conversation, he secured Mohan Singh's transfer to better quarters in a comfortable bungalow, where he spent the duration of the war. Bose told Shah Nawaz it would be inadvisable to bring Mohan Singh out as he was unwilling to accept a position under Bhonsle, chief of staff, and did not wish to accept a position secondary to anyone. Mohan Singh as commander of the first INA had superseded officers superior to him in the British-Indian Army.[66]

Bose made no move either to attempt to secure the release of N.S. Gill, who was also held in detention by the Japanese, under more trying prison conditions than Mohan Singh. Bose told Raju, however, that he would like to have the help of N.S. Gill.[67]

N. Raghavan, the lawyer from Penang, had left the IIL during the crisis with Rash Behari Bose, Mohan Singh, and the Japanese. It was understood between Rash Behari and Raghavan that he would henceforth be a liability to the movement, and he had returned to Penang to his practice. When *Netaji* arrived in Singapore Raghavan remained in Penang, and made no attempt to meet Bose until he requested it. The two men had a long conversation in Singapore. Raghavan told *Netaji* that he would do anything for his country but that he would remain outside the movement, as Bose would need Japanese help. Raghavan returned to Penang. Two months later Bose wrote Raghavan asking him to come for another meeting. Raghavan told Bose nothing had changed, and he was still better off outside the movement. "*Netaji* looked at me," recalls Raghavan, "and said, 'Raghavan, the position has changed." 'How?" I asked. 'It's like this,' *Netaji* continued, 'if I had to choose between you and the Japanese I'd choose you.'" Raghavan continued, recalling the impact of Bose on him, "It broke me down. I went with him and joined the government as a minister."[68]

Netaji's arrival infused new unity and life into the INA and independence movement in Southeast Asia. He announced plans to establish a Free India Provisional Government. This would be the next step forward in the march to Delhi and a free India.

VI BOSE AND FUJIWARA

Since he had been replaced by Colonel Iwakuro as *Kikan* chief in 1942, Fujiwara had had little opportunity to see his Indian colleagues. But he had followed closely the problems of liaison after the Mohan Singh crisis. With Operation U (as the Indian invasion plan was called) now at the tactical planning level, Fujiwara was again involved in liaison with the INA as intelligence staff officer of the 15th Army. Now that *Netaji* was in Singapore, Fujiwara looked forward to meeting him.

On 26 August 1943, Fujiwara was in Singapore attending an intelligence briefing sponsored by Southern Army Headquarters. Mutaguchi requested his chief of staff, Major-General Kunomura, to pay a protocol visit on Bose in preparation for the Imphal campaign. Fujiwara was ordered to accompany Kunomura, and old Mr Senda of the *Kikan* was to act as interpreter. Bose's official residence in the Singapore suburbs was surrounded by a well-tended garden. The red and yellow cannas were so brilliant they hurt Fujiwara's eyes and made a lovely contrast to the carefully trimmed lawn. Fujiwara saw several familiar smiling faces among the INA soldiers lined up to receive their Japanese visitors. He felt a twinge of regret that Mohan Singh was not among them. As Fujiwara watched, a huge noble figure emerged from the centre of the line smiling with dignified but casual assurance. It had to be Bose. He looked like a man men would follow. So this was the revolutionary all his Indian friends had begged be brought from Berlin! Bose's face bespoke confidence, friendliness, expectancy, and, Fujiwara thought, a touch of the philosopher. Fujiwara was impressed even before Bose spoke.[69]

Bose was introduced to General Kunomura first by old Senda. He then turned toward Fujiwara and gripped his hand warmly. His eyes and voice made a direct impact on Fujiwara. Bose invited Fujiwara to join him on the sofa. The INA officers followed every movement. Bose's first words to Fujiwara were, "Major Fujiwara, I've been looking forward to this meeting since Berlin." Fujiwara guessed he had been mentioned in Pritam Singh's communiqués to Berlin. Bose continued, "I have been given the revolutionary army I long hoped for. But it was you and Mr Pritam Singh and General Mohan Singh who gave birth to the INA. I want to thank you from the bottom of my heart on behalf of the Indian people." Fujiwara was equally warm but apologized for Pritam Singh's death in the plane crash and for Mohan Singh's imprisonment. Bose interrupted, "Don't worry about General Mohan Singh. I'll treat his case very carefully and deliberately. I feel very secure in the cooperation between India and Japan on the Burma front because of you."[70]

Bose then turned to Kunomura, who related in German the plan for the 15th Army operation. Bose listened intently. Fujiwara suddenly felt the burden of responsibility for the Mohan Singh crisis lift from his conscience. Fujiwara felt too a sense of destiny about the coming struggle of Japan and the INA in the offensive into India.[71]

CHAPTER EIGHT

Bose, the FIPG, and the *Hikari Kikan*

I BIRTH OF THE PROVISIONAL GOVERNMENT OF *AZAD HIND* (FIPG)

THE next step for Bose in Southeast Asia was the creation of the Provisional Government of *Azad Hind*. The Japanese had been reluctant to recognize the INA as an allied army, since it represented not a government but an organization, the IIL. The remedy, then, was to establish a government which could deal diplomatically on an equal basis with the Axis powers. The government would, Bose hoped, ultimately replace the British-controlled government in India when India became independent. This new government would gain prestige and status in international law for the independence movement.

The Provisional Government of Free India came into being at an inaugural meeting on 21 October 1943 in the Cathay cinema building, where the IIL had welcomed Bose to Singapore. Again Indians from all parts of Southeast Asia assembled. There was a capacity audience. Chatterji as general-secretary for the IIL read a brief history of the League.

Netaji next rose to speak. He announced the formation of the government and the composition of its first cabinet.[1] "It will be the task of the Provisional Government of *Azad Hind* to launch and conduct the struggle that will bring about the expulsion of the British and of their allies from the soil of India. It will then be the task of the Provisional Government to bring about the establishment of the Permanent National Government of *Azad Hind* constituted in accordance with the will of the Indian people and enjoying their confidence," [2] he proclaimed.

Bose read a Proclamation of Independence on behalf of the cabinet of the new government. He praised the heroes of the independence movement, tracing their deeds back to 1757 when they first fought British power in Bengal. "British rule in India has forfeited the good will of the Indian people altogether and is now living a precarious existence. It needs but a flame to destroy the last vestige of that unhappy rule. To light that flame is the task of India's Army of Liberation," Bose exhorted his audience. "The Provisional Government is entitled to, and hereby claims, the allegiance of every Indian. It guarantees religious liberty as well as equal rights and equal opportunities to all its citizens."[3] When Bose had read the independence proclamation he took an oath of allegiance to India as Head of State, Prime Minister and Minister for War, Minister for Foreign Affairs, and Supreme Commander of the INA. Each member of the new cabinet followed Bose's example, taking the oath to liberate India. Bose repeatedly wiped his eyes with his handkerchief during the ceremony.

In Tokyo, IGHQ and the cabinet had already been informed through the *Hikari Kikan* of Bose's plans to establish a Free India Provisional Government. In a Liaison Conference on 9 October it was decided that when Bose should establish the FIPG it would be recognized by Japan "in order to strengthen the propaganda offensive in its India policy".[4] Bose, informed of this assurance of Japanese recognition, had in turn hastened preparations for creation of the new government.

Following the birth of the FIPG by only two days, the Japanese Government on 23 October announced its recognition. At the same time, the Imperial Government declared, it would give "the utmost help for the achievement of the objectives of the Provisional Government".[5] Japan's recognition of the FIPG was followed immediately by eight other governments: Germany, Italy, Croatia, Manchukuo, Nanking, the Philippines, Thailand and Burma. Eamon de Valera, President of the Irish Free State, sent his personal congratulations to Bose.[6] With his fascination for Irish history, Bose had been a special admirer of de Valera. Within both the *Gaimushō* and IGHQ, however, some highly placed officials and generals felt Japan's recognition was not full diplomatic recognition, since the government was only provisional.[7] This opinion was not publicized at the time.

The next day, the FIPG declared war on the United States and Britain. Bose as chief of state and commander of the INA ordered the INA to begin its attack. Bose proclaimed the declaration of war to a rally of fifty thousand Indians on 24 October in a rousing cry: "I want you to demonstrate to the world that you are resolved as one man to follow up this declaration with action that will show to the world that you mean bloody war when you declare war.... So when I say 'war' I mean WAR—war to the finish—a war that can only end in the Freedom of India."[8] This declaration of war had to await the Japanese offensive in Imphal to be implemented. It was something over two months before the fighting began. But Bose had worked his audience into a frenzy. He continued, "I want you to ratify this declaration. ... If you are ready to sacrifice all you have in this world and to lay down your lives, then stand up and raise your hands...." [9] The audience rose instantly, cheering, raising rifles in the air, and shouting, *"Netaji Ki Jai! Inqilab Zindabad! Chalo Delhi!"* This appeal and others in the next few days netted the new government over thirteen million dollars from Indians in Singapore and Malaya. The money was spent almost as soon as it poured in.[10]

II THE GREATER EAST ASIA CONFERENCE

In November 1943, delegates from Japanese-supported governments in East and Southeast Asia assembled in Tokyo at the invitation of the Japanese Government. The Greater East Asia Conference had been planned much earlier in an Imperial Conference on 31 May "to establish the Greater East Asia Co-Prosperity Sphere to complete the war."[11] The Japanese Government then helped prepare the way for the conference by declaring the independence of Burma on 1 August, of the Philippines on 14 October, and recognition of the FIPG on 23 October.

The Greater East Asia Conference was presided over by Foreign Minister Shigemitsu. Prime Minister Tōjō, Navy Minister Yonai, and Greater East Asia Affairs Minister Aoki also appeared in the assembly. From Greater East Asia came Wang Ching-wei and Chou Fu-hai representing the Nanking Government, Premier Chang Ching-hui of Manchukuo, President José Laurel of the Philippine

Republic, Prime Minister Ba Maw of Burma, and Prince Van Vaidyakorn representing Thai Premier Phibun Songgram. Indonesia was still directly under Japanese rule and nationalist leader Sukarno did not receive an invitation.[12]

Bose was invited to the conference, but he attended as an observer rather than as a delegate. Japan had not announced that India or the FIPG were to be included in the Greater East Asia Co-Prosperity Sphere. Nor did Bose wish to commit the FIPG or the people of India to any decision which might be reached in Tokyo.[13]

Bose broadcast from Tokyo in Hindustani on 3 November, shortly after his arrival. He told his Indian audience that he had come to Tokyo to thank the Japanese Government personally for its recognition of the FIPG and for its promise of support in the Indian struggle for liberation. He added that he wished to strengthen further friendly relations he had established with the Japanese Government during his first visit. This personal contact was proof to the world of the friendship between Japan and the FIPG. Bose felt enemy propaganda which had misrepresented Japan's attitude toward India had been foiled.[14]

The conference in Tokyo continued for several days, with speeches by delegates from East Asian governments and statements by Japanese officials. Indian independence was a theme in several speeches. Ba Maw of Burma spoke eloquently in support of the FIPG on 6 November. "In my view Asia cannot be free unless India is free.... If we wish to destroy anti-Asiatic imperialisms, we must drive them out of their Asiatic stronghold which is India. The British Empire cannot be broken until and unless the British domination of India is broken," said Ba Maw.[15] Delegates unanimously passed a motion introduced by Ba Maw to give moral and material support to India in her fight for independence.

Netaji spoke next. He reviewed the Indian struggle for liberation and his own role in it. He related how he had been imprisoned, had fasted, kept a vow of silence, and finally escaped India, determined to get outside help in the struggle against the British. He thanked the nations of Greater East Asia for their sympathy and help. Referring then to Japan's leading role, Bose said, "This is not the first time that the world has turned to the East for light and guidance.... I believe that history has ordained that in the creation of a new, free and prosperous East, the Government and people of Nippon should play a leading role. This role for the Government and people of

Nippon was carved out by history as early as 1905 when, for the first time an Asiatic nation stood up to resist Western aggression. ..."[16] Bose cited the precedents of Buddhist and Islamic Pan-Asian ties. He called for creation of regional federations like the Greater East Asia Co-Prosperity Sphere. "The establishment of the Greater East Asia Co-Prosperity Sphere will pave the way towards a Pan-Asiatic Federation." Further, it would ultimately produce world federation, Bose believed.[17] The fate of all Asia was linked, and India's fate was linked with Japan's, Bose reiterated. This was the opportunity India had been awaiting. It might not come again for another thousand years. Assured of Japanese support Bose concluded, "We shall go to battle fully confident that the day of our salvation is at hand."[18]

The delegates on 7 November issued a Greater East Asia Declaration condemning aggression and exploitation by the US and Britain in Asia. The statement, drafted by the Japanese delegation, contained five principal points: 1) condemning Anglo-Saxon domination and calling for a restoration of Asia to Asiatics; 2) calling on Asia to rise and create a new East Asia of sovereign and independent countries; 3) pledging the signatories to defence of already liberated areas; 4) asserting insistence on free access to natural resources, freedom of communication and trade, and unrestricted cultural interchange; and 5) demanding that "principles of equality and reciprocity should be extended to govern international relations throughout the world", and condemning race prejudice.[19] This Japanese-inspired appeal to Asian nationalist opinion against colonial rule was well calculated. It served Japan well repeatedly in Southeast Asia.

One of Bose's aims in going to Tokyo was to ask the Japanese Government to turn over to FIPG the captured Andaman and Nicobar Islands in the Indian Ocean.[20] Gaining these islands as territory of the FIPG would have several advantages. First, the islands were of symbolic importance as the place of exile for Indian political prisoners of the British. Prisoners accused of conspiracy against the British had long been sentenced to penal servitude in these islands. Furthermore, the FIPG had no territory of its own. In order to become an independent government recognized in international law the FIPG needed territory. In addition, the Andamans and Nicobars would presage the liberation of all India. This Bose hoped for when he went to Tokyo.

III   THE FIPG ACQUIRES TERRITORY

The Andaman and Nicobar Islands lie in the Bay of Bengal some six hundred miles east, off the coast of Madras and at the closest point some one hundred miles south of the Irrawaddy delta in Burma. The Japanese Navy occupied the islands in the early months of the war. Bose met with Tōjō in a private interview on 1 November, the day after his arrival in Tokyo. During the interview Bose made a number of requests, one of the most important being the transfer of the islands to the FIPG. Besides enhancing the prestige and status of the FIPG, this step, Bose pointed out, would further attest to the sincerity of Japan. Tōjō demurred. The islands were strategically important for Japan, and the Navy would certainly object. At length Tōjō consented to a sort of compromise: he would announce before conference delegates that Japan was ready to place the islands under jurisdiction of the FIPG in the near future.[21] The decision was not Tōjō's alone; it was made in a Liaison Conference. According to the decision, "It has been decided to announce in the Greater East Asia Conference on November 6 preparations for the reversion of the Andaman and Nicobar Islands now under occupation by the Japanese Navy to the FIPG."[22]

Tōjō kept his promise. He appeared before the conference on 6 November and made the announcement. "I take this occasion to declare that the Imperial Government of Japan is ready shortly to place the Andaman and Nicobar Islands, now under the occupation of the Imperial Japanese forces, under the jurisdiction of the Provisional Government of *Azad Hind*, as the initial evidence of her readiness to help in India's struggle for independence," he proclaimed. Continuing, he reiterated earlier promises of Japan's "determination to extend all-out cooperation to India in her fight for freedom".[23]

This was a declaration of intent by the Japanese Government, not a *de facto* transfer. The distinction was significant, for the next step—actual transfer of administration—was never taken by the Japanese Government. On 10 November a Liaison Conference discussed implementation of the decision. Results of the discussion attached important qualifications to the status of the islands. The 10 November decision read:

1. The time for reversion of the Andaman and Nicobar Islands to the FIPG will be decided later, and we will make the following arrangements for the time being:

a. to the extent that there are no obstacles to the various policies concerning this in the operational sphere, we will allow the advance to the area by necessary personnel of the provisional government, and they will participate in the government of the specified places.
b. the scope of the above administrative participation will be gradually widened and we will do our best to satisfy the aspirations of the Provisional Government, under the leadership of the local commanding Navy officer.
c. it is approved that the Provisional Government shall use the reversion of the armed places for propaganda purposes abroad as an accomplished fact.
d. even after the reversion of the above islands to the Provisional Government, concerning their defense, we will make arrangements which will satisfy all the requirements of the Imperial Government.[24]

The Japanese Government clearly had no immediate intention of ceding the islands outright to the FIPG. Rather, the aim was to make a gesture which would quiet Bose's demands and at the same time serve both Japanese and FIPG propaganda purposes. But the administration of the islands was never completely Indianized, not "owing to a lack of sufficient trained men",[25] but because the Japanese had no intention of relinquishing ultimate administrative authority of the Japanese Navy.[26]

Secret arrangements were made by the Japanese Navy to have Bose visit the islands during December, as he wished. Publicity regarding the trip, however, would await completion of arrangements. The propaganda position of the Japanese Government was that the Government was already completing measures for the "speedy and smooth transfer of the islands". To Bose's request that an INA contingent be sent to the islands, however, the Japanese Navy responded that "since the time and method of carrying out this measure must be made to fit in with the conditions prevailing on the islands, an answer on this point will be given later after further consideration. There would, however, be no objection to the dispatch of two or three military liaison officers." The communiqué further pointed out that transportation and communication facilities were only sufficient for Japan's military needs.[27] Consequently, no INA contingent was sent.

Bose's visit to Port Blair in the Andamans eventually materialized, and in late December a ceremonial transfer of the islands took place; Bose hoisted the Indian National Tricolour over the newly named *Shahid* (Martyr) and *Swaraj* (Independence) Islands.

Following the ceremony, Bose named Lieutenant-Colonel Loganadhan, an officer in the Medical Services, as chief commissioner in charge of civil administration of the islands. Loganadhan was, from the Japanese viewpoint, "to co-operate fully in the military administration of the Islands under the direction of the Naval Commandant there".[28] Loganadhan and a small staff assumed their duties at Port Blair. He wrote Bose in the summer of 1944 that he was adviser to a Japanese civil government section which had authority over the civilians on the islands. Under this section, Indian advisers were attached to education, finance and propaganda, and police units. Bose's correspondence with Loganadhan indicated he was not satisfied with the lack of progress in transfer of the actual administration to Loganadhan's organization.[29] Bose was never willing to accept the limited Japanese interpretation of the transfer of the islands. He continued to press for a *de facto* transfer to match the Japanese and FIPG propaganda position.

Bose in his meeting with Tōjō made several other demands. He asked that the INA be used as a single spearhead unit in the Indian campaign, rather than be fragmented among Japanese units as General Terauchi had planned. Bose complained too about the *Hikari Kikan*. Relations between Yamamoto and Bose had become strained, and Bose no longer felt Yamamoto was representing his position adequately as intermediary between the FIPG and the Japanese Government.[30]

From the time of his arrival in Southeast Asia, Bose had been unhappy about having to deal with the *Hikari Kikan* rather than directly with Tokyo. *Kikan* officials were curious, and their inquisitiveness made Bose even more reluctant to take them into his confidence. Even before the organization of the *Azad Hind* Government Bose had kept details of his plans from *Kikan* officials and communicated instead with officials from Tokyo whenever possible. Yamamoto could not have been pleased with Bose's attitude.

Bose also mentioned the old issue of abandoned Indian property and the desire of the FIPG to issue its own bank notes. To the latter Tōjō did not object. Bose also pointed out the FIPG needed transportation facilities to cover its scattered territories. Tōjō obliged by offering Bose an eleven-place plane for his personal use, complete with Japanese crew. Bose wanted to replace the Japanese crew with Indians, but Tōjō did not agree. Bose had to be content with having the Indian National Tricolour painted on both sides of the nose of the plane, with the INA emblem of the springing tiger in the centre of the flag.[31]

Bose also exacted concessions from Army Chief of Staff Sugiyama. The INA would rank as an allied army under Japanese operational command in the India offensive. Sugiyama agreed to raising a second INA division and planning a third. Cadets for the INA might be trained at the War College in Tokyo.[32] Japan would finance ex-POWs in the INA if Bose would pay the civilian recruits. Equipment would continue to come from captured British stocks. By the time Bose left Tokyo on 18 November for Southeast Asia, he felt he had again made progress. FIPG Headquarters would shortly move to Rangoon in anticipation of INA participation in the campaign on the Indo-Burmese border.

IV THE *HIKARI KIKAN* AND FIPG IN BURMA

In December Bose moved FIPG Headquarters and the INA from Singapore to Rangoon. The second division was being organized and trained. In January 1944 the *Hikari Kikan* also moved to Rangoon, and Colonel Yamamoto was replaced as head of the *Kikan* by Lieutenant-General Isoda Saburo. At the same time Yamamoto was promoted to major-general. Several things prompted the replacement of Yamamoto by Isoda and Yamamoto's relegation to a secondary position in the *Kikan*. First, Bose had complained in Tokyo of Yamamoto's lack of understanding. Bose wanted INA strength increased to three divisions; Yamamoto balked at more than ten thousand.[33] Second, the offensive into India was pending, and it would be logical to have a higher-ranking officer as chief of the *Hikari Kikan*. Furthermore, Isoda was as benign a general as anyone could ask for, and he would be able to placate Bose, even though Japan could not always agree to Bose's insistent demands. The only person unhappy with the new arrangement was Yamamoto, whose relations with Bose continued to deteriorate.

The orders of the reorganized *Hikari Kikan* were virtually the same as for its predecessor. The *Kikan* was to maintain liaison during the forthcoming campaign between the Southern Army, the newly created Burma Area Army under it, and the 15th Army below the BAA on the one hand, and the INA and FIPG on the other. The *Kikan* would deal with the old IIL too. Problems of liaison were compounded as preparations for the campaign progressed. Special sections were added to the *Kikan* to handle administrative, medical, and weapons supply problems with the INA.[34]

Fujiwara had established the first contacts with the Indian POWs, helped strengthen the IIL, and ushered the INA into being. Under Iwakuro the *Kikan* had been mainly a political and propaganda organ. Under Yamamoto, most of the political appointments of the *Iwakuro Kikan* were replaced by military men, and the *Kikan* took on an increasingly military character. Now under Isoda the *Kikan* was called on to function as a military liaison unit during the Imphal campaign.

Isoda was immediately plunged into problems of maintaining liaison and co-operation between the BAA-15th Army Headquarters and the INA in the midst of the campaign. Liaison requirements were much more urgent than they had been under Isoda's predecessors. Issues arose at all levels of co-operation, from chiefs of staff down to the fighting man in the jungles around Imphal. Isoda was at Bose's side during meetings with General Mutaguchi, commander of the 15th Army, to which INA units were attached, meetings with General Kawabe, commander of the Burma Area Army, and meetings with Field-Marshal Terauchi of the Southern Army. Isoda watched as agreements were concluded regarding administration of captured territory which was to be handed over to the INA, and for the operation of the INA First Division under command of the 15th Army and ultimately under the BAA. The agreements were sanctioned in each case by the 15th Army command, the BAA command, and IGHQ in Tokyo. At the outset of the Imphal campaign in January, relations between Bose and the Japanese commanders appeared to Isoda to be good. Optimistic pronouncements about the liberation of India were issued by Bose and Tōjō at the start of the campaign.[35]

Two issues precipitated conferences in March 1944 between Bose and *Kikan* officials. Each series of conferences lasted at least three days, with threats and counter-threats. Each series ended finally in *Netaji* winning his point when the *Kikan* reluctantly conceded. One issue was the establishment of a National Bank of *Azad Hind* in Burma. Bose had already been assured of necessary capital and of Burmese approval for the project. He would not concede Japanese objections. The second issue was over the appointment of a Japanese military officer as chairman of the proposed Indo-Japanese War Co-operation Council to function on Indian soil after entry of the INA and Japan into India. Bose refused to consider the Japanese suggestion. Whenever *Kikan* officials hinted that high-ranking officials in Tokyo would be upset at Bose's stand, Bose threatened to cable Tōjō or Sugiyama himself. This was an effective counter-threat which Bose used on more than one occasion in dealing with the *Hikari Kikan*.[36]

There were also incidents between Bose and high *Kikan* officials over matters of protocol and courtesy as symbolic of the equal status of the INA. Bose's bargaining power in these cases was the threat to absent himself from functions if Japanese officers did not carry out formalities as agreed. The threat of the loss of Bose's leadership was his most effective bargaining weapon, since the Japanese realized their dependence on Bose would be great if they entered India.[37]

By the end of April the Japanese were obviously bogged down in the Imphal campaign, and IGHQ sent staff officers from Tokyo to review the situation on the spot. Bose was at the same time pressing Isoda for better liaison and more supplies. By May, Bose decided to visit Rangoon and Bangkok to build the morale of the INA and FIPG. Isoda accompanied him. To Isoda the campaign already appeared to be in serious trouble, but there was no hint that Bose was discouraged. Even after the withdrawal from Imphal, Isoda was hard put to persuade Bose to leave Rangoon. Isoda pleaded with *Netaji* repeatedly, but Bose would not leave until he was sure transport had been arranged for all INA units, including the Rani of Jhansi Regiment, toward which he felt a special responsibility.[38]

While the Imphal offensive was in progress, relations between the Japanese and INA fighting men deteriorated. Under battle conditions in the midst of monsoon jungle, with no supplies, tempers were short. Each side accused men of the other side of arrogance. Protocol regarding saluting was the immediate cause of numerous incidents. Isoda and his *Kikan* staff were called on to assuage the wounded pride of the Indians.

From the INA standpoint, Japanese-INA cooperation was a relationship between equals. The INA had been recognized as an allied army before the fighting began. And the INA was the army of a government now legally recognized in international law. From the Japanese standpoint, however, and especially in the eyes of some fighting men, prejudice remained because the INA was composed largely of POWs. Surrender had no legitimate place in Japan's long military tradition and ideal. The INA therefore suffered from a taint of disloyalty from the Japanese viewpoint. Furthermore, to many Japanese who dealt with the INA on an operational level, it seemed that INA demands often far exceeded reason and reality. When

Japanese supply officers were pressed to extend one day's rations to three days, Indian fighting men were likely to insist on their right to consume the rations in one day. Japanese often felt Indians were prone to insist on rights when the business of fighting was more pressing.[39] Furthermore, Japanese who dealt with Indians on a day-to-day basis did not always understand Japan's India policy.

Again, from the standpoint of the INA, the campaign was an all-out struggle to the finish for Indian liberation, while for Japan, Imphal was a limited holding operation defending Burma while the higher priority campaigns in the Pacific were being fought. The Pacific theatre had first claims on Japan's fast-diminishing supplies. Just as there were no limits to the INA objective, Indian demands for material support were insatiable. No degree of assistance the Japanese could give would satisfy Indian requirements. And the Japanese capacity for response was decreasing rapidly. The gap would never be closed.[40] Despite General Isoda's gentle nature, Bose grew increasingly insistent and could not be placated.

Indian leaders felt the difference among Japanese in the degree of understanding shown toward the independence movement. S.A. Ayer, Minister of Publicity and Propaganda in the FIPG, classified the liaison officers into three types: 1) the "Manchurians"—"the arrogant, obstinate type who had reduced the people of Manchuria to virtual serfdom. They did not see much point in Japan offering all-out aid to *Netaji* except on condition of something concrete in return—say, at least a promise of military, economic or political concessions to be given to Japan in Free India. They suffered from a fit of racial superiority", 2) "the true sincere but rather impotent group of juniors who went out of their way to help us, to encourage us, and to apologize for the short-sighted attitude" of the first group, and 3) "the colourless group which fully endorsed Tokyo policy, but would only pray and hope that the INA would somehow win India's independence, even in spite of the 'Manchurian' group". Further, Ayer charged the Manchurians "tried hard to pick puppets from among insignificant Indians and also to play off one man against another".[41]

Arriving in Rangoon following INA and Japanese withdrawal from the Imphal front, Bose on 9 July thanked Japanese authorities for their help, "without which the transfer of our Provisional Government from Shōnan to Burma would have been quite impossible".[42] At the same time, Bose was of course dissatisfied with the handling of the military situation at Imphal. If the INA had been built up to full strength of three divisions and used as regular fighting units rather than in guerrilla operations and for intelligence, he felt the outcome might have been different. These problems would have to be remedied.

Bose was still unhappy too about having to deal with the *Hikari Kikan* rather than directly with the BAA and the Japanese Government. He regarded the liaison agency as an unnecessary hindrance and cause of misunderstanding. Furthermore, he felt Japan's strategy had been at fault. Japan and the INA should have made an immediate attack on Chittagong. This would have sparked the anti-British revolution in Bengal which would have spread rapidly all over India.

There were also questions regarding military discipline. Bose was adamant that INA soldiers not be subject to Japanese military jurisdiction even though they were fighting under Japanese commanders. A compromise was arranged whereby Japanese military jurisdiction and discipline would prevail in cases of emergency only. But at the lower echelons there were many disputes over the authority of Japanese military policemen.[43]

Another problem was the transfer of captured territory to FIPG Commissioner Chatterji. Agreement provided for the transfer of captured territory to the FIPG, but the territory would be in Burma, and Premier Ba Maw objected. This created problems for the *Hikari Kikan* in dealing with the Burmese Government. There was behind the immediate dispute accumulated hostility of Burmese toward Indians, who were often successful businessmen in Burma.

Bose also looked toward India, as he did repeatedly during his struggle in East Asia. The homeland should never be lost sight of. On 6 July he broadcast a long message to India, addressing himself personally to Gandhi. He proclaimed the high esteem in which Gandhi was held by Indians abroad and acclaimed Gandhi's stand in the August 1942 "Quit India" resolution. Bose explained the rationale of his own actions outside India in the struggle for freedom, especially in seeking Axis help. After visiting Japan, Bose said, "I was fully satisfied that Japan's policy toward Asia was no bluff but was rooted in sincerity." He reasserted to India the determination of all Indians in East Asia to continue the struggle until freedom became a reality.[44]

In July, following announcement of the disaster of Saipan, came news of the fall of the Tōjō Cabinet. The military outlook for Japan grew darker. Bose's talks with Kawabe and other Japanese officers confirmed his fear that the new Koiso Cabinet might change its policy toward the INA. Bose was now more than ever dissatisfied with having to deal through an intermediary. He wanted direct diplomatic and military relations with Japan, rather than having to use the *Hikari Kikan* to discuss both political and military problems. Direct dealings Bose felt would eliminate some misunderstandings. It all added up to the need for Bose to visit Tokyo again. Bose had already been pressing Japanese authorities to send him to Tokyo again. His proposal was not approved by agencies on the spot, however, and Bose was unable to leave until several months later.[45]

Bose had a talk with the naval attaché in Burma, Rear-Admiral Nakado. Nakado made a secret suggestion to Bose. In view of the pressing military situation, Bose might abandon his strategy of liberating India from the east and instead seek Soviet co-operation to liberate India from the north through central Asia and Samarkand. Bose was interested. Major-General Yamamoto had also hinted at the idea when Imphal had become a fiasco. Bose indicated he would be willing to try the new approach if Tokyo agreed. For Bose it did not matter from which direction help came. The only thing that mattered was that India be freed and that Indians themselves fight for their freedom. But Tokyo's consent to the new plan did not come in 1944. Bose was still of propaganda value to Japan.[46]

Meanwhile Bose had complained bitterly about the *Kikan* in a letter to Foreign Minister Shigemitsu. In it he asked for the elimination of the *Kikan* and for a Japanese diplomat accredited to the FIPG. His letter concluded with the threat that, unless he received a favourable reply, he would resign from leadership of the FIPG and INA, and lead a suicide squad into India.[47] This use of Bose's own leadership was a successful stratagem; he went to Tokyo.

V BOSE PAYS A THIRD, FINAL VISIT TO TOKYO

On 31 October, Bose flew to Tokyo with Chatterji, Lieutenant-Colonel Kiani of the INA 1st Division, and Vice-Chief of Staff Major Habibur Rahman. Isoda, Shigemitsu, and a delegation of Indian students and IIL representatives were on hand to meet them. Tokyo had changed since Bose's last visit. And as Bose's plane was approaching the city, about one hundred American B-29 bombers were also screaming toward Tokyo to begin the first of a series of devastating air attacks. The Indians were escorted to the *Gaimushō* guest house, where they stayed for ten days. They then moved to the Frank Lloyd Wright Imperial Hotel. It became an action-packed month. Bose on his first day in Tokyo called on the new Prime Minister Koiso. He called also at the Foreign Ministry, the Army and Navy Ministries, and the Finance Ministry to renew old acquaintances.

Indians in East Asia interpreted Bose's visit as preparation for a new India offensive. Bose encouraged this impression when he announced over Radio Tokyo on 8 November, "I have come to Tokyo to see General Koiso and other Japanese Ministers personally, as I want greater collaboration on military matters and wish to discuss military affairs with Japanese military officials."[48] Bose also spoke on 3 November, sounding more as if the Imphal campaign were in the offing than a recent defeat. "The battle for Chittagong and Imphal will be much more than a local battle," said Bose. "It will be in essence and in substance the battle of India. In other words, the future fate of India will be decided in the hills and in the jungles which bar the way to Chittagong and Imphal."[49] Bose was ready to push ahead with a fresh assault into India, while Japan was already beaten on the Indo-Burmese border and fast losing islands in the Pacific.

Prime Minister Koiso gave a state dinner for Bose and reaffirmed Japan's pledge to aid the cause of Indian independence. He also renewed Tōjō's earlier promises that Japan sought no territorial, economic or military gains in India. Japan was repaying an ancient cultural debt to India, said Koiso. Another dinner was given by Bose's old friend. Foreign Minister Shigemitsu. Bose was sorry to hear of the death just two days earlier of Tōyama Mitsuru, Rash Behari Bose's old protector. Rash Behari was by this time seriously ill, and *Netaji* paid him a final visit. Bose met many other friends, including the poet Noguchi, who had been a friend of Rabindranath Tagore. And Bose was honoured by an audience with Emperor Hirohito, who knew of Bose's exploits.

There was a mass meeting at Hibiya Hall under joint auspices of the Imperial Rule Assistance Association and the Japan-India Society at which Bose addressed a mixed Indian-Japanese audience. Bose talked without pause—except for applause—for two hours about Indian independence. Those who were unable to enter the jammed auditorium reported Bose's booming voice could be heard outside the hall.[50]

Bose got down to the business at hand. He held several conferences with members of the cabinet. There were negotiations with Army Chief of Staff Umezu Yoshijirō, Army Minister Sugiyama, Navy Minister Yonai Mitsumasa, and Naval Chief of Staff Oikawa Koshirō. Present at most of the meetings were Isoda, General Arisue, chief of the Second Bureau (Intelligence), IGHQ, and Lieutenant-General Sato Kenryō, chief of the Military Affairs Bureau of the General Staff.

Bose made several demands during the negotiations: an expansion of the size of the INA by at least fifty thousand, an ambassador accredited to the FIPG, a loan agreement, better weapons including tanks, planes, and guns to supplement captured British stores, distribution of propaganda literature written by himself, and transfer of all Indian POWs to the INA. Bose reiterated his view that the only way out of problems like those encountered at Imphal was to enlarge the INA. Finally, it was decided that the INA would be expanded by forty thousand, which was far less than Bose hoped.[51] He felt the lack of weapons had contributed to the fiasco in Imphal; he was assured that arms, ammunition and supplies would be forthcoming. But Japan's productive capacity was so reduced that Sugiyama and Umezu could only promise one bomber and some munitions when pressed for figures.[52] Till the end of the war Bose could never reckon with Japan's diminishing productive capacity.

Bose pushed hard for a loan agreement and for a Japanese diplomatic envoy. Under existing arrangements, whenever the Japanese Government loaned money to the FIPG, the FIPG issued IOUs. Bose wanted a more formal agreement so that Japan would be unable to exert any form of pressure on India after independence.[53] In a speech from Burma on 1 July 1944 Bose stated, "All our finances are based on the cardinal rule: Indians stand on their own legs; they refuse stilts lent by others. This has given us a lot of independence in our dealings with the Japs. Also it has prevented our worst enemies from pointing a finger at the smallest item in our programme to say that we have bartered the future of our country."[54]

Shigemitsu and Greater East Asia Minister Aoki were willing to send a diplomat, but Lieutenant-General Satō was unwilling unless Bose gave a *quid pro quo,* by which he did not mean an opposite number. A tentative agreement was reached whereby Japan would appoint Hachiya Teruo, chief of the Foreign Department in Taiwan, as Japanese Minister to the FIPG. In return, although not announced at the time, Bose agreed to put the INA under Japanese command during the defence of Malaya and Burma.[55] On the day of Bose's last meeting with Japanese military authorities seventy B-29s bombed Tokyo, forcing the meeting underground.

Bose was entertained during the remainder of his stay by cabinet members and IGHQ officers. He visited Indian students in Tokyo to bolster their morale. He inspected the Military Academy, the War College where some Indians were in training, and the Air Force Training School. He talked with Rama Murti, chairman of the Tokyo IIL since Rash Behari Bose's illness. In return for Japanese hospitality Bose gave a party at the Imperial Hotel before leaving Tokyo.

Bose had a final wish in Tokyo: to interview Soviet Ambassador Malik. Bose sought an introduction through the good offices of Shigemitsu, but this avenue was unsuccessful. He then wrote directly to the Ambassador; again Malik refused to see Bose. But Bose's idea of securing Soviet aid persisted and motivated his last act at the close of the war.[56]

VI RETURN TO RANGOON

Bose left Tokyo for Southeast Asia on 29 November, having done everything he could in Tokyo. He stopped in Shanghai, Taihoku, Saigon, and Singapore, meeting INA-IIL branch heads and Japanese authorities at each stop. In Saigon Bose talked with Terauchi about his Tokyo discussions.[57] He returned to Rangoon at the end of the year.

The status of Hachiya Teruo, new Minister to the FIPG, was equivocal. Shigemitsu had been especially concerned about the crisis in relations between the INA and *Hikari Kikan* and persuaded the Army to agree to the sending of an envoy. The Supreme War Conference on 21 November reached the decision to "send a diplomatic representative to the Indian Provisional Government". According to the decision, however, "Concerning India policy, as heretofore, IGHQ is in charge and all agencies concerned shall co-operate." Further, "The diplomatic representative mentioned above shall be under the aegis of the India policy agency of IGHQ regarding India policy."[58] This decision and the policy for implementing it were anything but regular diplomatic protocol. The decision was, in the first place, a military one. It was never contemplated that the envoy would be a regular *Gaimushō* appointee. In Southeast Asia he was to remain under military purview, that is under the *Hikari Kikan* in the chain of command.

When Hachiya arrived in Rangoon in February 1945, it was immediately apparent to Bose and the FIPG that something was awry in protocol. When Hachiya asked for an interview with Bose, Foreign Minister Chatterji asked Hachiya for his credentials. But Hachiya had none, for he had not been provided any in Tokyo. Hachiya told Chatterji there was no precedent for the Japanese Government sending an accredited diplomat to a provisional government.[59] Bose accordingly refused to see Hachiya until such time as he could present proper credentials as an accredited diplomatic representative. Hachiya immediately communicated his dilemma to Tokyo, asking that he be provided with credentials as soon as possible. But before this glaring omission could be remedied, the war had ended. Japan never did send an accredited envoy to the FIPG, and Bose never realized his desire of circumventing the *Hikari Kikan* and dealing directly with both the Japanese Government and IGHQ.

The sending of a diplomatic envoy, then, was another tongue-in-cheek attempt to meet Bose's demands in form but not in substance. Perhaps it was assumed that, since Bose had no experience in dealing with diplomats, he would accept Hachiya without credentials. This was the third time Japan used these tactics in dealing with the FIPG. In the first case, Japan's recognition of the FIPG immediately after its formation was not full diplomatic recognition. It was viewed even by the *Gaimushō* as conditional recognition of a provisional government which would probably not be binding in the event that India became independent.[60] The second instance was the announcement of the transfer of the Andaman and Nicobar Islands to the FIPG. In fact, as noted above, final authority for administration of the islands remained with the Japanese Navy.

On 23 January 1945, Bose's birthday, there was a large meeting of Indians in Rangoon. Bose was ceremonially weighed against gold, but rather than dispensing gold in the traditional manner of Indian kings, the FIPG collected the gold as revenue from those at the rally. With the presentation of jewels and money to Bose, he reaffirmed the dedication of all efforts and resources to the cause.[61]

The military outlook for Japan had dimmed since Bose's absence in Tokyo. English ships were close to Bengal, Japan's 28th Army had withdrawn nearly to Rangoon, and the INA was retreating with the 15th Army to the right bank of the Irrawaddy. The Japanese defence line had reached Mandalay, and enemy forces were dashing toward the Irrawaddy. The situation grew tenser by the day. All these things Bose knew.

Bose accordingly announced several INA promotions: Chatterji, Bhonsle, Kiani and Loganadhan to major-general; Shah Nawaz, Gulzara Singh, Habibur Rahman, Aziz Ahmed, G.R. Nagar and S.A. Alagoppan from lieutenant-colonel to full colonel. Chatterji as Foreign Minister was also called on to negotiate with Burma regarding Indian property there.[62]

Bose spent the early months of the new year inspecting the front lines near Meiktila where INA men were fighting. If he was discouraged the troops got no hint of it.[63] Isoda watched Bose as he encouraged ragged Indian soldiers in what Isoda felt was a hopeless situation. INA troops were exhausted but unable to rest. They avoided roads and skirted houses, fearing discovery by British scouts. Bose used spare moments to refresh himself by reading Irish history, which sustained his hopes.

Isoda's assignment was to urge Bose to retreat south of Meiktila as the enemy pressed on Meiktila from the north with tanks and planes. It was a difficult assignment, for Bose cherished every inch of territory and demanded reconnaissance reports on the defensive situation. He issued a statement: "I have been reading a history of Irish independence. Although the independence fighters were nearly all killed, seven or eight years later their prayers were answered.... We must fight to the death led by the 1st Division. Then our hopes for independence will be realized for the Indian people."[64] Isoda had to use all his ingenuity to persuade Bose to withdraw to Rangoon where it was safer for the moment. Bose urged Japanese commanders not to abandon Rangoon.

By mid-July the end of the war for Germany was imminent. Bose turned his attention now from the Japanese Army to the Navy. He sent a letter to Southern Task Force Commander Vice-Admiral Fukutome, advising, "The Japanese Navy should adopt more positive strategy towards the Indian Ocean."[65] It was unclear how Bose's advice could be carried out, Vice-Admiral Fukutome remarked.

Bose's resolve was reflected in the faith of the INA staff officers. Gulzara Singh, vice-chief of staff, Shah Nawaz and Sahgal discussed the requirements for maintaining the INA position. But Bose was saddened on arrival in Rangoon to hear of the desertion of four senior officers of the 2nd Division. He asked Shah Nawaz Khan to select his own replacements for these men. Bose also issued an order that any who retreated would be given the death penalty.[66] But the INA and Japanese both were hopelessly short of ammunition and other supplies. The enemy had crossed the Irrawaddy at several points. The defence of Meiktila was hopeless. Enemy landings on the coast dealt another blow to Japanese hopes to defend any of Burma. It was evident that the battle of Burma had been lost.[67]

Yet another blow to Japanese and Indian hopes was the defection of the Burma Independence Army to the British. The BIA, commanded by General Aung San (Defence Minister in the Ba Maw Cabinet), had been encouraged and trained by the Japanese, much like the INA. Now, however, the BIA turned against the Japanese and co-operated with advancing British forces. The BIA had completely lost faith in the Japanese. The BIA harassed the Japanese Army with guerrilla tactics, further weakening the Japanese supply system until it collapsed.

On 20 April news of the retreat of BAA commander General Kimura from Rangoon was reported to Bose. Bose refused the order for retreat but hurriedly arranged for evacuation of the Rani of Jhansi Regiment. Finally Bose left Rangoon for Moulmein secretly by car the night of 23 April. He left Major-General Loganadhan in Rangoon to take charge of evacuating other Indians.

In December of the previous year some of Bose's advisers suggested moving the headquarters of the FIPG and INA to Bangkok or Saigon, but Bose had prevaricated. He was preoccupied, for one thing, by news from Bengal of his mother's death. Now there was no choice, and Bose's car was joined by nine others to transfer FIPG and INA headquarters eastward. It was the end of another chapter of an epic.

Imphal Setting—Terrain

CHAPTER NINE

To India or Not?

I   THE JAPANESE PERSPECTIVE

The Imphal campaign in India became the vortex of all the forces in the Indo-Japanese co-operation: the impact of the charismatic personality of Bose on IGHQ Tokyo, the problem of delineating Japan's policy aims toward India, Japan's logistics and military dilemma in Burma, differences over military protocol and command arising between the INA and the Japanese Army, and the Japanese attitude toward the INA and the Free India Provisional Government. The fate of Imphal determined the course of Japan's cooperation with the Indian independence movement in Southeast Asia. Imphal loomed large in the whole defence of Burma and the westward boundary of Japan's Greater East Asia Co-Prosperity Sphere. From the Japanese standpoint the military stakes at Imphal were critical. For the INA it was one real chance to break through the border and ignite the Indian revolution. At Imphal Japan and the INA at last cooperated in a military campaign, but with cataclysmic results.

The battle of Imphal was a major disaster in the military annals of the world and is still one of the most controversial Japanese campaigns of the entire Pacific War. A total of five Japanese generals-in-command and numerous staff officers were dismissed during and immediately following the action in an unprecedented attempt to fix blame for the fiasco. One staff officer in the supply section committed suicide; one general threatened to.

Japan's lightning dash through Thailand and Malaya had taken the British aback, especially with the successful capture of Singapore after a startlingly brief fight. When the Japanese Army overran Burma in 1942 there was a longer struggle, and the stakes were even higher. Burma in Japanese hands meant the severing of the all-important supply lines between China and India through which British and American support was funnelling to Chiang Kai-shek's forces. The only alternative to the legendary Burma Road from Mandalay through Lashio in Burma over the mountains to Kunming, China, was to airlift supplies from Indian airfields over the unmapped "Hump" into China. This was the mission of the swashbuckling Major-General Claire Chennault.

The end of 1942 saw the Axis everywhere successful. Rommel was in Egypt, the German invasion of Russia had gone smoothly. Nationalist China was on her knees, and India and Australia were expecting a Japanese invasion. Prospects for the Allies were dark in the Pacific, and the Rising Sun was at its zenith from Japan to the Bay of Bengal. If Japan could take Australia the imperialism of the white races would be purged from Asia, and India could soon gain independence. Britain was unable to dispute with the Japanese Navy, and there were not enough British and Indian troops in India to assure its defence. Even air protection was inadequate.[1]

A Japanese carrier-borne attack was launched on Colombo and Trincomalee in April 1942, and bombs were dropped on the southeast coast and on the Bay of Bengal, closing British shipping for a time. A follow-up of the Japanese attack would have been impossible for the British to repulse. Luckily for the British and Indians the attack was not renewed.[2]

Japanese forces had not pursued retreating British troops beyond the Chindwin River in Burma in May 1942, allegedly because "an invasion was likely to arouse ill-feeling amongst the Indian masses".[3] By mid-1942 there was a definite desire in Tokyo to heed the political import of Indian opinion for propaganda purposes. So the Japanese remained east of the Chindwin River, leaving British-Indian forces to build up their strength in the Imphal plain.

The British momentarily expected the Japanese to cross the Chindwin and strike into India, but during 1943 the Japanese failed to resume major fighting in the sector. The only British attempt to counter Japanese strength east of the Chindwin came in February 1943, with an unorthodox long-range thrust into Japanese territory by Brigadier-General Orde Wingate's specially organized and equipped Chindits. Though the conception of the operation and the dramatic personality of Wingate appealed to the Allied Press, the Chindits remained in Burma only two months, and did little damage to Japanese positions other than temporarily disrupting the Mandalay-Myitkyina railway.

But the idea of a long-range operation into enemy territory without a secure line of communications made a singular impact on at least one Japanese, Lieutenant-General Mutaguchi Renya, who had the onerous duty of mopping up after the Chindits and who was soon appointed commander of the 15th Army. Mutaguchi was to reverse his earlier opposition to the idea of invasion of north-east India on the ground that what the British could do, the Japanese Army could do better.

By the end of June, ground and air reinforcements had begun to reach India, and though the British fleet was still unable to dispute for command of the Bay of Bengal, British anxiety over the defence of India was allayed, and by late 1943 there was still no sign of a Japanese thrust into India.[4]

British intelligence had it that the Japanese were planning a "full-scale invasion of India".[5] This British assumption had no basis in Japanese operational plans. Tōjō, to be sure, had said in the Diet in 1942 that Japan was planning to strike a decisive blow against British power and military establishment in India. But this was a policy statement made for propaganda impact. It did not reach the stage of operational or even strategic planning on such a sweeping scale. The strategic and operational objectives of the Imphal campaign were much more limited. British anxieties over a full-scale Japanese invasion of India were generated perhaps more by Britain's psychological heritage in India than by reality.[6]

By mid-June Wavell was able to report that the military posture in India required re-evaluation and that "we can now begin definitely to plan the recapture of Burma, which has been in my mind ever since it became obvious that I was likely to lose it."[7]

At midnight on 15-16 November 1943, the Southeast Asia Command was created and Acting Admiral Lord Louis Mountbatten became Supreme Allied Commander. Mountbatten took over from General Sir Claude Auchinleck, commander-in-chief in India, responsibility for conducting all operations against Japan which were based on India and Ceylon.[8]

The first British plan called for a limited offensive into upper Burma "with the object of confirming the Japanese of our intentions to attack in Burma".[9] British strategy of clearing north Burma first

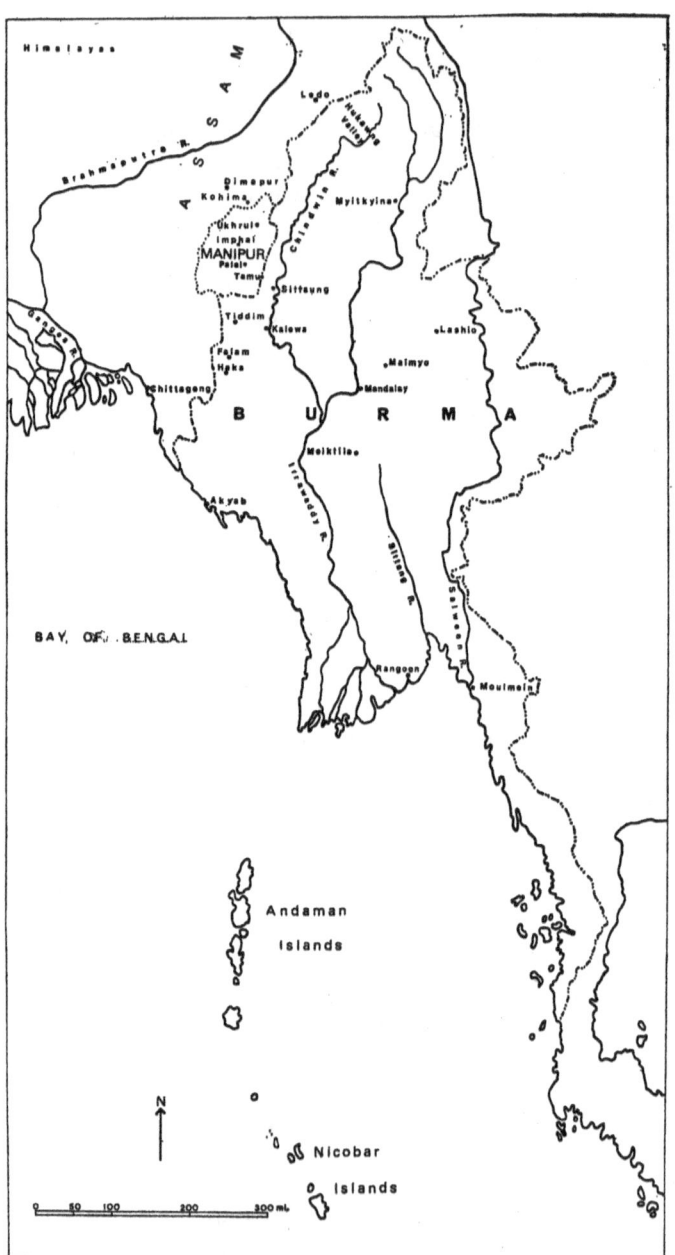

Imphal Setting

would allow "Vinegar Joe" Stilwell, American chief of staff to Chiang Kai-shek, to build a new Burma Road north of the old one and closer to west China airfields. The British choice for the new route was Ledo through Myitkina and the Hukawng Valley. Myitkina was also a good staging airfield for a shorter route over the Himalayas to Kunming which would mean a saving on valuable fuel. Furthermore, Myitkina was an important rail-head in north Burma. A British advance down the Hukawng Valley and from Imphal across the Chindwin River could combine with a Chinese push south from Yunnan. The British never doubted that the tide would turn eventually and Burma would be cleared of the Japanese Army.

British reopening of the Burma Road would have to follow reconquest of north Burma. Retaking north Burma would have other advantages too. Long-range B-29 bombers based west of Chungking, China's wartime capital, could strike at Japanese cities. By the spring of 1943 plans were being mapped by both British and Japanese chiefs of staff for a Burma-India offensive. Imphal was thought by the British to be the best possible staging area for reconquering Burma from the north. It was also the Japanese-INA choice for a strike at British power in north-east India. Imphal was thus the battlefield chosen by both sides.

II THE SETTING

The Imphal plain is one of the most forsaken spots in the world. India and Burma are separated by the Chin Hills of the Arakan mountain range[10], which is an extension of the Himalayan roof of the world. The mountains form such an effective barrier that communication between the two countries has traditionally been by sea instead. Three great river systems—the Chindwin, Irrawaddy, and Salween—wend their way roughly north-south through the mountains and provide important communication through the mountainous jungle terrain. The main entrance to the valley was an all-weather road which wound its way northward through spectacular scenery along precipitous mountainsides to Kohima and Dimapur. Other than this there was virtually no contact overland. There had never been a Burma-India rail connection, and until 1942 there was no east-west road worthy of the name. Until British and Japanese army engineers hewed out roads there were only jungle tracks used by animals and hillmen, and then only in dry weather. These were the tracks followed by the British and Chinese troops in their retreat from Burma to India, and later by retreating Japanese troops.

Imphal is the capital of the state of Manipur, just inside the Indian border. It lies on a flat, nearly treeless plateau some three thousand feet high, surrounded on all sides by impassable mountains. Peaks in the Zybew range east of the plateau are from two thousand to four thousand feet high above the plateau, and from thirty to fifty miles across. This range stretches some five hundred miles along the eastern edge of the plain. To the west and south are the Chin Hills of the Arakan range, an equally formidable stretch of inhospitable terrain. The jungle surrounding this enclosed basin is not really neutral; it is hostile to human habitation.

The northern access to the plain from India and Assam lies through Dimapur and the steep Kohima Road. From Dimapur a single-track railway sweeps west through Bengal and Assam. This was the nearest rail-head to Imphal and was an important military objective for both armies.

The Manipuris and Naga hillmen inhabiting the region are people of Mongoloid stock. Hinduism was imposed on the Manipuris in the eighteenth century, but their social structure differs from the Indian caste system and relates them more closely to the Nagas. The Nagas were head-hunters by reputation, many of them now Christian, and throughout the war these proud people refused to aid the Japanese.

By the end of the dry season, usually sometime in May, the plains of Imphal like most of north India are parched and cracked. The temperature has risen to 120°F in the hottest time of the summer. Lassitude overtakes all forms of life. Abruptly the monsoon breaks in May or early June. The plains are drenched and the sky filled with black cumulus clouds. In contrast to the menacing sky, relief and hope appear on men's faces. Life is possible again for another year.

The monsoon rains in this part of India are among the heaviest in the world. Between June and September the local hill people say not even tigers can travel. Army engineers cajoled roads out of the mountains during the height of these monsoon rains. As soon as they were built they were swept away by torrents. But Japanese sappers and navvies without bulldozers worked doggedly, and roads were completed through the Arakan and Mintani mountains and out onto the plains.

Cumulus cloud cover reduces air operations to almost nil during the monsoon season, with visibility down to less than a mile. The clouds, torrential rains, heat and accompanying disease meant the campaigning season was normally limited to the eight "dry" months of the year between October and May.

Even during the eight "dry" months the jungle is scarcely habitable, for there are hazards even in peacetime. Malaria was the greatest cause of casualties among British and Japanese troops alike. The Japanese monopoly of the world quinine supply gave them some initial advantage, but this was more than counterbalanced by other problems by the time of the Imphal battle. Dysentery, typhus and dengue fever ravaged both armies. Leeches incessantly drained human blood and maggots preyed on wounds. Though leeches may lower the resistance of tired and hungry men, even more horrifying was an infection called the Naga sore, caused by inexperienced tearing off of the leech, leaving the head embedded in the flesh. The infection spreads from a small blister to a large putrefying sore, destroying skin, muscles and tendons. Thousands of retreating malnourished Japanese soldiers fell victim to this potent killer in 1945.[11]

Added to these very real physical hazards was the psychological effect the jungle produced on the fighting man. The macabre atmosphere of the terrain and climate plus the strain and uncertainty of battle made the men "jungle happy". The condition was progressive, and there was no real cure so long as they remained in the jungle under battle conditions. For the British and Indian troops there was the added fear of the superior jungle fighting ability of the Japanese soldier.

III THE BRITISH PERSPECTIVE

Japanese success in Malaya and Burma in 1942 conjured in the minds of the British soldier an image of the Japanese soldier as an invincible jungle fighter. Behind the image was the reality of specialized training in jungle fighting, against which British training had proven relatively impotent. This was a major concern for Mountbatten as Supreme Commander in Southeast Asia and for Lieutenant-General Slim as commander of the 14th Army, as for all British and American commanding officers in Southeast Asia. The indoctrination of centuries of military tradition contributed too to make the Japanese soldier one of the fiercest fighters in the history of warfare.

Another British anxiety was over Japanese intelligence, whose detailed knowledge of British positions in Burma had facilitated the Japanese advance with the least possible exposure to enemy fire. India Command dispatches from 1943 onward referred to the use of "JIFs", the Japanese-inspired fifth column, which was the British name for the Indian National Army. British reports expressed little concern over the use of JIFs as agents and saboteurs, however, since "up to June of this year (1943),... in spite of much advertisement and publicity on the part of our enemies, their results were thought to have afforded them little encouragement".[12] This was before the Imphal campaign began. British intelligence also noted an increase in the number of civilian as compared to military agents used by the Japanese. This change was thought by the British to reflect Japanese mistrust of Indian POWs and the influence of newly arrived Subhas Chandra Bose as JIF leader.

IV   JAPANESE STRATEGIC IMPERATIVES

India formed the western perimeter of the Greater East Asia Co-Prosperity Sphere, which included Burma. At least by 1941 Imperial General Headquarters and the Cabinet had begun to consider India's place in the Southeast Asian scheme of things. By contrast with crucial tin and rubber supplies in Malaya and Indonesia, however, India was of no economic consequence to Japan's war machine and industrial establishment. Many of India's resources, such as iron ore deposits, lay undeveloped. But India loomed important in the thinking of Imperial General Headquarters for other reasons. India formed the defence perimeter to the west of Burma. Securing this border against further Allied offensives was one imperative. The problem was where to establish the line of defence. At least three alternatives were suggested during discussions of Imphal strategy in 1943.

Another strategic imperative for Japan was to disrupt land communications between China and India through which Chiang Kai-shek's forces were being supplied by Allied support from India. This aim was significant not only for defence of Burma but also for the total war picture in Southeast Asia and the Pacific. The India-China route by land and air was the sole life-line for American-Chinese forces in Chungking.

Still other policy considerations for Japan were political and military aims in India. A complete defeat of Britain and the Allies in Asia presupposed expelling Britain from India. There were two ways to approach India, politically and militarily. The problem could clearly not be solved by military means alone. The Indian independence movement in Southeast Asia had the common aim with Japan of ending British colonial rule in India. Tokyo had long recognized the desirability of encouraging the anti-British independence movement, but this was a political rather than a military problem. Securing the cooperation of the INA and IIL had been the task of the *Fujiwara Kikan* and its successors, the *Iwakuro* and *Hikari Kikan*.

V   OPERATION 21

Genesis of the idea for an invasion into India can be traced to 1942. The Burma Area Army had not yet been created. A bold plan for a combined land and air operation was conceived with the object of advancing into east Assam to confront the main force of the British-Indian Army, at the same time severing air communications between India and China. This would avert a British counter-attack in Burma and at the same time disrupt the only connection the British and Americans had with China, the dangerous five-hundred-mile Hump route over the Himalayas to Kunming. The rationale for Operation 21, as it was called, was to follow up Japan's initial success in capturing Burma by moving across the border into India to take the strategic and political initiative there.[13]

For Tokyo there was also a general policy objective of uniting with Germany in a drive against British India from both directions. This aim of co-ordinating strategic planning in Tokyo and Berlin for Asia, however, never went beyond the stage of informal talks. A German-Japanese naval agreement was reached to the effect that the Indian Ocean should be divided at 70° E. longitude between the German and Japanese navies.[14]

The Japanese calculated a British counter-attack in Burma would begin in October after the monsoon and would be primarily in the air. The first operational objective should therefore be to defeat the British in the air and disrupt the Hump airlift. Any ground operation ran the risk of becoming mired in an air war of attrition. General Sugiyama warned of this danger in his report to the Throne in July 1942. Vice-Chief of Staff Tanabe on 20 July 1942 wired the chief of staff of the Southern Army to report by the end of August on the following matters: 1) measures for avoiding a war of attrition in the air, 2) guiding principles for an air operation directed against India, and 3) measures to cut the air route between India and China. This telegram was the germ of the Imphal operation of 1944.[15]

On 11 August Southern Army Operations staff officer Lieutenant-Colonel Hayashi Akira took the Southern Army proposal to Tokyo. The Southern Army staff suggested enlarging the defence area in the north-east border of India because of the enemy air force based in Calcutta, threatening the western perimeter of Greater East Asia and also hindering a blockade of the Hump route. But an air operation against Calcutta presupposed an air base at least in the Indo-Burmese border sector. Imphal and Chittagong must therefore be captured. These were the objectives envisioned in the 6 August operational plan drawn up by the Southern Army staff. The operation was to begin in early October, to be completed within one month, and to engage the 18th and 33rd Divisions, air units under the 15th Army, and units from the 25th Army. Ground, sea and air operations were to be co-ordinated in the offensive. The plan included detailed instructions for deployment of troops. It was calculated that British troops, particularly Indian units, had lost all will to resist. The operation could also take advantage of the unstable political situation within India. Supply lines would be a big problem; food would have to be captured within enemy sectors. The long wall of the Arakan range was envisaged as the permanent defence line.[16]

The Southern Army plan was opposed locally by Lieutenant-General Iida Shōjirō, 15th Army commander, who viewed it as impossible. Lieutenant-General Kuroda Shigetoku, Southern Army chief of staff, tried in vain to win Iida over to the idea. Kuroda had more success with the commanding generals of the 3rd and 5th Air Forces, Lieutenant-General Sugawara Michio and Lieutenant-General Ōbata Eiryō. Kuroda stated later that if the operation had been carried out in 1942 when first conceived, rather than in 1944, it would have succeeded. General Tōjō stated in the spring of 1945 that he regretted Japan had missed this opportunity in 1942.[17]

At Headquarters in Tokyo Colonel Hattori, Operations Bureau chief, questioned Lieutenant-Colonel Hayashi about enemy strength. Hayashi replied that it was five divisions at most, with no large buildup anticipated. On 22 August IGHQ accordingly issued Army Directive no. 1237, ordering the Southern Army to prepare for an operation into north-east India "to attack and secure important strategic areas in north-east Assam state and the Chittagong area and to facilitate the air operation, and at the same time to try to cut the air supply route to Chiang Kai-shek." An order for execution of the operation was to follow once preparations were completed.[18]

In connection with an India offensive three problems were of primary concern to IGHQ. First, Indian public opinion was regarded as anti-fascist and pro-Allies, and there was thus the danger of Japan being regarded as the invader. In this case a compromise between Britain and India might be reached which would generate a national Indian war against Japan. Second, there was the possibility that British military power in India might be increased following Axis reverses in north Africa. Third, once the Japanese Chungking offensive began, there would be no prospect of increasing strength in Burma. The planned Ceylon offensive would also have to be coordinated. IGHQ also suggested more active and effective use of the INA and more effective propaganda toward India.[19]

Indian opinion was thus a major concern of the Operations Bureau in IGHQ at this time. On 5 September the Intelligence Bureau made an evaluation of India for the Operations Bureau. In the judgement of the Second Bureau, as the Japanese Army advanced into east India, the danger of British-Indian compromise would increase. British propaganda would attempt to divert nationalist animosity against Britain to Japan. There was also the possibility of American mediation between Britain and India which might secure Indian independence. The Operations Bureau was also warned that carrying the war into India would surely result in a war of attrition in the air. Air bases in north-east Assam should be captured, but the total operation should not penetrate India deeply. Guerrilla units of the INA should be used in Assam and Bengal, and also in Nepal. The *Kikan* should expand its *bōryaku* operation.[20]

The IGHQ directive was transmitted through the Southern Army to the 15th Army on 1 September by Lieutenant-Colonel Hayashi. Iida, dismayed, told Hayashi the task of the 15th Army was to defend Burma with as small a force as possible. Iida asked Hayashi if the directive was an order. Hayashi said yes, Iida had to accept it. Iida's concerns were practical: the terrain, the impenetrable jungles, the monsoon, and the problem of building roads which could serve as supply lines. Iida decided to try to kill the plan by carrying it to ridiculous extremes. He ordered his staff to plan an offensive to the Ganges River. They replied that this would be going too far. A compromise was devised.[21]

Iida had no choice but to make strategic plans for Operation 21. 15th Army divisional commanders studied the problem from the standpoint of supply, topography, climate and deployment of troops. Some staff officers, unlike Iida, had begun to dream soon after the capture of Singapore of pushing their success westward, into India. When all Burma came under Japanese control six months later, others who had thought an India offensive too visionary also began to dream.

In September Colonel Katakura Tadasu of the Kwantung Army was ordered to Rangoon as staff officer of the 15th Army. In Katakura Iida found an ally. Katakura was a cautious, realistic staff officer with a brilliant record of service in IGHQ, the Army Ministry, and the Kwantung Army, in Manchuria. Staff Officer Takeshita, a recent convert to the India plan, was assigned to meet Katakura's plane and bring him to headquarters. He did his best to explain the strategy in outline to the colonel from Tokyo. This was the beginning of Katakura's association with Burma. He was later appointed to the staff of the new Burma Area Army and gained a reputation as the redoubtable "Tiger of Burma". Katakura immediately called a staff conference in the operations room.

Officers hoping for Katakura's approval were taken aback by his gruff manner and abrupt questions. Katakura's round head, stocky physique, and stubborn expression suggested an iron will. His objections sounded disappointingly logical. It was true that there were no adequate lines of communications for supply and transport. It was also true that Japanese troops were exhausted after the Burma campaign and that Japan's combat potential for such an offensive should be questioned. There was no doubt that road building and further study were called for. Certainly there was the problem of malaria, which had felled as many as sixty per cent of the 55th Division in north Burma and seriously impaired the morale of the Japanese troops. Still, there were staff officers, including Lieutenant-Colonel Hayashi and Major-General Isayama, 15th Army chief of staff, who were disappointed that Katakura had pointed these things out. They continued to study their maps after Katakura left to report to Tokyo.[22]

But Katakura discovered opposition to the plan not only from Iida but also from division commanders on the spot. Lieutenant-General Mutaguchi Renya, commander of the 18th Division, was not taking the plan seriously and had no intention of doing so. The idea was impossible, Mutaguchi argued, because of the problem of building supply roads.[23] Mutaguchi's attitude was recalled by some six months later when he generated the Imphal campaign plan. The commander of the 33rd Division was similarly opposed to Operation 21 from the standpoint of combat potential and timing. Katakura asked General Terauchi, Commander of the Southern Army, to visit the Burma front to inspect the situation at first hand. As a result of his tour Terauchi agreed with Katakura that the operation should be postponed.[24]

On 21 September the 15th Army view was submitted to Southern Army Headquarters and from there it was forwarded to IGHQ. Colonel Iwakuro had already advised IGHQ that the plan should be postponed pending completion of preparations for the India project and until four conditions were guaranteed after the monsoon: 1) the anti-British mood within India should continue; 2) pro-Japanese sentiment should be fostered within India; 3) supply preparations should be completed; and 4) Japan should be able to use the INA with confidence.[25] Katakura also reported to Tokyo that Burma could not be defended with less than ten divisions.[26] And the Southern Army too seemed to be moving toward caution and postponement, following Terauchi's visit to the front.

Iida was relieved when on 5 October a telegram arrived from IGHQ through Southern Army Headquarters ordering that the operation be postponed. The date for a future operation was pushed back to February. Further study and preparation should be made with the new date in mind. Iida knew IGHQ was faltering after the earlier mood of urgency. 15th Army Chief of Staff Major-General Isayama Haruki reiterated Iida's concern at a top-level meeting in Tokyo in October. Sugiyama and Vice-Chief of Staff Tanabe listened sullenly as Isayama enumerated the difficulties Operation 21 would encounter. The following day General Tominaga, chief of personnel in the Army Ministry, told Isayama that Tanabe was very dissatisfied with this report. After Isayama returned to Rangoon he was notified on 27 November of his transfer to the 26th Infantry Group in north China.[27]

Pessimistic reports from the south plus doubts in Tokyo were reinforced by the reversal in Guadalcanal in December and a British counter-offensive in Akyab. On 23 December IGHQ ordered preparations for Operation 21 halted. At the same time the Southern Army was ordered to re-examine the plan for a land operation into India. It was generally understood that Operation 21 was indefinitely postponed. However, IGHQ Army Directive no. 1237 was neither cancelled nor amended; IGHQ had not entirely abandoned hope of an India offensive. This hope was revived in the Guiding Plan for the Imperial Army in the Southwest Area for 1943, drafted by IGHQ in February 1943. According to this plan, "When the general situation permits, a ground offensive will be carried out in north-east India or the Chittagong sector. Enemy operational bases near the border will be disrupted or occupied."[28]

VI   TOKYO RECONSIDERS OBJECTIVES

Given this state of mind in Tokyo and the Japanese aim of encouraging the independence movement as a political weapon against Britain, Tokyo was already predisposed to listen to Bose when he arrived in Japan in the summer of 1943 to plead for Japanese aid to the INA in its proposed thrust into India. Tōjō, initially reluctant to meet Bose, by September 1943 had become, if not a champion of Bose, at least receptive to his requests and willing to contemplate again a campaign into north-east India for both political and military reasons. Bose had injected a non-military influence into the planning of Tōjō and IGHQ, and the Imphal campaign became Japan's "political campaign" of the Pacific War.

Within India British procrastination in the face of Congress demands for independence led Gandhi to sponsor a Congress resolution in August 1942, demanding immediate British withdrawal from India. The British responded to the "Quit India" demand by throwing Gandhi and most of the other Congress leaders into jail once more. That Gandhi had abandoned his more moderate stance encouraged Indian civilians and the INA throughout Southeast Asia to accelerate the demand for independence. Bose's arrival further ignited Indian patriotism, and this in turn had repercussions on Japanese policy toward India and Burma. These forces were all converging in 1943.

Other problems were pushing up the timetable for Imphal. The British plan for an eastward offensive to recapture Burma was known to Japanese strategists. The old military adage that the best defence was offence gave rise to pressure for a Japanese surprise attack as soon as possible.

But by 1943 the general war situation showed signs of deteriorating for Japan. The failure of Germany at Stalingrad and the Japanese fiasco at Guadalcanal reversed Japan's earlier optimistic perspective. Other losses in the Pacific followed. Not only the Army but the public at home in Japan needed a morale-boosting "positive campaign". Something spectacular was called for to reverse the tide and raise spirits. Prime Minister Tōjō needed success too for political reasons. But the place for the new campaign—and there could be only one such success—had not been decided by May 1943.[29]

By the end of February 1943 IGHQ had completed its guiding operational principles for the year. IGHQ abandoned the idea of passive defence and began to prepare for a counter-offensive in the Southern Area. Influenced by Operation 21, thinking at this time included the idea of an advance into north-east India "if general conditions permit". The India-China airlift to Chiang's forces was escalating daily. Japan's relative sea and air power were diminishing daily the hope of any pressure on India by sea. The border would be defended with a built-up strength in Burma of six or seven divisions. The operation was to begin "after the monsoon season in October".[30] This action was to be co-ordinated with a surprise attack by air to "destroy the enemy's air strength in the eastern part of India". An attack by sea was to be launched simultaneously. This was the general strategy.

The build-up of enemy strength on the Burma border made it increasingly obvious to IGHQ that a large-scale counter-offensive was in the offing. The British Army counter-attack to recover central and north Burma was expected to begin after the summer monsoon.[31]

Allied planning reached a final decision for a counter-attack in Burma in January 1943, but details remained to be ironed out at Casablanca, Washington, Quebec, and Cairo. While the Allies were trying to work out their differences, American forces pushed the Ledo Road eastward.

Beyond these considerations were the personalities of the men in command and their inter-relationships. The generals of the 15th Army and the divisions under it, of the newly created[32] Burma Area Army, of the Southern Army, and of Headquarters in Tokyo all played their roles in the working out of the Imphal strategy. This exceptionally complex network of relationships had ramifications beyond the Imphal campaign itself.

Though the plan for Operation 21 was abandoned in 1942, the breakthrough of Japanese lines by Wingate's Chindits in early 1943 forced the Japanese to re-evaluate the defence of north Burma and invasion of north-east India.

By early June 1943, Subhas Chandra Bose, the legendary *Netaji* awaited by Indians throughout Asia, had arrived in Tokyo and made his impact on Tōjō, Sugiyama, and Shigemitsu. With Bose in command of the Indian National Army a major fear of IGHQ—fear of alienating Indian opinion by sending Japanese troops onto Indian soil—would be allayed. Bose's leadership of the Indian independence movement would vindicate all the work of the *Fujiwara Kikan* and its successors and cement Indian cooperation with Japan. Bose's faith that when the INA stepped onto Indian soil total revolution would be ignited was unshakeable.

On 3 April 1943, just before the arrival of Bose, the Burma Area Army was created below the Southern Army and above the 15th Army to ensure the defence of Burma. Lieutenant-General Kawabe Masakazu, commander of the new army, had already conferred with Tōjō on the question of an offensive into India. IGHQ planned a general build-up of divisions in the new army over a year's time to full strength of six or seven divisions, rather than the ten Katakura suggested.

VII MUTAGUCHI'S *VOLTE-FACE*

Lieutenant-General Mutaguchi, who had refused to take Operation 21 seriously, was appointed commander of the 15th Army in March 1943. When Mutaguchi had been asked six months earlier for his opinion about an invasion of Assam, he had replied that it would be impossible. By late April 1943, however, angered by the Chindit operation across the Chindwin River, Mutaguchi mapped a plan for a Japanese counterpart. The association of Mutaguchi and Burma Area Commander Kawabe was an old one. In 1936 Kawabe was in command of the Infantry Brigade in north China, in which Mutaguchi served. Mutaguchi still felt personal responsibility for the Marco Polo Bridge incident and wanted to be exonerated. The Mutaguchi-Kawabe combination was now revived with the closeness of the old relationship. Kawabe admired Mutaguchi's aggressive spirit, and Mutaguchi was devoted to his former commanding officer. It could be a fruitful working relationship.

Mutaguchi had a good record on his own. He had been a regimental commander in Peking during the Marco Polo Bridge incident, later chief of staff of the 4th Army, the Kwantung Army, and when the Pacific War erupted he was commander of the 18th Division at Singapore. Mutaguchi now felt Japan was being encircled and hesitation meant death and, worse, defeat. The only way to break through the cordon, the only sector where Japan could fight back, was the route into India through Imphal. The enemy's offensive had to be forestalled. In a choice between offence and defence, Mutaguchi would choose boldly rather than ponder the uncertainties. There were staff officers in the Burma Area Army, the Southern Army, and IGHQ who felt as Mutaguchi did: the only defence of Burma was offence into India. Mutaguchi's plan was guaranteed a hearing.

When Mutaguchi broached the suggestion of an offensive beyond the Chindwin River to General Kawabe in late April 1943, Kawabe responded with a directive that the 15th Army make immediate plans for such an offensive. On 5 May 1943, Kawabe reported upward to the Southern Army on the need for an offensive to secure the defence of Burma. The Southern Army and Burma Area Army agreed to study the strategy for such a campaign in mid-June in Rangoon.[33]

Mutaguchi was known for his irascible temper. He looked the part. His mouth was drawn sternly downward and his bearing was so stiff that his chin doubled, though he was not obese. If Mutaguchi suggested an attack on Ledo or Imphal, his staff officers agreed to an attack on Ledo or Imphal. Mutaguchi was never challenged, especially by his own staff. There was one exception. This was Major-General Ōbata Shinryō, Mutaguchi's own chief of staff. When Ōbata mentioned problems of lines of communications, supplies, terrain, and climate, Mutaguchi lost his temper. Ōbata was summarily dismissed and transferred elsewhere. Mutaguchi continued to plan with yet another chief of staff, Major-General (later Lieutenant-

General) Kunomura Homoyo. This time it looked as if Mutaguchi had found an amenable chief of staff.[34] The campaign had not yet reached the strategic planning stage and two generals were already dismissed. It was a portent of an unprecedented shake-up in the chain of command during the campaign itself.

VIII   DELAY AND MODERATION

The above forces were all pushing for an early decision and processing of the campaign plan. But there were other forces working in the opposite direction to delay a final decision until early 1944, over a year after the initial strategy was mapped out. Tokyo Headquarters balked especially at the lack of Japanese operational strength in the Burma sector. The creation of the Burma Area Army was an attempt to strengthen Japan's operational power in the area. There was also the perennial but increasingly serious problem of supplies over such attenuated lines of communication. To go beyond Burma would push Japan to the limits of her weakening supply position. There were all the geographic hazards of the hostile mountainous terrain, torrential rivers, and tropical diseases. Then there was the area where the British were gaining undisputed leadership after Burma was captured by the Japanese—air power. This was the Achilles heel which in General Terauchi's calculations finally spelled Japan's defeat in Burma.

IGHQ was wary for all these reasons. Staff officers of the Southern Army, Burma Area Army, and 15th Army were called on again to justify their prognosis of Japanese success at Imphal. It was several months before they were able to tip the scales of Tokyo's caution in favour of a go-ahead signal for Operation U.

In early June the 15th Army staff studied the strategy of an invasion of India. The strategy was basically similar to Operation 21 which had been rejected a few months earlier. The plan in general called for a main thrust by the 33rd and 15th Divisions from the Kabaw Valley toward the road connecting Sittaung, Palel, and Imphal. When enemy opposition had been smashed in this sector a coordinated attack would be launched on Imphal itself. This basic plan, though it underwent minor changes during several map manoeuvres and war games, remained basically constant. Mutaguchi repeatedly emphasized the need to capture enemy transport facilities and arms and ammunition locally to compensate for logistics problems and insecure lines of communication. He counted on completing the operation within three weeks.[35]

In early July commander of the Southern Army Field-Marshal Count Terauchi sent his vice-chief of staff, Major-General Inada Seijun to Tokyo Headquarters to explain the plan for the Imphal operation and to ask for additional divisions for use in the campaign, including communications and supply units. In early September instructions for campaign preparations came back down through the chain of command. Burma Area Army commander Kawabe was ordered to prepare for the campaign into Imphal after October, again accounting for the monsoon.[36]

IX   BAA MAP MANOEUVRE

From 24 to 27 June 1943, the Burma Area Army held a map manoeuvre at Rangoon on Imphal campaign strategy, under the direction of Lieutenant-General Naka, chief of staff, BAA. Staff officers from the 15th Army and all divisions under the BAA participated. Observers came from Southern Army Headquarters and Imperial General Headquarters. From the 15th Army Mutaguchi was accompanied by his new chief of staff Major-General Kunomura and Major Fujiwara, who was now staff officer in charge of intelligence for the 15th Army, working on liaison with the INA during the operation in Imphal. Observers from Southern Army Headquarters were Vice-Chief of Staff Major-General Inada, Operations Staff Officer Yamada and Staff Officer Hayashi. From IGHQ Staff Officer Colonel Prince Takeda and Staff Officer for the South Major Kondo sat in.[37]

The operation would involve crossing two high mountain ranges and the Chindwin River, three hundred feet wide at the narrowest. Questions of supplies and lines of communications were raised again as in the case of Operation 21 strategy discussions. Many staff officers remained dissatisfied with the plan, but Mutaguchi overrode opposition and was able to get enough support in the right places. Terauchi tried to dissociate himself from the campaign, saying, "If the field armies think they can do it, let them."[38]

The problem was where to establish the Army line of defence. Mutaguchi favoured a thrust far into India by the main force in September, to a line connecting the Dimapur and Shillong plains and the Brahmaputra River, with an auxiliary operation from the Chittagong area. Mutaguchi's plan was almost a replica of Operation 21.

Katakura, who recorded the course of discussions in his diary, felt the whole operation would logically involve four stages: first, deployment of troops along the Chindwin River, second, crossing the river, third, advance into the mountains, and fourth, capture of Imphal and defence of the plain from the western mountain ridges.[39] Katakura felt Mutaguchi's plan was brilliant but not as sound as the plan favoured by the majority at Rangoon.

The Burma Area Army staff suggested two other alternative lines of defence. The first and more conservative view was to establish the line of defence on the west side of the Kabaw Valley or along the mountain range east of the valley. The second plan would advance the line of defence to the mountain range west of the Imphal plain, destroying the enemy's counter-attacking bases at Imphal. General Inada said if the operation involved the 15th Army in the sectors north of Imphal, the Southern Army would not approve the plan.

Discussion continued four days and nights. The consensus reached was that a defence line at the Kabaw Valley which ignored the enemy's main strength at Imphal would be insecure. Mutaguchi's more drastic plan was also rejected in favour of the plan to capture Imphal, make a co-ordinated series of sudden attacks, and establish the defence line along the mountain range west of the Imphal plain.[40]

X WHAT OF THE INA?

Since the Imphal campaign was conceived in part as a political campaign, problems other than military strategy had to be considered. In striking a political blow at India what should the role of the Indian National Army be? This question was discussed by IGHQ, Southern Army Headquarters, and Burma Area Army Headquarters. At all three staff levels there was some opposition to the idea of using the INA as a fighting unit at the front.[41] There were doubts about the combat effectiveness of the INA, about prospects for supplying the INA, and about possible trouble between the INA and Japanese forces once Indian soil were reached. General Iida was also opposed to having the INA advance into India when Burma was not yet independent. Within Burma Area Army Headquarters Colonel Katakura discussed the problem on 30 June with Chief of Staff Lieutenant-General Naka and later with Kawabe. They concluded the anti-British Indian independence movement could not be forced by Japan, nor could Japan engage in anything which appeared to the Indians as aggression. The spontaneous co-operation and goodwill of the Indian people were imperative. This had long been Fujiwara's contention. It was a political objective and could not be achieved by military means.

Katakura emphasized during the discussions that the first aim of the campaign was to stimulate anti-British sentiment and actions among the Indians. Toward this end the INA could be used in various ways: in intelligence, sabotage, supply, and personnel units, and perhaps as guerrilla fighters. New head of the *Hikari Kikan*, Colonel Yamamoto Bin, agreed with Katakura's suggestions. Yamamoto, Bose's old friend in Berlin, was now handling liaison with Bose.

When Bose arrived in Rangoon at the end of July he met Kawabe and BAA staff officers. He made it clear to Kawabe that he proposed to establish the Free India Provisional Government to carry out an armed revolution, refusing any compromise with the British. Further, Bose insisted again that INA men be the first to set foot on Indian soil, and that the INA fight as a unified army rather than as units within the Japanese Army.

When Bose had talked with IGHQ staff officers in Tokyo, he had requested arms and ammunition, two planes, and the transfer of all Indian POWs to the INA. Lieutenant-General Arisue had suggested to Bose that he make these specific arrangements with the general in command in Singapore. IGHQ placed "all matters, including both political and military affairs, concerning the INA and the FIPG in the Burma Area ... under the direct jurisdiction of the Burma Area Army".[42] When an INA unit moved through a Japanese operational zone, arrangements regarding its mission and zone of operation were made at a joint conference of INA and BAA staff officers. Then the INA unit was put under the command of a Japanese officer of equivalent or higher rank. Liaison with INA special duty and intelligence units was arranged through the *Hikari Kikan*, under Lieutenant-General Isoda Saburō, who succeeded Yamamoto at the time of the Imphal operation.[43]

The first request of the INA, to be advance echelon into India, was rejected by the BAA. Reasons given were that this would be the initial campaign for the INA, and for the Japanese it had to be a certain victory. The INA was small, trained for guerrilla warfare, and could not be used in regular fighting. Japanese forces would begin the operation, and just before final success the INA could cross the border onto Indian soil. This would fulfil Japanese propaganda objectives and also the INA desire to cross the border first. Bose asked Kawabe later, on 7 January, as he had before the campaign began, that the first drop of blood shed on Indian soil be Indian. He made the same request in conversations with Japanese Ambassador to Burma, Sawada.[44] Kawabe felt Bose's wishes in this matter had to be restrained, but not so much as to irritate him. Bose's desires had to be at least partly fulfilled for Japan to gain political advantage from the INA co-operation. It was a delicate balance.[45]

Some on the BAA staff felt the INA as a regular fighting unit would be more a hindrance than an asset. Nor were there supplies and food to spare. The value of Bose's three divisions was felt to be for guerrilla operations rather than in tactical strength in ordinary battle formation.[46]

The BAA began to plan the deployment of INA forces. Politically, the best use of Indian troops would be in a thrust from the south through Akyab to Bengal, where Bose was most likely to meet an enthusiastic reception. But Japanese forces could not fight at sea. Nor could Japan dispute Allied air power over Burma. For strategic reasons it would therefore be safer to use the INA in north Burma. It was decided to use a regiment of the 1st INA Division under Shah Nawaz Khan in the Haka-Falam area of the Chin Hills.[47]

XI THE 15TH ARMY PLANS

By July, the 15th Army felt approval for Operation U was forthcoming and was making all possible preparations for an offensive in early October. The deployment of troops was to be as follows: the 56th and part of the 18th Divisions were to crush the enemy in the Salween River area; the rest of the 18th Division was to advance into the Hukawng Valley sector and hold it against an American-Chinese counter-attack; the 31st Division was to take Kohima and prevent an enemy attack from Assam; and the 33rd and 15th Divisions from the north and south were to destroy the enemy in the Imphal Valley in a pincer attack.[48] The 15th and 31st Divisions were both to cross the formidable Chindwin River and establish the defence line in the ridges of the Chin Hills west of the Imphal plain.

Crucial problems of timing and supplies coincided. Supplies for three weeks were to be carried by each division. After the capture of the Kalewa-Tamu-Palel-Imphal-Kohima Road it was to become the main line of communications. One-third of the military strength available was allotted to Kohima. This was a key point in view of Mutaguchi's cherished hope for a longer thrust into Assam. There was not much emphasis on planning for unexpected eventualities. Mutaguchi counted on victory in three weeks.

On 7 August the order came from Southern Army Headquarters to the Burma Area Army "to complete preparations for a counter offensive ... to offset a possible large-scale enemy offensive", and more specifically, "the Burma Area Army will take the offensive in the direction of Imphal, with the main force disposed on the west side of the Chindwin River, will defeat the enemy in the vicinity of the border area, destroy the enemy in the Imphal area, and will establish a strong defence in the vicinity. Meanwhile, the armies on the other fronts will take measures to delay and pin down the enemy. It is expected that this operation will commence no sooner than the early part of 1944. Approximately seven divisions will be available for operations in Burma." These would include, besides the 15th Army, the 55th Division in the Akyab sector, the 18th Division in the Hukawng Valley, and the 56th Division against Chinese forces poised along the line of the Salween River.[49]

The Burma Area Army in turn ordered the 15th Army to advance to Imphal "before enemy preparations for a counter-offensive could be completed". The defence line was to be along the spine of the Arakan mountain range. Now it was up to the 15th Army staff to devise the operational plan for the capture of Imphal. On 25-26 August Chief of Staff Lieutenant-General Naka briefed division commanders at Maimyo on the tactical plan for Operation U.

By December the go-ahead order still had not come from Tokyo. Mutaguchi, however, held a map manoeuvre at 15th Army Headquarters in Maimyo. Staff officers from the BAA and Southern Army attended, including Vice-Chief of Staff Lieutenant-General Ayabe. After five days of discussion Ayabe was convinced that though supply and timing problems were serious Japan should go ahead. He reported favourably to Commander Terauchi in Singapore.[50]

XII CURTAIN RAISER

The curtain was raised for Operation U on 3 October with operations in the upper Salween and Yunnan sectors. Enemy forces were routed from the upper Salween area by the end of October by the 18th and 56th Divisions. The Hukawng Valley was another story. Before fighting began a reconnaissance unit of the 18th Division sent back reports of Chinese forces in undermined strength along the border. Together with the report came a description of the fearsome "Death" Valley. *Hukawng* is the word for death in local parlance, and the valley lives up to its name. Some thirty miles in length, it is bisected by a tableland into northern and southern sections. Each of the valleys is interlaced with river tributaries which snake their way through marshy, densely forested zones. The southern valley was sparsely peopled by Kachin tribes, who were heavily infected by cholera and malaria. Along the bordering north-eastern mountain range lived some of the fierce Naga hill tribes.

The Allied Army was hiding in the hill region in the eastern corner of Assam, still hoping to connect the Burma-China road to the Ledo Road. They built the serpentine road through several hundred miles of tortuous terrain, working into the rainy season in an attempt to push through to the rail-head at Myitkyina. Oil pipelines and fuel depots were also desperately needed in China. This was General Stilwell's dream.

The commander of the 18th Division, Lieutenant-General Tanaka Shin'ichi, was ordered to confront the Chinese 18th Division in the Hukawng Valley and annihilate it. But the Chinese 18th was a reorganized, self-confident, and well-equipped unit, unlike earlier Chinese divisions encountered by the Japanese Army. The operation was to begin on 15 December. Earlier in December Mutaguchi cancelled the operation to avoid diverting vehicles and supplies while he impatiently awaited the starting signal for Operation U. Lieutenant-General Tanaka was apprehensive about the Imphal operation but was no more successful in getting Mutaguchi to listen to him than others had been.[51]

The divisions of the 15th Army were all deployed into position along the east bank of the Chindwin River for the beginning of the offensive. Mutaguchi became distraught. It was necessary to start well before the onset of the rainy season, but by November, then early December, the order still had not come from Tokyo.

The balance of strength in the air was shifting rapidly in favour of the Allies. In December the Japanese 5th Airborne Division bombed Calcutta and Chittagong with 160 planes, doing considerable damage. By January 1944, however, it was no longer possible to speak of Japanese defence of Burma by air. Tokyo was showing cautious concern following the loss of the Solomon and Gilbert Islands. Chinese forces were deployed on the north-eastern border of Burma and British-Indian on the west. Despite growing pressures for a rapid decision, however, the starting signal did not come. Finally, at the end of December, Commander Terauchi sent his vice-chief of staff, Lieutenant-General Ayabe, to IGHQ to get the order. Ayabe had already been convinced several months earlier that the operation was feasible. But the final decision had to be Tōjō's.

When Ayabe arrived in Tokyo it was already dark. Colonel Nishiura Susumu, Chief of the Military Affairs Section and Secretary of the Army Ministry, rushed to Tōjō's residence, only to learn that the Prime Minister was in the bath. Tōjō, hearing the commotion, called Nishiura to the room, and through the bathroom window asked the following questions in rapid succession: 1) can the Imphal operation successfully counter possible landings by British-Indian forces on the southern coast of Burma from the Bay of Bengal? 2) In view of the increased length of the front which would result from the occupation of Imphal, is there a need to increase strength to guarantee defence of Burma? 3) Since our air strength is very inferior, will ground operations be feasible? 4) Will supply lines be adequate? 5) Is the 15th Army plan sound?[52] Tōjō had been contemplating an Indian offensive for some time and obviously had the key problems clearly in mind. Hearing the report of Ayabe's prognosis from the Southern Army staff, Tōjō now gave his assent.

CHAPTER TEN

The Rising Sun Unfurls; the Tiger Springs

I OPERATION U IS LAUNCHED

On 7 January 1944, IGHQ Army Directive no. 1776 was issued to the Southern Army "to capture strategic areas near Imphal and in north-eastern India, for the defence of Burma". One of Mutaguchi's divisions, the 15th, was late in arriving, and the launching of the offensive was postponed until March.[1] On 8 March all divisions were deployed according to plan. In mid-April the 31st Division occupied Kohima and the 33rd and 15th Divisions fell on the bottlenecks north and south of the Imphal basin respectively.[2] Among the Japanese troops a mood of optimism prevailed.

II THE INA IN ACTION AT LAST

On 24 January 1944, Colonel Katakura, staff officer of the Burma Area Army, met with *Netaji* to outline campaign strategy and the role of the INA in it. Colonel Shah Nawaz Khan was the third person at the secret meeting. When Katakura revealed the Japanese plan for a heavy bombardment of Calcutta simultaneous with the ground offensive, *Netaji* forcefully objected. Discussions finally yielded Bose's consent to the general plan, but not to the bombing. Bose gained his point that the INA fight in units of regimental size, not only in espionage and intelligence units attached to the Japanese Army.[3]

Bose three days later called in Shah Nawaz and told him that as his guerrilla regiment, the Nehru Regiment, would be the first INA unit to see action, it would be closely watched. Shah Nawaz would have to be the model for the whole INA. Bose briefed Shah Nawaz on the deployment of battalions and told him detailed orders would come from 15th Army Headquarters at Maimyo. Japanese officers would be attached to each battalion for liaison and to arrange for supplies and transport. INA intelligence units of eight to ten men would also be attached to various Japanese forces for intelligence, propaganda and interrogation of POWs.[4]

On 10 February Shah Nawaz met Mutaguchi at Maimyo for orders. Mutaguchi told Shah Nawaz his regiment was in charge of defence of the Haka-Falam sector in the Chin Hills against two British brigades (including Chins and Gurkhas) which might threaten Japanese supply lines. The object of the Shah Nawaz operation was to divert British attention from the main point of attack. Shah Nawaz objected and pointed out that the INA should not be allotted an out-of-the-way sector but rather should be the spearhead of the advance into India. Mutaguchi replied his orders were to first test the INA in a separate sector. Of this Bose had already warned Shah Nawaz. The sector would be hard to hold because of terrain and supplies, Mutaguchi cautioned.[5]

Shah Nawaz, still dissatisfied, met Fujiwara at 33rd Division headquarters in March. A year had elapsed since they last met. Fujiwara listened as the gentle-mannered Shah Nawaz, fingering two hand grenades around his neck, told Fujiwara the INA should be sent as an advance unit into Tiddim and Imphal. Fujiwara, impressed by the eagerness of the handsome Muslim, agreed. Two weeks later the 33rd Division was stalemated, Tiddim had fallen, and Fujiwara could not live up to his promise.[6]

Fujiwara also witnessed the first meeting between Bose and Mutaguchi at Maimyo headquarters in early February 1944. The two men were in remarkable harmony and spirits. They appeared to Fujiwara as if they had already taken Imphal and gained India. Mutaguchi's ebullience led him to promise Bose more than was included in the operation plan. He said to Bose, "The occupation of Imphal is only the beginning. The problem begins after that. The Japanese Army wants to advance to Dimapur, and, if the situation warrants, to the Brahmaputra River. The INA should go in at that time." *Netaji* responded jubilantly, "If the Japanese Army succeeds in the Imphal invasion and pushes the INA forward in the Assam plain, the Indian people, as well as officers and men in the British-Indian Army, will respond to the INA. This will spread all over India, especially in my home state of Bengal."[7] Both men had the same tenacious zeal for extending the Imphal operation into Assam. But the operational plan for Imphal called for a line of defence only at the Arakan mountain range. Mutaguchi was clearly speaking off the cuff to Bose out of his conviction that the Imphal campaign would reverse the whole course of the war for Japan.

At 11 p.m. when the dinner conversation between Bose and Mutaguchi broke up, Bose invited Fujiwara to continue the discussion at his guest house. The two men talked until nearly dawn. Bose's main concern was for the government of occupied areas during the campaign. He wanted the government of these areas to be entrusted at once to a committee of the Free India Provisional Government. Protection of lives, property, temples, and public buildings in the occupied areas should be handled by the committee. All Indian POWs should be turned over to the INA by the Japanese Army. Special currency issued by the Free India Provisional Government would be used rather than Japanese military currency. The INA should have priority in using captured arms and ammunition. Supplies of the Japanese Army for the INA should be improved. Bose had already brought up these problems at every meeting with Japanese staff officers. It was a formidable list, and Fujiwara was surprised at Bose's detailed military information, since Bose was without military experience beyond what he had gained in the Indian Legion in Berlin. In all these matters, Bose sought Fujiwara's help. Fujiwara felt himself thrown again into his familiar role of liaison and cooperation with Indian revolutionaries.[8]

III SHAH NAWAZ IN BATTLE

The Nehru Regiment faced the hard fighting and serious supply problems of the rest of Japanese forces. But Shah Nawaz had been sceptical of Japanese sincerity from the time of the surrender at Singapore. He had stood aloof from the INA at first, trying to decide the best way to protect Indian lives and property in Southeast Asia. Shah

Nawaz came from a military family with a long tradition of service in the British-Indian Army. He was a graduate of the military academy at Dehra Dun. He had to work out his personal conflict of loyalties before he could volunteer for an army dedicated to exterminating British power in India. Once he resolved his conflict, he became commander of the largest of three guerrilla regiments of the 1st Division of the INA, a unit of approximately three thousand men.

When Shah Nawaz and his regiment met with short supplies in Burma he was convinced that the Japanese were deliberately shortchanging the INA. He wrote later:

> The Japanese could, if they wanted to, help us in this respect, but they did not do so and I am of the opinion that they did it deliberately. They had seen the spirit and determination of our men and had realized that they would stand no nonsense from the Japanese. The actual fact was, as Field Marshal Terauchi had told Netaji long before in Singapore, the Japanese did not want large formations of the INA to come to the front and now that they were there the Japanese wished to break their spirit and health by putting impossible obstacles in their way. All that they wanted to do was to break the morale of the INA and tell Netaji that his army could not face the rigours of a hard campaign.... The Japanese were putting us through a terrible test indeed.[9]

Shah Nawaz saw his alternatives by April as either 1) to leave a large force at Haka and risk its starvation, or 2) to leave a small force and risk its annihilation by the enemy. The main force would have to withdraw. He and his staff chose the second course. Shah Nawaz realized it was already too late for Japanese victory. A new order came on 16 May for his regiment to support the 31st Division in its strike at Kohima. This was a move of several hundred miles from the spine of the Chin Hills through the Kabaw Valley, followed by an attack on the 10,000-foot ridges inhabited by Naga tribesmen.

The guerrilla unit had no field supplies and was to rely on Japanese supplies, which were non-existent. But the regiment was elated at the opportunity to advance beyond Kohima and into Assam. Hospitalized soldiers volunteered. By this time the 31st Division was confronted by four British-Indian divisions and was being bombarded night and day. The men had been without fresh supplies of rice or ammunition for sixty days. They were eating dry-field rice grown by Naga tribesmen mixed with jungle grass. The Shah Nawaz regiment, advancing into this sector under daily increasing rains, reached the south of Kohima by early June. By the time they arrived, however, Kohima was not tenable and the Shah Nawaz unit had to retrace its tortuous steps back through the mountain trails. The only consolation for the men was that they had seen Assam and stood on Indian soil.[10]

Shah Nawaz on 4 June met the division commander who gave him an order to retreat to Ukhrul. Shah Nawaz protested that he could not retreat from Indian soil. He was then told, in what he regarded as a "false pretext", that there was to be a renewed attack on Imphal and that he could choose his role there. After Imphal was taken he could advance again. A few days later Shah Nawaz was told at division headquarters that the situation had deteriorated further and the division was falling back to Tamu and Sittaung to get supplies via the only route left, the Chindwin River. Shah Nawaz was sure he had again been taken in by false orders. Irate, he demanded his regiment be transferred to join the main force of the INA 1st Division. His request was granted on 22 June.

Arriving at Tamu, Shah Nawaz was told his regiment could not join the 1st Division as its orders had been changed. Shah Nawaz and his staff felt they had once more been betrayed. Given his initial suspicion of Japanese motives, Shah Nawaz was ready to interpret any order or change of plan as a deliberate plot against the INA. From his viewpoint, the evidence was almost overwhelming.[11] Japanese commanding officers were of course motivated by urgent military considerations which often had little relation to INA objectives.

Officers under Shah Nawaz were all now equally convinced that further obedience to Japanese orders would be dishonourable. They determined to attack the enemy and die fighting. A Japanese liaison officer who uncovered the plan sent a frantic message to Bose. *Netaji* in turn ordered Shah Nawaz to withdraw to Kalewa. Shah Nawaz did not change his belief that the heavy INA casualties and the failure to take Imphal were caused by Japanese non-cooperation.

During the retreat Shah Nawaz reported several serious clashes between Japanese and INA men. He thought it likely Japan had designs on India and wanted to prevent the INA from becoming too powerful, for fear they might one day turn on the Japanese, as the Burma Independence Army did.[12] This concern of the BAA and IGHQ was confirmed by Lieutenant-Colonel Ozeki Masaji, who during the war was in the 8th Section of the Second Bureau, IGHQ.

The final Japanese collapse in Burma Shah Nawaz saw as affected also by the revolt of the Burma Independence Army under General Aung San in 1945. Shah Nawaz reported the BIA rebels remained friendly to the INA even after they turned against the Japanese. One INA crossing of the Irrawaddy in late April 1945 was aided by BIA troops. Shah Nawaz reported a change in the customary Burmese hostility toward Indians because of *Netaji* and also because of the Japanese presence in Burma. In a later evaluation of the fiasco. Shah Nawaz recognized the British counter-offensive, the monsoon rain and mud, disease, and impossible supply situation as cogent causes of the abandonment of Imphal.[13]

On April 20 the main force of the INA 1st Division under General Kiani was ordered to join both wings of the Yamamoto Detachment near Palel. The Gandhi Regiment under Colonel Kiani (the commander's cousin) joined the southern wing of the detachment, and the *Azad* Regiment under Colonel Dhillon joined the northern wing. Because the senior adjutant of the Yamamoto Detachment was killed and because of Fujiwara's long association with the Indian independence movement, he was detailed to the detachment with the main force of the INA for over two months. He couldn't have asked for more. Fujiwara was grateful that two officers with great sympathy for the INA were also assigned to liaison, Major Ōgawa and Major Kemawari. Both these men, however, were killed in action with the INA.[14]

The Kiani regiment was ordered with the Yamamoto Detachment to attack the Palel air base, beyond the Kabaw Valley, deep behind enemy lines. The valleys and the steep Chin Hills reverberated with the chattering of hundreds of monkeys. Through the cover of darkness, Fujiwara heard the familiar cry, "*Chalo Delhi! Chalo Delhi!*" He knew his Indian friends were close at hand.

But the Yamamoto Detachment and Kiani regiment were stopped by superior enemy weapons at the steep mountain pass of Tegnoupal. Lacking any air cover, the regiment was forced to retreat to the southern wing of the detachment. But for eighty days the INA regiment and Yamamoto Detachment held their ground in the drenching rain without supplies. To Fujiwara it seemed an impossible feat.[15]

IV   LIAISON PROBLEMS

Bose's optimism and ebullience before and during the Imphal campaign posed problems for his own publicity staff and for Japanese censors. Bose had declared at a huge public meeting in Singapore in the summer of 1943, "Before the end of this year we shall stand on Indian soil." *Kikan* officials, pushing through the delirious audience, frantically asked Japanese correspondents to kill the statement about standing on Indian soil before the end of the year. "That was not in the original draft," they complained. The Japanese censors then confronted S.A. Ayer and told him the speech could not be broadcast unless that sentence was deleted. Ayer was in a dilemma. How could he eliminate the most sensational statement Bose had made during the speech? He telephoned Bose and suggested that he broadcast the speech himself. Bose readily agreed.

Ayer informed the censors that *Netaji* himself would make the broadcast. The censors then approached the *Kikan* and Southern Command Headquarters attempting to solve the problem. A compromise was reached just before Bose went on the air. Bose might broadcast the speech as he wished but Japanese broadcasts would delete the statement about standing on Indian soil. Similarly, the Indian Press might publish the speech in full but Japanese papers and *Dōmei* (the Japanese news agency) would carry a censored version. The compromise was accepted and *Netaji* announced over *Azad Hind* Radio the electrifying news of the march to India.

After the broadcast, Ayer's staff met with Bose and waited for him to tell them about the military strategy for the Indian campaign. The staff was disappointed. Bose mentioned no campaign. Finally, in response to questions from the journalists, Bose said, "Oh! It was such a huge crowd and I felt towards the end of the speech, that it was expecting something from me, something more than what I had already said. I hope what I said is perfectly all right—about our standing on Indian soil before the end of the year."[16] Bose's statement had no connection with Japanese strategy.

When Operation U was under way Bose and Kawabe, BAA commander, met several times. The two men respected each other, though their viewpoints did not coincide. Kawabe felt a strong sense of responsibility to Bose and the INA throughout the operation. On 18 March when the campaign was going well Kawabe told Bose they would next meet in India. April 6 Kawabe warned Bose not to allow British propaganda to make use of him. The following day both men agreed that the word "Provisional" in the name "Free India Provisional Government" should be dropped. Bose again made his appeal that the INA be used primarily as a fighting force. Kawabe was impressed once again with Bose's determination and judged him a trustworthy ally.[17] The Bose-Kawabe dialogue continued into May, when

Bose again requested by wire that the size of the INA be expanded and greater efforts be made to push the Imphal offensive to victory. Kawabe was troubled on both counts. It was impossible to answer Bose without reference to the whole situation in Burma.[18]

On 22 June as Operation U was hopelessly mired Bose and Kawabe met again. Kawabe had just inspected the battle front and could not encourage any optimism in Bose. Bose asked that the Rani of Jhansi Regiment be sent to the front immediately.[19] Even had the campaign continued longer than it did, it is extremely doubtful that the Burma Area Army would have taken this request seriously.

In a September meeting of Bose and his regimental commanders in Mandalay dissatisfaction with the *Hikari Kikan* was unanimous. It was agreed that the INA would rather deal directly with the Japanese Government in Tokyo and with the BAA Headquarters in military matters. In October Bose's Cabinet suggested the exchange of diplomatic representatives. General Chatterji was appointed Foreign Minister and a twelve-man War Council was created, with a supply department for future operations.[20] Bose again demanded Tokyo send an accredited diplomatic representative to the FIPG. He was not satisfied with the replies from Tokyo. He wanted a clear separation of diplomatic relations from military liaison with the Army. Tokyo had already sent a specialist from the *Gaimusho* to the *Kikan*. Now Tokyo would have to go all the way and send a diplomatic envoy, a minister if not an ambassador. This was done at length, but in a backhanded way and too late to establish relations before the war came to a close.

Netaji made his third and last visit to Tokyo in November 1944, after the collapse of the Imphal campaign. He had already heard a rumour that IGHQ wished to confer on him the Order of First Merit of the Rising Sun. He refused; Japanese authorities were taken aback. When the day of Indian independence arrived, Bose and his staff would be happy to receive the decoration, but for the present he could not accept.[21]

V OPERATION U BOGS DOWN

For about a month Operation U went according to plan. Enemy forces were successfully encircled in the Imphal basin. A mood of elation and self-confidence prevailed in 15th Army Headquarters. There seemed every reason for the 15th Army to look for complete success by 21 April.

Suddenly, in the middle of April, the military balance began to shift against Japan and the INA. On 5 March Wingate's airborne unit had already begun to attack from the air over Burma. By 24 March the 33rd Division, which enclosed the long line of the British 17th Division in the narrow passes around Tonzang, was stalemated and hesitated to continue to Imphal. British forces were being supplied by airlift into Imphal, and reinforcements were also beginning to flow in. British forces were being sent into Kohima to the north by both rail and air.

On 8 April 15th Army commander Mutaguchi ordered the 15th Division to capture Dimapur and the main part of the INA 1st Division to assemble in the Kabaw Valley for an offensive into the Assam plain. But General Kawabe, Mutaguchi's old commander, countermanded the order to advance to Dimapur. Mutaguchi was stunned; he commented later, "Kawabe was slow and lacking in determination."[22]

Japan had no spare air power with which to strike back at enemy air operations and was forced to fight a two-dimensional operation against a British three-dimensional operation. As soon as the Imphal offensive got under way Lieutenant-General Tazoe, commander of the 5th Airborne Division in Burma, asked Mutaguchi to stop the campaign. He had then visited BAA headquarters with the same request. Kawabe responded, "Even if the Area Army should consent, IGHQ won't agree."[23] Tazoe felt the situation was hopeless. All remaining air strength had been diverted to the Pacific. Japanese troops had no anti-tank weapons. The 31st and 15th Divisions carried food and ammunition for only three weeks and had no way of replenishing supplies. A steady stream of telegrams requesting ammunition and air cover reached 15th Army Headquarters daily. By the end of April every division's battle strength was decreased forty per cent. By now the time for success by surprise attack had already passed. Japan gradually took the defensive.[24]

Then the monsoon broke. Roads and valleys became muddy streams. Streams became rivers, and rivers swirling torrents. All supply routes were cut off as roads became impassable. There were no spare supplies to transport anyway. Tanks and ammunition were lost. Cows and horses were killed by the heavy rains. Nearly every man had malaria, cholera, dysentery, beriberi, or jungle sores. Most had a combination of diseases. Rice mixed with jungle grass became standard rations for enervated Japanese troops.

Forty days of desperate fighting by the 33rd Division had not taken them any closer to Imphal. Vast amounts of military supplies were now being flown in to the beleaguered British forces in the Imphal plain. British lines were holding firm and the Japanese advance was stopped. There was no longer any army organization of men with any ideas.

VI INSUBORDINATION IN THE CHAIN OF COMMAND

By early March Mutaguchi already felt harassed by problems of supplies, munitions and food, the onset of the monsoon, and the lack of progress following initial success. Finally in mid-March he relieved Lieutenant-General Yanagita from command of the 33rd Division, charging that he lacked fighting spirit. This despite the 33rd Division's reputation as the toughest and most aggressive of all Japanese divisions in Burma. When Mutaguchi had ordered the 33rd Division to take Imphal it was with the injunction: "The fate of the Empire hinges on the result of this battle. Imphal will be taken at all costs." Yanagita asked Mutaguchi to reconsider the order, but Mutaguchi stood firm. Then Yanagita, passing the order on to his troops, added, "You will take Imphal, but the division will be annihilated."[25] This was hardly failure of spirit. But in Mutaguchi's calculations the operation should have been completed within three weeks. Yanagita should have pursued the retreating 17th Division rapidly despite its heavier equipment. It was now closer to three months. Someone was to blame.

Yanagita was a man who respected reason and calculation above all else. The Imphal operation had never been to his taste. He felt from the beginning that without air power and secure supply lines the outcome was obvious. Kawabe hesitated to agree to Yanagita's replacement but finally relented and appointed Lieutenant-General Tanaka Nobuo in his place.

On 15 May Lieutenant-General Yamauchi was also relieved for failure of morale in the 15th Division. He died shortly thereafter of tuberculosis in the hospital at Maimyo and was replaced by Lieutenant-General Shibata Uichi. Yamauchi and Satō Kotoku, 31st Division commander, were both graduates of the 25th class at the Military Academy; they both sympathized with Yanagita, who had graduated the year before them.[26]

The division commanders had grievances of their own against Mutaguchi. It was enough that they were fighting under impossible conditions and without any of the supplies they had been promised. At the end of January as the operation was about to be launched, Mutaguchi called a staff conference at Maimyo headquarters. He summoned division chiefs of staff and operations staff officers, but division commanders were notably omitted. They felt they were being called on to fight without full knowledge of the scope of Mutaguchi's plan.[27]

After 15 May only one of the three original division commanders was left. This was Lieutenant-General Satō Kotoku, commander of the 31st Division. His task was to take Kohima. Satō was hard pressed by reinforced enemy troops and had no chance of getting supplies or reinforcements. In late April Mutaguchi ordered Satō to send a regimental group to Kanglatongbi to support the 15th Division in a renewed offensive on Imphal. Satō knew if he complied, he would have no chance of capturing and holding Kohima against reinforced British troops. He ignored the order. By now Satō felt that to remain stalemated on the spot any longer would mean certain destruction of the whole division. Most of the men were sick, and casualties had been heavy in desperate fighting.

Satō asked Mutaguchi for permission to withdraw to a position which could be supplied from the Chindwin, the only supply line left. Mutaguchi flatly refused, still believing Imphal could be recaptured with perseverance. Satō cut off communications with 15th Army Headquarters in an unprecedented action, and began the withdrawal, countermanding Mutaguchi's order. It was insubordination in the chain of command of the Imperial Japanese Army.

On 19 June Chief of Staff of the Burma Area Army, Lieutenant-General Naka Eitarō, came to Satō with an order. General Naka pulled a piece of paper from his pocket and, holding it with trembling hands, said, "I have an order to have the chief legal officer investigate you." As Naka read the order sweat streamed down his face and dripped onto the paper. Satō, holding himself in check, replied calmly to Naka, "Sit down. Don't hurry away." Naka, responding in turn to

Satō's aplomb, tried to reassure him. "Don't worry," Naka said. "The chief legal officer is Colonel Sakaguchi, who was with you once in Hokkaido." Satō was satisfied when Colonel Sakaguchi later promised to base his report on one Satō had already written describing his division's plight.[28]

Satō as he retreated left Major-General Miyazaki's detachment behind to try to intercept the Kohima Road. It was a sacrificial mission; it failed. Satō's retreat opened the Imphal-Kohima Road for the British. British troops disgorged from Kohima into the Imphal basin on 22 June. And the Mutaguchi-Satō clash had set in motion an endless chain of acrimonious arguments and counter-arguments which still continues.[29]

General Satō, returning to 15th Army Headquarters, encountered Staff Officer Colonel Kato and Colonel Tsunematsu, chief medical officer of the *Retsu* (Satō's 31st) Division. Tsunematsu told Satō he had been ordered to certify that Satō had suffered a nervous breakdown. The chief medical officer of the 15th Army had suggested to Tsunematsu that this might be a way to avoid an embarrassing court martial for Satō. Tsunematsu complied.[30]

General Satō's return to headquarters was delayed by piles of corpses along the road, which he ordered staff officers to bury. When Satō arrived neither Mutaguchi nor Chief of Staff Kunomura was there to meet him. Satō thundered at Colonel Kinoshita, a staff officer who was instead sent to him, "Do you realize the situation of the *Retsu* Group? 15th Army Headquarters sent me orders but no food or ammunition. How can we fight with no food or ammunition ?"[31] Satō demanded food, shoes and supplies be sent immediately to the 31st and 15th Divisions and that lines of communication be established. Kinoshita agreed to see what he could do but both Satō and Kinoshita knew it was hopeless.[32]

VII DECISION TO RETREAT

Reports of trouble in Burma were reaching Tokyo. In May IGHQ sent Vice-Chief of Staff Lieutenant-General Hata Hikosaburō and Staff Officer Colonel Sugita Ichiji to inspect all fronts of the Southern Army, including Burma. General Kawabe briefly reported his faith in Mutaguchi and his determination to continue and take Imphal. Kawabe had his own reasons for believing in success at Imphal. It was more than a military campaign; it was also a campaign for the independence of 350 million Indians. Kawabe had become a great admirer of Bose. The faces of the Indian troops were haunting Kawabe, and it was now impossible for him to be objective. As Kawabe said, "In this operation there was a big factor beyond my range of vision. So long as there remains any step to take we must persevere. The fate of both Japan and India depends on this operation. I said to myself that I would commit double suicide with Bose."[33]

Other BAA staff officers made pessimistic reports separately to Hata and his staff. Major Ushiro Masaru, BAA staff officer in charge of supplies, said to Colonel Sugita, in the presence of Kawabe and Chief of Staff Naka: "Considering the battle strength, supply potential on both sides and fighting spirit of the enemy, there is no possibility for capture, independent surrender or retreat of the enemy.... Judging from the comparative military power of both sides, the supply situation, and the influence of the rainy season, the limit for continuing the operation is the end of May. Full strength offence should be continued for the time being, but it must be over by the end of May, whether it succeeds or not."[34] This was the first glimmer of anxiety Sugita found in BAA Headquarters. Sugita wired IGHQ of the crisis in Imphal.

Hata and his staff returned to Tokyo, where on 15 May Hata was to make a verbal report to the regular morning meeting of senior staff officers. Meanwhile Tōjō received from Southern Army Headquarters a written report on the Imphal operation which suggested there was still a glimmer of hope. This optimistic report from Southern Army Headquarters was based on a report by three staff officers: Major Kaizaki, operations staff officer of the Southern Army; Lieutenant-Colonel Yamaguchi, supply staff officer of the Southern Army; and Lieutenant-Colonel Kurahashi, supply officer of the Burma Area Army and senior to Major Ushiro. Ushiro, on the other hand, was only a twenty-nine-year-old major. Despite this handicap, Hata and Sugita had listened to his evaluation and reported it to Tokyo.[35]

When Hata began his report to Tōjō and staff officers in the operations room, he spoke of the monsoon and suggested prospects of success were uncertain. Colonel Sugita pointed out that staff reports from the Southern Army were not coming directly from the front lines in Burma. Tōjō reprimanded Hata, saying, "How is it you have returned believing what one young staff officer reports?" At the same time Tōjō ordered forty plane-loads of anti-tank weapons and car parts to Imphal. Major Ushiro in Burma regarded this token shipment as useless when enemy forces in Imphal were receiving one hundred plane-loads of supplies daily.[36] A second telegram from Southern Army Headquarters had just arrived from the front in Burma reporting the situation as desperate; the second telegram forced Tōjō to send supplies.

Next morning the meeting in the operations room resumed. When Hata began his report Tōjō abruptly stopped Hata and asked, "Where is the operation unsuccessful?" Tōjō then changed the subject. But optimistic Southern Army reports were not the only reason for Tōjō's apparent diffidence. Listening in the operations room was Prince Mikasa, the Emperor's brother and a major in the Second Bureau, IGHQ. Prince Mikasa might report to the Emperor, and this would bode political ill for Tōjō. He had to make it appear the operation was going well. Tōjō was really talking not to Hata but for the benefit of Prince Mikasa.[37] The operations room fell silent, and the meeting was dismissed. Operation U would continue.

On 5 June Kawabe met Mutaguchi and heard a discouraging report on the plight of the 33rd Division. Kawabe's face had become haggard and his eyes bloodshot. He realized the situation would not improve. Kawabe was half tempted to call a halt to the operation. He had decided that, if Mutaguchi requested it, he would agree. But Kawabe realized at the same time that this was something Mutaguchi could not ask, and Kawabe's impulse to make a decision was quelled. Kawabe noted in his diary on June 7 that he had a strong feeling there was something Mutaguchi wanted to say but could not. "Though I had such an impression, I didn't try to discover what it was openly, but departed",[38] Kawabe recorded in his diary. Mutaguchi later recalled of the same meeting: "I fully realized that General Kawabe had come to sound out my opinion on continuing the operation. But there was no way of expressing my feeling frankly. I just wanted him to judge from my appearance."[39]

This psychological impasse was in sum the psychology of Japan's Pacific War. Kawabe then visited 33rd Division Headquarters and sent a request to Southern Army Headquarters—by now moved from Saigon to Manila—requesting reinforcements in air and ground strength. He did not suggest an immediate halt to the operation.[40]

Major Ushiro at Burma Area Army Headquarters felt that with the transfer of Major-General Katakura in April to 33rd Army chief of staff, decisive leadership in BAA Headquarters was lost. Katakura, he felt, could have controlled opinions of other staff officers and would have brought about a decision when the situation demanded. Ushiro visited Operations Staff Officer Lieutenant-Colonel Fuwa three times to see if he would expedite the decision to halt the operation. His visits were unavailing.[41]

At the end of June 1944 when Fujiwara returned to 15th Army Headquarters after fifty days at the Palel front he was called in to Commander Mutaguchi's tent. Mutaguchi turned to Fujiwara and ordered: "I want you to report in concrete detail to BAA Headquarters all about this difficult problem of the cessation of the 15th Army's lines of communication for supplies. The BAA doesn't realize the desperate predicament of the Army." Mutaguchi continued in a lower voice: "When BAA Headquarters makes the decision I will decide what to do, assuming complete responsibility for the failure of this operation. What do you think about this?" Fujiwara judged from Mutaguchi's tragic expression and tone of voice that he was contemplating *harakiri*. Fujiwara answered, "In this time of crisis when the 15th Army is facing destruction at any moment it is irresponsible for an army commander to think about what he should do himself. At present the only choice is to make all efforts to save the army and the situation. I sincerely hope you will be prudent."[42] Fujiwara's eyes were moist as he talked, and he saw tears glistening on the general's face. There was no witness to the conversation.[43]

It was not until 26 June that Mutaguchi finally was able to bring himself to recommend to Kawabe a halt to the offensive—or defensive—and a "shift of the line of defence to the Chindwin River". This time it was Kawabe who rebuked his former subordinate: "At present we have no orders from Southern Army Headquarters. It is unprecedented for an Army to report such a strong view. We are expected to push forward with one accord to succeed in our duty." At the same time Kawabe at last sent a request to Manila for an order to halt the operation. Kawabe's request, which was to go by plane to Manila on 29 June, was delayed by bad weather until 3 July. On 4 July Kawabe's request was forwarded by Southern Army Headquarters to Tokyo. Tōjō could no longer avoid the inevitable. On 8 July Tōjō issued the order to halt the operation.[44]

Among 15th Army staff officers there was a belief that Mutaguchi was not reconciled to the retreat even after the order came from Tokyo. He ordered his staff to assemble on a mountain top early on the morning of 13 July. Here Mutaguchi had prayed for his Army daily in a simple Shinto shrine surrounded by a bamboo fence entered through a *torii*. White sand covered the ground in the centre of the shrine. Mutaguchi turned to his waiting officers and said:

> General Satō countermanded an army order and withdrew from Kohima. He retreated, saying there was no food. Is this the Imperial Army? The Imperial Army must fight even without food. If there is no ammunition or food this is still no reason for abandoning the battlefield. If there is no ammunition there are bayonets. If there are no bayonets they still have their bare hands. If they have no hands they have their feet. They can kick. If they lose their legs they can bite. Don't forget, we have our 'Yamato Damashii' [Japanese spirit]. Japan is a divine country. The gods will protect Japan. Japan can never be defeated.... We must fight until the last minute even if we have no food. Don't forget, the Japanese Army will never be defeated.[45]

Many officers fainted while Mutaguchi's hour-long lecture continued. For a malnourished officer, standing under the blistering sun was too great an effort.

All three division commanders of the 15th Army had been relieved in the course of the operation. At the end of the Imphal fiasco all top-level staff officers in the 15th Army were also transferred elsewhere. General Mutaguchi was transferred to the reserve, recalled to Tokyo, and replaced by General Kitamura Shihachi. Mutaguchi was later appointed commandant of the Military Academy, causing some military eyebrows to rise. And General Kawabe was replaced as commander of the Burma Area Army by General Kimura Heitaro. It was the largest-scale reshuffling of top-level command in Japanese military history. Responsibility was being charged to all commanding and top staff officers in the 15th Army and Burma Area Army.

VIII RETREAT

The retreat began as soon as the decision was made. Japanese and INA troops were bottled up in the Kabaw Valley, between the Chin Hills to the west and the Chindwin River to the east. The retreat of the 15th Army through the Kabaw Valley was a glimpse of hell. The sad procession south was led by division commanders and guards with jeeps or horses, followed by officers and those who looked strongest. Next came supply, communications and medical services, such as they were. Behind them came thousands of stragglers, trembling in the rain with fever and malnutrition, their rotting flesh covered with rags. Of those who still had spirit and guns but no strength, many shot themselves. Others with no strength or will or weapons simply slumped into the mud. Corpses accumulated along the roads with no one to bury them or carry out the wounded. There was no such thing as a healthy man. The sorry procession could not move by day for fear of being spotted from the air. It was a macabre march. Of 220,000 Japanese troops who began the Imphal campaign, only 130,000 survived, and of these only 70,000 remained at the front for the retreat. INA casualties were also estimated at over fifty per cent.[46] Rangoon became a field hospital for Imphal troops.

When Bose heard the order to retreat he was stunned. He drew himself up and said to Kawabe in ringing tones: "Though the Japanese Army has given up the operation we will continue it. We will not repent even if the advance of our revolutionary army to attain independence of our homeland is completely defeated. Increase in casualties, cessation of supplies, and famine are not reason enough to stop marching. Even if the whole army becomes only spirit we will not stop advancing toward our homeland. This is the spirit of our revolutionary army." Kawabe, impressed once again by Bose's fervour, tried to placate him by saying they would think of a plan for the future of the independence struggle.[47] Kawabe was pained that there was nothing he could do for Bose. But Kawabe's sense of responsibility toward Bose and the independence movement had already delayed his decision to retreat.

First Regiment commander Kiani voiced the same determination. Kiani told Fujiwara the INA would leave the Japanese Army and follow *Netaji* to India. Fujiwara could not find words to reply. It was only an order from Bose that finally induced INA officers and men to retreat, and relieved Fujiwara of the burden of attempting to persuade Kiani. Fujiwara took steps to expedite the INA retreat two days before the Yamamoto Detachment withdrew.[48] This was the only means he had of showing his goodwill to his old comrades whose hopes were shattered. Fujiwara wept as he watched the retreat of the Indians, clothed in rags and leaning on sticks as they staggered through the mud. The sides of the road were clogged with decomposing corpses, already becoming white bones in the tropical heat and rain. Bodies of men who collapsed on the banks of the Chindwin were thrown into the river in a Hindu parting gesture.[49]

When Bose had arrived in Singapore in 1943 he had promised all Indians in Southeast Asia he would stand on Indian soil before the year was out. This promise even before the launching of the Imphal campaign seemed very optimistic to some military strategists. Bose was not able to keep his promise by crossing the border overland, but he did visit the Andaman and Nicobar Islands in December 1943, thus redeeming his pledge in a sense.

In an article in *Azad Hind* on 6 November 1944, after the retreat from Imphal, Bose was reported to have "reiterated his firm conviction that the final victory in this war would belong to Japan and Germany ... that a new phase of war was approaching in which the initiative would again lie in the hands of the Japanese".[50] Bose's consistent repetition of this faith throughout and even after the Imphal campaign raises the question of the soundness of his military judgement.

There were at least three cogent reasons for Bose's statements. First, as leader of a revolutionary movement he could not destroy the hopes which sustained it, however dismal Japan's military prospects. Second, he must have regarded the propaganda value of his voice, both within the INA and in India, as warranting some departure from grim reality. Third, he continued to uphold the faith in an Indian revolution once INA troops could cross the border, even without Japanese military success. Bose felt he had prepared the ground in India through radio broadcasts from Berlin, Tokyo, and Southeast Asia. Even his most intimate associates among INA staff officers and the FIPG Cabinet report that Bose never expressed any personal or private loss of faith in a Japanese-INA success.[51]

In the final withdrawal of Japan from Rangoon, Lieutenant-General Isoda, last chief of the *Hikari Kikan*, offered Bose trucks for himself and the Rani of Jhansi Regiment to evacuate Rangoon. Bose refused, unless all INA troops were sent out first. Isoda entreated Bose to leave by car. Again he refused on the same grounds. At last he did leave by car but only after ascertaining that all INA units were safe.[52]

IX RETROSPECT

There were as many causes for the failure of Operation U as there were reasons for undertaking it in the first place. Each commander in Burma had his own analysis. For Mutaguchi it was a problem of chain of command and differences between Kawabe and himself and between Satō and himself over whether to try to take Dimapur and Kohima. For Terauchi it was lack of air power which spelled defeat. For Colonel Hattori, Major-General Katakura, and several staff officers it was dispersal rather than concentration of forces during the campaign which contributed to failure. For Bose it was timing with respect to the monsoon. He felt the only chance to take Imphal was before the rains came. Most strategists agreed on this score. He also counted lack of air support among the causes.[53] For Shah Nawaz it was lack of adequate support by the Japanese for the INA, probably as a matter of intent.

For Fujiwara the fiasco at Imphal was not inevitable. It could have been avoided had it been undertaken a year earlier when British power was less able to repel Japan's offensive. The delay Fujiwara saw as caused by the late arrival of Bose in Asia; if Bose had been brought earlier the crisis of the first INA and the arrest of Mohan Singh in turn might have been averted. Fujiwara never ceased to regret these events.[54]

Chain of command, personnel, logistics, topographical, climatic, timing, and operational causes all contributed to the failure of a fantastic gamble. If Mutaguchi was too eager for success, so were Kawabe and Tōjō. The psychology of the decision contributed to the magnitude of the fiasco. Politically Japan had to gamble for a big military success somewhere at the time. Victory would have meant, too, a secure line of defence for Burma west of the Chindwin River, halting of the Allied counter-offensive in Burma, a base of operations within India, interception of India-China land communications, and great propaganda value within India. These were the stakes. Failure in Imphal was in microcosm also the defeat of Japan in the Pacific War.

Lack of air power and secure supply lines were telling factors, but these problems were recognized at all levels of command before the decision to launch Operation U was made. Political realism and military judgement were temporarily thrust aside.[55] "It was an impossible campaign, but the Japanese like such campaigns," commented General Inada.[56] The grim human cost was not counted in a campaign which perhaps proved a "taste for war".[57] And the psychology of military commitment, like an "escalation machine" in any war, was cumulative.

This campaign, so difficult to embark upon, was even more difficult to bring to a halt. As the political advantages of cooperating with the INA in an offensive into India weighed heavily in the first decision, so the obligation to the INA was a heavy burden on Kawabe's conscience in the final decision. It was not a purely military campaign either in conception or in execution. It could not be so judged.

CHAPTER ELEVEN

A Plane Crash

I DEPARTURE FROM BURMA AND THAILAND

Bose and his INA party arrived at Moulmein by car on 1 May. Bose's plan was to move the FIPG and INA headquarters to Bangkok. He wanted to see General Kimura of the BAA, whose headquarters was temporarily at Moulmein, but was refused on grounds of security precautions. Bose then endeavoured through Isoda to arrange rail and steamship transport for everyone to Bangkok. When arrangements were completed Bose went on by car, arriving in Bangkok on 12 May.[1]

Bose had in the back of his mind the old plan to contact the Soviet Ambassador and arrange for transportation to the Soviet Union to get help for the liberation of India from the north. Field-Marshal Terauchi, who was also in Bangkok, hoped Bose would consent to follow headquarters of the Southern Army to Saigon. But Bose was hoping to move headquarters north to China with INA units, and ultimately to the Soviet Union. At length Bose agreed to go with the Japanese Army, meanwhile ordering the strengthening of the INA-IIL in Shanghai preparatory to going to Soviet Russia.

But first Bose wanted to go to Singapore, last headquarters of the FIPG and INA. In Singapore Bose got news of the offer of the British Government through Lord Wavell to reorganize his Viceroy's Executive Council, adding Indians to it. Bose broadcast his opposition to the offer from Singapore on 18 June, saying, "It is crystal clear that any acceptance of Wavell's offer will be tantamount to a voluntary shedding of precious Indian blood and draining our resources in fighting Britain's imperialistic war. But what would India gain in return? Nothing, except a few jobs on the Viceroy's Executive Council."[2] He appealed to Indians inside and outside India not to give up the struggle, never to compromise.

By this time it was early August. Isoda cabled Bose urging him to hurry to Saigon. Chief of Staff Bhonsle also advised Bose of the urgency of completing preparations to move to Saigon. After Bose received a final telegram on 16 August with news of Japan's acceptance of the Potsdam Proclamation, he returned to Saigon.[3]

Not to be distracted from his single-minded purpose, Bose immediately visited Field-Marshal Terauchi and requested transport to Soviet Russia. Terauchi cabled IGHQ for instructions. The reply came back—negative. It would be unfair of Bose to write off Japan and go over to Russia after receiving so much help from Japan. Terauchi added in talking with Bose that it would be unreasonable for him to take a step which was opposed by the Japanese. Nevertheless Terauchi was determined, on his own responsibility and for motives which cannot be fully fathomed, to comply with Bose's desires. Terauchi made arrangements for a plane to fly from Saigon to Dairen, Manchuria, and from there Bose would be able to reach Russia.[4] The war was over, and perhaps Terauchi wanted simply to make a final friendly gesture to Bose, to help him escape interrogation by British or Americans.

Colonel Rahman, S.A. Ayer and Colonel Pritam Singh had flown with *Netaji* from Bangkok to Saigon on 16 August. Bose hoped to take these three men and Devnath Das, Colonel Gulzara Singh, and Major Abid Hassan to Russia with him. Bose's party was irate when they heard the plane could carry only Bose and one other Indian. He asked his party to wait for the next plane when they could all follow him. He chose as his travelling companion his trusted secretary and aide. Colonel Habibur Rahman. The others were flown to Hanoi two days later; S.A. Ayer was flown to Tokyo.

The plane was ready for the secret flight on 17 August. There was an hour's delay at the Saigon airport. News of *Netaji's* departure had leaked out of the cordon of secrecy, and a gift of treasure contributed by local Indians was presented to Bose as he was about to board the plane. The two heavy strong-boxes added overweight to the plane's full load. At noon the twin-engine heavy bomber (Sally type) took off, winging eastward for Taihoku (Taipei), Taiwan, where it was to refuel en route to Manchuria. Aboard the plane were *Netaji*, his secretary Rahman, a Japanese crew of three, and several

Japanese Army and Air Force officers, twelve or thirteen men in all. *Netaji* was sitting at the left over the wing, to the rear of the cockpit of the bomber.

II DESTINATION

The Indians who saw the plane take off wondered where it was really bound. No one had openly stated the destination of the secret flight. But each member of Bose's staff standing at the Saigon airport thought he knew, and that Bose knew he knew. How many times had Bose discussed with his Cabinet his cherished hope to seek Russian help when the Japanese cause looked hopeless. *Netaji* had tried unsuccessfully during his visit to Tokyo to contact the Soviet Ambassador. Returning from Tokyo via Shanghai in November 1944, Bose had visited Anand Mohan Sahay and asked him to try to contact the Soviet Ambassador. There seemed no doubt that the destination was Dairen, not Tokyo. What more could Tokyo do for Bose and the INA now? Bose had already despaired of any further aid from Tokyo. He had written Shigemitsu in May 1945, pleading again with the Foreign Minister to use his good offices to contact the Russians and ask for transport for Bose and his staff to Russia. The reply was negative, as before. And Bose had often asked Isoda for information about the Japanese position in Manchuria and north China.[5]

As highest-ranking Japanese officer aboard the plane. General Shidei was (according to testimony of witnesses examined by the Indian Government committee in connection with the crash) to be the key figure in negotiating with the Russians in Manchuria and to help Bose cross over from Manchuria into Soviet territory. The plane was to stop off in Dairen, allow Bose and Shidei to deplane, then return to Tokyo with the other Japanese passengers.[6]

III THE CRASH

The plane had had a late start, and the pilot decided not to go on the same day to Taiwan. The plane landed at dusk at Tourane, on the northern coast of Indochina to refuel and give the passengers a chance to spend the night in a hotel. While the plane was on the ground at Tourane the pilot and co-pilot, judging the plane to be overloaded, relieved the plane of some five hundred pounds of weight.⁷ The plane took off again at dawn on the morning of the 18th for Taihoku, Taiwan. At noon on the 18th the plane landed at Taihoku airport to refuel again. There was a scheduled two-hour layover while the plane's tanks were filled and passengers and crew lunched. At 2 p.m. the plane was ready to leave.

There was some discussion between the chief pilot and ground engineer about the functioning of the left engine; it was tested several times. Then the pilot revved up the engines, tested the controls, and taxied onto the runway. A few mechanics watched on the ground as the plane became airborne. Less than five minutes later, as the plane was leaving the pattern, something fell from the left wing (it turned out to be the propeller and engine!), the plane careened to the right and dived into the ground, cracking in half. It was soon engulfed in flames from the engine. Several figures staggered from the door of the plane. One of the men had become a flaming torch. It was Subhas Chandra Bose.

Habibur Rahman groped his way toward Bose and beat out the flames which nearly enveloped *Netaji's* body. A truck which served as ambulance rushed Bose and the other passengers to the Nanmon Military Hospital south of Taihoku, where Bose soon lapsed into a coma. A few hours later he was dead of third degree burns. General Shidei and the two pilots also died in the crash. It was not until 23 August that *Dōmei*, the Japanese news agency, announced the news of the crash and Bose's death.

Bose's remains were cremated two days later and his ashes flown to Tokyo to the Army Ministry on 7 September. On the 8th the ashes were turned over to Rama Murti, president of the Tokyo IIL, and on the 14th there was a memorial service. The ashes were entrusted to the Reverend Mochizuki, priest of the Renkoji Temple in Suginami-ku, Tokyo. Fittingly, it was a temple of the militant nationalist Nichiren Buddhist sect. It was the only place Rama Murti had been able to find for Bose's ashes to rest.

IV   THE MYTH

But Bose had become a myth in his own lifetime, dating from the time he eluded house arrest and escaped from India to Afghanistan and Europe. Thousands of Indians refused to believe he was dead.

Man is very mortal but myths die hard. Accordingly the Indian Government, hoping to lay the myth to rest forever, in 1956 appointed a three-man commission to go to Tokyo to interview eye witnesses to the plane crash. Members of the commission were Shah Nawaz Khan, S.N. Maitra, and *Netaji's* brother Suresh Chandra Bose. After interviewing sixty-seven witnesses in Japan, the first two members of the commission issued a report concluding that Bose had in fact died in the plane crash and recommended that his ashes be sent from Tokyo to India. Bose's brother Suresh Chandra Bose refused to accept the findings of the other two members and issued his own *Dissentient Report*,[8] concluding that Netaji had not died in the crash but had succeeded in reaching the Soviet Union, where he had gone into hiding. Bose's brother contends that the evidence of the eye witnesses was so conflicting as to constitute reasonable doubt about the circumstances of the crash. Whatever Mr Bose's motives in issuing his minority report, he has helped to perpetuate until the present the faith that Subhas Chandra Bose still lives.

There are several theories current in India about the secret flight and the crash. One is that it was the Japanese plan to have Bose and General Shidei fly to Dairen and enter Soviet Russia, after which the Japanese Government would announce simply that *Netaji* had "disappeared". It would then be impossible for the British to interrogate or try him. Some Japanese witnesses examined by the inquiry committee corroborated this plan.[9] This version of the plan was not inconsistent with the conclusions of either the majority or minority report.

Another version, that the "crash" was prearranged, also had the virtue that the Japanese could announce Bose's "death", whereupon he would disappear from view. With both of these theories one could postulate that Bose was still alive and had not after all died in the crash. According to Devnath Das, a Japanese staff officer told him the news of the crash was only a story! Bose's staff were not to believe it but should continue to act according to plan. Devnath Das subsequently went underground to continue his activities and did not emerge until May 1946.[10] The secrecy and delay with which the Japanese Government announced the news of the crash was taken by many as additional evidence that the story was fictitious.

Stories persist that *Netaji* has become a *sannyasi* (holy man) and has been seen in the Naga hill country of Assam; that he was a member of a Mongolian trade delegation in Peking; that he lives in Russia;

that he is in the Chinese Army. There were reminders of the strain of renunciation in Bose's early character, when he talked of going to the Himalayas to seek salvation. Pictures have been produced to prove that *Netaji* is still alive. Bose's family have announced at various times that he is still in hiding and will return to India when the time is right. In February 1966, Suresh Chandra Bose announced in the Press that his brother would return in March. To date, however, Bose has not reappeared to contradict the evidence that he died in the crash on Taiwan. But the myth lives on.

CHAPTER TWELVE

A Trial in the Red Fort

I THE VICTORS DISPOSE

After the war INA officers and men in Southeast Asia were repatriated to India. An organization called the British Combined Services Detailed Interrogation Centre interrogated the returned prisoners in the Red Fort. The fort had an illustrious history. It had been the seat of Mogul rule and the focal point of fighting toward the end of the Indian Mutiny in 1857. It became during the war the goal of Netaji and the independence movement. Now a new drama unfolded there as thousands of Indian freedom fighters arrived as prisoners. Fifteen hundred had been captured at Imphal. In September seven thousand surrendered in Malaya and Bangkok. Over ten thousand INA soldiers were returned from Rangoon between May and October 1945. Not until March 1946 were all repatriated.[1]

Thousands were interrogated within the walls of the historical Red Fort. Some were simply returned to their regiments. Others were sent to "rehabilitation centres" before being returned to the Army. Still others were held in custody, adjudged too "indoctrinated" to be safe within the Army again.

On all sides arose popular support for the returned heroes. Sympathy for the patriots spread to the Army and Navy. Nehru spoke of the men on 20 August:

> Now a very large number of officers and soldiers of the I.N.A.... are prisoners and some of them at least have been executed. At any time it would have been wrong to treat them too harshly, but at this time—when it is said big changes are impending in India, it would be a very grave mistake leading to far-reaching consequences if they were treated just as ordinary rebels. The punishment given them would in effect be a punishment on all India and all ndians, and a deep wound would be created in millions of hearts.[2]

Nehru's attitude was remarkable in view of his former antagonism to Bose and his 1942 declaration that he would resist any armed invasion of India which Bose might lead for the liberation of India.[3] News of *Netaj's* death, reaching India at this time, further enhanced popular sympathy for the INA. The British had cause for concern.

The problem for the British was what to do with all these men. From the standpoint of the British every man in the INA was guilty of treason, an offence legally punishable by death. But it was obviously impossible to execute all these men, now acclaimed by most Indians as heroes. On the other hand, considering the rest of the British-Indian Army who had remained loyal, neither could the British ignore the actions of the INA. It was an impossible dilemma. Court martial was the answer, but it was decided for political expediency to limit the trials as much as possible. Proposals were made to the Government of India by the interrogators. The Government in turn forwarded the suggestions to the Secretary of State in London, who accepted them.[4]

It was decided to classify all those interrogated either as Blacks, Greys or Whites according to the following criteria:

a) Blacks—men who appeared, after interrogation, to be so imbued with enemy propaganda that they remained actively hostile to the present Government of India and, if released forthwith, would constitute a danger to the reliability of the Army and to the peace and order of the country.
b) Greys—men who were considered to have been misled, rather than to have been active leaders in co-operating with the enemy, but nevertheless were thought to have been imbued to some extent with enemy propaganda so that they would not be regarded as reliable.
c) Whites—a man was classified White who was able to prove that he had not been tainted by German or Japanese propaganda and that his fidelity to the oath he took when joining the Army was beyond question.[5]

Of the Blacks, it was further decided that the only ones who would be court-martialled would be "a) Any person actively instrumental in causing the death of any British or Allied subject whether in or out of battle", and "b) any person responsible for the brutal treatment of any British or Allied subject". Other Blacks would simply be dismissed from the service. Greys would be dismissed with forty days' leave with pay.[6]

The Government of India announced that by these criteria the rank and file of the INA would be treated leniently; only a few officers would actually be court-martialled. The All-India Congress Committee in September attacked the trial and expressed the hope that all would be released. A Congress fund was set up to handle any cases brought to trial. Congress defence was significant because the INA had transgressed the principles of non-violence and opposition to the Fascist powers.[7] Public opinion had already judged the men heroes and patriots, innocent of any crime. If the officers were convicted they would become martyrs.

As Nehru recalled in the foreword of the proceedings of the trials:

> The legal issues were important enough, involving as they did questions of that rather vague and flexible body of doctrine known as International Law. But behind the law there was something deeper and more vital, something that stirred the subconscious depths of the Indian mind. Those three officers and the Indian National Army became symbols of India fighting for her independence. All minor issues faded away, even the personalities of the three men being tried for an offence involving a death sentence became blurred in that larger picture of India. The trial dramatised and gave visible form to the old contest: England versus India.[8]

II THE TRIAL

The trial began on 5 November 1945 in the Red Fort. It was originally suggested that the trials be held in a remote place where they would not attract attention. But General Auchinleck was so sure the crimes charged against the defendants would horrify public opinion that he gave orders for the trials to be public, in an accessible place. The Red Fort was chosen because it was near New Delhi and because the Press and a limited number of spectators could watch. But the choice had several major drawbacks from the British standpoint that were overlooked.[9] The Red Fort had for centuries been the seat of Mogul rule in India. During the war it was the goal of the INA struggle. It was thus both the symbol of foreign rule and of Indian national aspirations. To Indians it appeared that the British, in selecting the Red Fort for the trials, were arrogantly flaunting Indian opinion.

Case for the prosecution was presented by Advocate-General for India Sir N.P. Engineer. The defence was led by Mr Bhulabhai Desai, a barrister from Bombay. Though Nehru and *Netaji* had been political antagonists, Nehru could not remain aloof, and he appeared in court in barrister's gown to assist the counsel for the defence. Also aiding were Sir Tej Bahadur Sapru, Dr K.N. Katju, Rai Bahadur Badri Das, Mr Asaf Ali, Sir Dalip Singh, Sir Tek Chand, and Mr P.K. Sen. Colonel F.C.A. Kerin was Judge Advocate.[10]

The charges brought by the prosecution were two: waging war against the King, and murder and abetment of murder. There were three defendants: Lieutenant Gurbaksh Singh Dhillon, charged with the murder of four persons; Captain P.K. Sahgal, charged with abetment of murder of the same four; and Captain Shah Nawaz Khan, charged with abetment of murder of two persons. All three were also charged with waging war against the King, that is, treason.[11] The prosecution called thirty witnesses and the defence called twelve. The trial continued until 31 December.

The defence challenged the legality of the trial and the jurisdiction of the tribunal. The defence argued principally that the acts for which the defendants were being court-martialled were acts committed as members of the army of the Provisional Government of Free India, that the INA and FIPG were independent, not under control of the Japanese. The defence argued further that, in view of the above, the defendants could not be tried under the Indian Army Act and Criminal Law of India for their individual actions.[12]

The defendants themselves testified that they had committed no offences for which they could be tried by a court martial or any other court, since they were acting as members of the fighting forces of the Provisional Government of *Azad Hind*, waging war for the liberation of India according to the rules of warfare which applied to the status of belligerents.

The defence counsel also contended that the INA was not a puppet army of the Japanese but was acting independently. Evidence was introduced of the recognition of the FIPG by Japan, of Japan's transfer of the Andaman and Nicobar Islands to the FIPG, and of the dispatching of Mr Hachiya as Japanese Minister to the FIPG.[13] Defence counsel also cited the agreement between the FIPG and Japanese military authorities to turn over captured Indian territory to the FIPG. The FIPG actually administered the region of Zeawaddy in Burma and part of Manipur state in India, according to evidence introduced by the defence.[14] These actions were adduced as evidence that Japan did in fact recognize the independent existence of the FIPG and its army, the INA.

The defence further argued that the FIPG was a functioning government, that it was entitled in international law to wage war and did wage war for the purpose of liberating India.[15]

As the defence saw the court martial, "What is on trial before the Court is the right to wage war with immunity on the part of a subject race for their liberation."[16] This right the defence sought to uphold by citing precedents in international law and by examining witnesses who testified to the independent action of the INA and FIPG. The defence counsel maintained that the ratio of INA to Japanese troops was irrelevant to the question of the independence of the INA.[17]

Indian witnesses called by the defence cited instances of the independent action and status of the *Azad Hind* Government. S.A. Ayer, for example, testified that the Japanese had attempted to appoint a Japanese chairman for the War Co-operation Council, but Bose had successfully resisted this demand as he had others.[18] Ayer also testified that INA broadcasts were made independently of any Japanese control or coercion.[19]

Shah Nawaz in a preliminary statement to counsel stated that, in a conversation with Colonel Iwakuro during the crisis of the first INA, Iwakuro agreed that no coercion would be used and that Indians would be able to continue in the INA or leave of their own volition.[20] This supported another contention of the defence, that Indian POWs were not coerced into enlisting in the INA, contrary to the suggestions of the prosecution. Shah Nawaz also had told the men under his command on the eve of battle in the Imphal campaign that the INA was in no way subservient to Japan, and "If and when India is made free and the Japanese who are now helping us try to subdue us, we shall fight them."[21]

Colonel Sahgal in an interview with J.P. Chander, also reaffirmed the independence of the INA. "When we started the INA movement we firmly believed that if the Japanese withdrew their support or did not agree to our terms, we should be in a position to attain enough strength to follow our course of action independently, and, if need be, to oppose them.... We were determined not to be dictated [*sic*] by any outsider."[22]

Sahgal referred to numerous instances when the Japanese had acceded to INA demands. In one case Japanese officers asked the INA to vacate barracks in Rangoon for use by Japanese troops; Sahgal refused, threatening use of force, and the Japanese backed down. During the Imphal campaign, in May 1944, Sahgal refused to move a company unless adequate boots were provided; despite acute supplies shortage, the boots were provided.[23]

Some Indian statements, however, contradicted the defence case for the independence of the INA. Lieutenant Gurbaksh Singh Dhillon, in a preliminary statement to counsel, stated "I was a Japanese tool which I hated to be ... receiving orders from a Jap liaison officer with whom I was always at loger heads [*sic*]".²⁴ Lieutenant Dhillon at one point had ordered the officers and men under him to have no direct dealings with the *Hikari Kikan* or with any Japanese officers, but to report to headquarters in case they were approached by a Japanese.

The defence counsel called five Japanese witnesses. These were men who had been involved with the Indian independence movement and particularly with the INA. Japanese witnesses subpoenaed for the defence were: Mr Ōta Saburō of the *Gaimushō*; Mr Matsumoto Shun'ichi, Vice-Minister of Foreign Affairs; Mr Sawada Renzō, Vice-Minister of Foreign Affairs and ex-Ambassador to Burma; Mr Hachiya Teruo, Japanese Minister to the FIPG; and Lieutenant-General Katakura Tadasu of the Burma Area Army.

The Japanese delegation which left Tokyo on 10 December was faced with a dilemma: what posture should they adopt in the court martial of the three INA officers ? The INA had actually been fighting under Japanese command at Imphal. But Bose had always claimed, and the defence was now maintaining, that the INA had been an independent army. The Japanese delegation opted to testify according to the wishes of the defendants.²⁵ Testimony given by Japanese witnesses supported the defence contention that the INA was an independent army of an independent government. Although Japanese support of the FIPG had in at least three instances been mostly for propaganda purposes, this did not affect the Japanese testimony. Japanese witnesses had no desire to see the Indians with whom they had cooperated convicted of treason against their British colonial masters.

Mr Ōta Saburō of the *Gaimushō* introduced documents as evidence that Japan recognized the free and independent status of the FIPG and wished to render all possible assistance to it. Mr Matsumoto, who was Vice-Minister of Foreign Affairs and chief of the Treaty Bureau during the war, testified in court that the Japanese Government had helped Bose and the INA for two reasons: primarily to promote Japan's own war aims but also to help India achieve independence, which was in turn one of Japan's war aims. Regarding the meaning of independence, Matsumoto testified that though Japanese troops were present in Manchukuo, Nanking, and the Philippines, the Japanese Government recognized those governments as independent.²⁶

Mr Sawada, Vice-Minister of Foreign Affairs when Hachiya was appointed Minister to the FIPG, testified that when Hachiya was appointed "credentials were not issued solely because the Government was provisional. But at the instance of Mr Subhas Chandra Bose, credentials were issued later."[27]

Lieutenant-General Katakura testified that the "INA were allotted a separate operational role in the battle of Imphal under the control of the Japanese. When there were no operations in progress the INA and the Japanese were independent. When an operation was in progress they came under the command of the Japanese higher command." He testified also that captured territory was to be turned over to the Provisional Government of *Azad Hind*, under an agreement signed by Terauchi and Bose. Further supporting the independent status of the INA, Katakura testified that the Japanese Army never used the INA as labourers. This contradicted other statements by Shah Nawaz Khan. Further, Katakura stated the Japanese and INA saluted each other.[28]

The testimony of Japanese witnesses in court was brief: six pages in all.[29] The burden of Japanese evidence supported the defence claim that the FIPG and INA were independent both politically and militarily, and that Japan had recognized this independence during the war. This Japanese testimony gave moral support to the INA defendants and to Indian aspirations for independence. Japanese testimony and role during the war were reported favourably in the Indian Press.

III FUJIWARA COMES TO THE TRIAL

On 15 August as the Emperor's historic announcement accepting Allied terms of surrender was broadcast, Fujiwara lay ill with malaria at a hospital in Fukuoka. Fujiwara was expecting revenge by the British and Dutch for his role in Southeast Asia. He asked the nurse for potassium cyanide, and waited for the summons. In mid-October a subpoena was presented to Fujiwara, not as a POW but as a witness in Delhi. The subpoena had come from Allied Army Headquarters in Southeast Asia. Ex-Premier Tōjō, Foreign Minister Shigemitsu, Navy Minister Shimada, Southern Army commander Marshal Terauchi, and Burma Area Army commander General Kawabe were also designated. But these men, all suspects as class A war criminals, were detained in Tokyo. Fujiwara was anxious to testify in Delhi on behalf of his INA and *F Kikan* comrades. He would attest that his Indian friends had risen to fight for Indian independence, not as Japanese puppets. This was the only way he could fulfil his obligation to his friends.[30]

Still, Fujiwara was apprehensive as he lay in bed; he might be blamed by the Indian National Congress for encouraging the INA to violate the principles of non-violent disobedience, or he might be charged by the British with violation of rules regarding treatment of POWs in wartime. Or he might even unwittingly cause embarrassment to his superiors. But as Fujiwara prepared to leave for Delhi he threw away the cyanide. He would accept his responsibility and suffer the consequences, whatever they were.[31]

Once again Fujiwara was aboard a military plane bound for Southeast Asia; this time it was an American plane. Fujiwara was aggrieved as he looked down on the battlefields of Burma from the air. Approaching the high red walls of the Red Fort in Old Delhi, Fujiwara felt acutely that this macabre enclosure was symbol of the sad history of the Indian people. The gate of the Red Fort might as well be the gate of hell. Inside was the headquarters of the British military might needed to hold India.[32]

Inside the fort, encamped in a barbed wire enclosure, Fujiwara's anxiety was dispelled as he talked with General Isoda and other Japanese officers. He began to feel the tense atmosphere that surrounded the trial, and the acclaim with which Indian opinion hailed the INA patriots. Fujiwara realized then that the struggle was still continuing. Again he was thrust into the midst of it. He felt the outcome would be as significant as the Indian Mutiny of 1857, and more so. At stake was the loyalty of the British-Indian Army which guarded the British Empire in India.[33]

The court martial was a gross British miscalculation. Fujiwara watched as Gandhi and Nehru took advantage of the blunder to mobilize anti-British opinion. It was as if Congress had laid a snare and the British had been caught.[34]

Fujiwara had a dramatic reunion with his old Indian friends who greeted him with warm embraces and cries of "*Jai Hind*, Major Fujiwara!" He was elated by the confidence and high spirits of the Indians. Fujiwara, feeling somewhat embarrassed, asked, "Will the trial go well?" Lieutenant Dhillon assured him, "Don't worry. India will gain independence within a year. If they punish any one of us no Englishman will leave India alive." Fujiwara noted with admiration from the corner of his eye that the British officer standing guard did not bat an eyelash.[35]

Fujiwara was introduced to Bhulabhai Desai, chief counsel for the defence. Fujiwara was impressed by the tall, venerable, white-bearded lawyer. Desai's words of greeting to Fujiwara were in gratitude for Japanese aid to Asian independence. Desai apologized for not being able to accord better treatment to the Japanese guests. Fujiwara was gratified at the words of sympathy for Japan. He was relieved that his apprehensions about Congress attitudes toward Japan were groundless. Relatives of Fujiwara's old INA friends visited him daily, bringing necessities and liquor. Even the guards greeted Fujiwara with the salutation *"Jai Hind!"* Each morning Fujiwara awoke to strains of an INA song which the British authorities were unable to silence. Fujiwara felt at home again in the midst of Indian friends.[36]

Most memorable of all was Fujiwara's reunion with Mohan Singh. The two met with a barbed wire fence between them. They looked at each other long and intently in silence, then shook hands warmly. Fujiwara recalled with a twinge their last meeting at old Senda's house during the crisis of the first INA. Each man offered the other his help now. Fujiwara was thankful it had not been the end of the INA, that the Army had been able to go on to Imphal. The operation had been a miserable military failure, but now Fujiwara was watching the political aftermath. After all, the independence struggle was ending in victory.[37]

As the court martial continued Fujiwara could feel the rage of Indian opinion, now transformed like a charging elephant. The court martial in effect was finally trying the British for their actions in controlling India for the past two hundred years. Newspapers and meetings reflected the public accusations of a united Indian opinion. Protest demonstrations were held in Delhi, Calcutta, Lahore and Madras as the trial began. In Madras the demonstrations erupted in violence. In Calcutta several hundred were killed and wounded in a general strike lasting from 21 through to 26 November. The strikers were led by students of Bose's alma mater. Demonstrations spread along the Ganges to Patna and Lucknow. Even Bombay was enveloped.[38]

The British authorities were reminded of 1857 as the Red Fort itself was surrounded by hundreds of thousands of shouting Indians. Fujiwara and his friends within the walls waited breathlessly as they heard the sound of gunfire. The shouts became roars. Fujiwara's Indian bearer whispered to him excitedly: "Some have been killed, some wounded! The Post Office has been burned! The Police Department is burning!"[39] The clamour continued until dark. An appeal by Nehru finally calmed the demonstrators, but not until one hundred had been killed or injured.

The whole history of Bose and the INA unfolded daily in the Press. Fujiwara read of his own role in the Farrer Park transfer of the British-Indian prisoners at Singapore.

IV   THE AFTERMATH

The defendants were convicted as charged, but by this time the British realized that the day of independence for India was at hand. They could no longer ignore the overwhelming Indian sympathy for the officers on trial. And in Bombay in February 1946, following the Calcutta riots, the Navy mutinied, protesting against the INA trials and also demanding better food and pay and more rapid demobilization. The mutineers seized control of twenty ships, tore down Union Jacks, wrote INA slogans on walls, and attacked British personnel.[40] If there were any Englishmen who still doubted the questionable loyalty of the Indian services, they were now convinced.[41]

The court convicted the accused and sentenced them to life imprisonment, then immediately commuted the sentences to dismissal from the Army, and released the men.

Though the first trial concluded at the close of 1945, the trials of other INA defendants continued into early 1946. On 24 April 1946, Nehru issued a statement warning British authorities of his opposition to new trials. There were no further trials, and the defendants were all released.[42]

If Bose had remained alive to return to India the atmosphere surrounding the trials—public support for the accused, Congress reaction, and the British response—would have been intensified several times. As it was, Congress had had to support public opinion, and the British in turn completed the preliminaries for the transfer of power to India and Pakistan in 1947. By 1947 the aims of the long struggle of Bose and the INA were realized. India was independent.

CHAPTER THIRTEEN

Retrospect

INDIA was an intriguing problem for Japan on the verge of war in Southeast Asia. The tentacles of the British empire were athwart most of the sea routes in Southeast Asia, and the British-Dutch-American military and economic agreements in the Indies had created a blockade which Japan had to break through to reach vital sources of oil, tin, and rubber. India was, in addition, the stronghold of Britain's power in Southeast Asia. Geography dictated confrontation.

India lay west of the expanding periphery of Japan's wartime Greater East Asia Co-Prosperity Sphere. But nowhere in the most extreme versions of the Co-Prosperity Sphere was there any notion of incorporating hundreds of millions of Indians into the Japanese empire. It would not have been militarily feasible or economically advantageous for Japan to have envisioned a Japanese regime in India. Nevertheless, some Indians in the independence movement feared the Japanese were planning the conquest of India, using the INA to soften the blow to Indian opinion.

Instead, the nationalist aspirations of the Indian independence movement became a natural target for a Japanese propaganda offensive, a logical counter against Britain. Anti-British sentiment in India could be converted into a political and hence military asset for Japan. There was no need for Japan to create an Indian independence movement; she could co-operate with and foster the movement which had existed for nearly a century. This co-operation fitted also into Japan's pattern of a drive against Western imperialism in Southeast Asia.

This possibility occurred to some highly placed Japanese by early 1941 when the portents of war in the Pacific were unmistakable.

Diplomatic communiques from Calcutta to Foreign Minister Matsuoka described the Indian independence movement, particularly in Bengal. The attention of the *Gaimushō* was drawn to Subhas Chandra Bose, Indian revolutionary exile in Berlin, by both Calcutta and the Japanese Embassy in Berlin.

Imperial General Headquarters in Tokyo also took some notice of the independence movement in 1941. The Japanese military attaché in Berlin was instructed to contact Bose and submit a report on him. At nearly the same time, a young major was sent to Bangkok by the Intelligence Bureau of Headquarters on a three-pronged intelligence mission. He would contact and co-operate with Malay groups, overseas Chinese organizations, and Indians organized for the independence struggle. Beyond this IGHQ took no action and made no concrete plans for India. There were no India experts in IGHQ. There was no overall plan at the time or later for a large-scale invasion of India. A strong tradition in the Army dictated that the best staff officers be assigned to north China to guard especially against a military threat from Soviet Russia. Major Fujiwara, setting out on a small-scale intelligence mission to Bangkok, could find no accounts of India in IGHQ archives. At the same time, he was instructed by Chief of General Staff Sugiyama to keep in mind the problem of India in relation to the total Greater East Asia Co-Prosperity Sphere. Fujiwara's instructions were very general, allowing him much leeway in the use of his own initiative, in line with Japanese Army policy of assigning important projects to middle-ranking officers.

Two events forced India on the attention of IGHQ once hostilities broke out in the Pacific: Japanese military successes in Malaya and Thailand, particularly the capture of Singapore and with it thousands of Indian POWs, and reports by Major Fujiwara of the creation of a revolutionary Indian army eager to fight the British out of India. Fujiwara presided at the birth of the Indian National Army, together with a young Sikh, Captain Mohan Singh. Two generals sent by IGHQ to review Fujiwara's project reported favourably on his proposals to step up intelligence activities through the civilian and military arms of the independence movement.

Tōjō and Chief of General Staff Sugiyama took passing notice of India, while the campaigns in the Pacific were piling up impressive victory after victory for the Japanese. In the first four months of 1942 Tōjō several times in the Japanese Diet called on Indians to rise and shrug off the oppressive grip of British rule. IGHQ called

Indian representatives from Southeast Asia to Tokyo in March for a conference on the means to encourage the independence struggle.

Fujiwara's proposals for expanding the India operation were implemented with the appointment of Colonel Iwakuro, heading a greatly enlarged liaison agency. Iwakuro and his staff lent political acumen and greater influence to the whole India endeavour. Iwakuro was founder of the Army Intelligence School, and among his staff were numbered two Diet members. Iwakuro had so much power in the Army that Tōjō, attempting to remove Iwakuro from the Tokyo scene, had appointed him a regimental commander in the crack Konoe Imperial Guards in Malaya.

Indo-Japanese co-operation in Southeast Asia drew on a cultural nexus of ancient origins. For Japan, India was the birthplace of Hinduism, of the historical Buddha, and of the modern saint of nationalism, Gandhi. As the source of inspiration for centuries of artistic, literary, and philosophical expression, India attracted devout Buddhists and literary figures. Okakura Tenshin and Rabindranath Tagore both celebrated Asian spirituality as a heritage which was distinctively Asian.

For Indians, as for many other Asians, Japan was a source of encouragement for aspirations for freedom from colonial rule. Japan's unexpected victory over the Western colossus of Russia in 1905 infused hope into Asian nationalist movements. Japanese patriotic societies and individuals had for over two decades protected revolutionary exiles from many parts of Asia from the authorities of colonial regimes. Bose and other Indian revolutionaries during World War II, therefore, responded readily to Japan's call for "Asia for the Asiatics", for ridding Asia of Western imperialist control.

The Iwakuro mission marked a testing of the limits of Japan's India-INA policy. How far would Japan's support of the INA actually extend? Neither Fujiwara nor Iwakuro received any specific instructions delineating the limits. In both cases they relied on their own interpretations and ingenuity. Clearly Iwakuro's was chiefly a propaganda mission, and Iwakuro was the master plotter in Army intelligence. When Iwakuro was confronted by Indian demands for response to a series of specific requests he balked. He read the mood of Tokyo as unwilling to go beyond a general statement in principle of Japanese support. Iwakuro read Tokyo well. The only point to emerge clearly was that the India project was part of a secret war which would be fought chiefly with the weapons of propaganda and espionage. Under Iwakuro Japanese-sponsored intelligence schools burgeoned throughout Southeast Asia, training Indians for infiltration behind enemy lines.

1943 brought re-evaluation of Japanese support of the Indian independence movement. The whole military outlook in the war had altered for Japan. Subhas Chandra Bose was brought to Asia from Berlin. The independence movement was faltering under Rash Behari Bose's leadership, particularly following the incarceration of Mohan Singh. Subhas Chandra Bose revitalized Indian hopes and urged Tokyo to take seriously a discarded earlier proposal to push a military offensive into north-east India. This thrust would cut Allied communications between Chungking and India and simultaneously defend Burma against an Allied counter-offensive.

Beyond these military objectives, the rationale which dictated the Imphal offensive included the political imperative of providing the Japanese public with one victory in the midst of successive demoralizing defeats, and the propaganda aim of encouraging Bose and the independence movement. Opinion in India was judged by the Japanese to be anti-Japanese, and Bose had as his chief bargaining counter his own leadership of Indians in Southeast Asia.

If the decision to begin the Imphal campaign was long in coming, the decision to retreat in failure was equally protracted and painful. Political and propaganda considerations and repeated defeats had clouded the judgement of strategy planners at top staff levels. In retrospect Fujiwara and many others regretted the campaign into India had not been undertaken a year or more earlier when it was first suggested. Bose also grieved that he had not been able to reach Asia over a year earlier, at the time of his first visits to the Japanese Embassy in Berlin. These two events might have pushed up the Japanese timetable in Burma to put victory within reach. Psychology combined with bad timing prevailed over realism at Imphal to produce a military debacle still debated in Tokyo.

Militarily, Japan adjusted to Bose's arrival in Asia also by appointing, first, Colonel Yamamoto Bin, then Lieutenant-General Isoda Saburō as chief of the *Hikari Kikan* liaison agency. The political propaganda staff which had served under Colonel Iwakuro was largely replaced by military personnel in anticipation of the Imphal offensive. Isoda outranked Iwakuro and was besides a gentle, mild-mannered man, whose appointment was calculated to appease Bose.

For the Indian independence movement, Bose's arrival in Asia from Berlin meant several things. The divisive elements which had plagued the independence groups stopped bickering and united behind Bose's charismatic leadership. Civilian-military rivalries and antagonisms between Indians in Tokyo and those in Southeast Asia were subsumed under a common goal. The IIL and INA were no longer isolated groups but now represented a government-in-exile. Indian unity and Bose's leadership also meant Japanese reassessment of policy toward the INA and reconsideration of the plan for an India offensive. Though Bose was unable to manipulate the Japanese timetable as he wished, he did carry some weight in Tokyo. But other factors affecting Japanese decisions diluted Bose's influence on Tōjō, Sugiyama, and Shigemitsu.

Bose and the *Azad Hind* Government made requests of the Japanese Government for recognition, for ceding the Andaman and Nicobar Islands, and for an accredited diplomatic representative. In each instance the Japanese Government was willing to concede the form but not the substance of Bose's demands. The *Azad Hind* Government was recognized, the islands were ceded, and a minister was sent, but in every case the action was formal rather than substantive. Before Bose was able to elicit the substance of his requests, hostilities stopped and he turned instead to Soviet Russia for help in liberating India.

Japan at no time planned a major invasion of India or incorporation of India into the Greater East Asia Co-Prosperity Sphere militarily. Bose had not changed that. Tōjō's declarations in the Diet in early 1942 regarding the liberation of India reflected a propaganda goal rather than a strategic military objective. The best time for an invasion of India would have been during the spring and summer of 1942, when British forces would have been helpless against it.

Japan's aim in aiding the INA remained to foster anti-British sentiment. All Japanese policy decisions regarding the INA pointed toward this goal. The major Japanese thrust throughout the war was to encourage proliferation of Indian intelligence activities throughout Southeast Asia. Even during the Imphal campaign and the engagements in Burma, the Japanese Army was reluctant to see the INA evolve into a large fighting force. Japan had questions about the possible actions of the INA once the Indian border were crossed, problems about equipping a large INA, and doubts that the INA would be a real military asset to Japan. The manner in which Japan recognized the Azad Hind Government, transferred to it the Andaman and Nicobar Islands, and sent a diplomatic representative also revealed this major propaganda goal.

Japanese objectives in assisting the INA were strictly limited. Japan's major military concern was the overall strategy and prosecution of the Pacific War, in which India was a peripheral concern. INA objectives in co-operating with Japan, on the other hand, were unlimited. For Indians, military co-operation with Japan brought the goal of independence within the realm of possibility. Alone the INA could not have harboured a realistic hope. But there could be no compromise with the struggle for independence, no wavering from the goal of Indian freedom. The bond of a common enemy did not carry the co-operation as far as the INA hoped in the face of this disjunction in basic goals.

The period of greatest success in the Indo-Japanese co-operation was under the *F Kikan,* when Fujiwara and Mohan Singh were both excited by the possibilities of the INA, which they were ushering into being. Friendship and idealistic enthusiasm were important ingredients in their early success. Though IGHQ listened to Fujiwara's proposals, he always felt the gap between his own views on India and those of IGHQ, even within the 8th Section handling Indian matters. The war in the Pacific had just begun and Japan's star was bright. By the time of Iwakuro's appointment, however, the prognosis for Japan had darkened considerably, and Iwakuro was a very different man from Fujiwara. The intelligence activities of the *Kikan* were greatly expanded, but there was little of Fujiwara's idealistic sympathy for Indian independence. By the time Isoda took charge of INA liaison, Japan's military situation had deteriorated still further, and the Imphal campaign was launched out of desperation. There was little room for concession to Bose's increasingly persistent requests. But even in the midst of military fiasco men like General Kawabe hesitated when it came to disappointing Bose.

Was the INA then a puppet or a genuine revolutionary army? The question has several dimensions. Was the INA an independent army in Japanese intent, in international law, and in INA aspiration?

Japanese intent was itself a variable. Policy was formulated and implemented at several different levels, and at each level it was transformed by the biases, experiences, personalities and predilections of the men in charge. There was also a chronological evolution in Indian policy throughout the war. Japanese attitudes were affected at any given moment by the course of the war and the dictates of military necessity.

From the standpoint of international law too the answer is ambivalent. During the court martial of INA officers in Delhi after the war, counsel for the defence argued that the INA was an independent army representing an independent government, that the officers were therefore immune from charges of treason. Japanese witnesses called by the defence supported the case for the independent status of the INA, hoping thus to relieve the defendants of charges of treason. This Japanese testimony, however, was contradicted by Japan's actions toward the FIPG and INA during the war. The stand of Japanese witnesses in 1946 was a separate phenomenon from Japanese aims and actions during the war. In 1946 Japanese witnesses had no desire to see leaders of the Indian independence movement convicted by British colonial power. Furthermore, there is no body of evidence on Japanese policy as an occupying power, since apart from the case of the Andaman and Nicobar Islands there was no military administration over Indian territory. This meant also less chance for confrontation over formulation and execution of occupation policies than, for example, in the Philippines and Indonesia.

Is the conclusion then that the INA was a genuine revolutionary army? The answer hinges partly on the subjective aims and emotions of officers and men of the INA. No one can dispute the character of Bose as a revolutionary in every sense of the word. Even Gandhi and Nehru, who had broken with Bose over the use of violence against the British, conceded during the INA trials that Bose was a true patriot. For Indian opinion there was no real onus of treason or taint of collaboration as in the Philippine case. The INA had fought the British for Indian freedom; that their allies were Japanese was incidental.

Mohan Singh, co-founder with Fujiwara of the INA, was a revolutionary of a different order. Before Fujiwara's eyes Mohan Singh became transformed into a revolutionary, unwilling to compromise with the Japanese when other Indians advised caution and moderation. He went to prison rather than compromise with his convictions.

Most of the INA officers, including Mohan Singh, felt a conflict of loyalty when first confronted with the prospect of fighting Britain for independence, in co-operation with the Japanese. These officers were all professional soldiers, many of them from families with traditions of long and loyal service to the British-Indian Army. Training and experience could not be disavowed overnight. Once they resolved their personal conflicts, however, they fought doggedly for Indian independence, refusing in many cases to retreat when ordered to do so. At the opposite end of the spectrum there was also professionalism and even opportunism among some of the officers and men. The material inducements to volunteer for the INA were attractive, irresistible for many.

The answer to the original question is therefore equivocal, from both the Japanese and Indian viewpoints. For many staff officers in IGHQ, particularly in the Operations Bureau, and for some staff officers in the field, the INA was a puppet army to be used for propaganda functions according to Japanese requirements. For others, at the top, like Sugiyama and Arisue, the INA was a revolutionary army so far as the Indians were concerned, but it had to be subordinated to Japanese military and political objectives. For still others, mostly young idealists in the field like Fujiwara, the INA was a genuine revolutionary army which should receive real and sympathetic support from Japan.

The logic of geography in Southeast Asia and the common enemy, Britain, made some form of co-operation between Japan and the Indian independence movement natural. Although wartime policy toward India was a peripheral Japanese concern, it was one which drew her into ever-increasing involvement. As events of the war continually tested the limits of Japan's policy objectives, the goals themselves were affected. As Japanese military occupation and administration spread westward through Southeast Asia, the boundaries of the Greater East Asia Co-Prosperity Sphere were stretched to accommodate more of Southeast Asia.

Despite the military defeat of Japan and with it the INA, popular support for the INA ultimately helped precipitate British withdrawal from India. Japan's interest in the Indian independence movement, begun as a small-scale intelligence mission in Thailand and Malaya, developed into a complex propaganda and espionage network designed to foster anti-British sentiment, and finally burgeoned into limited support of and cooperation with a government-in-exile and revolutionary army.

There is another dimension to the INA experience—what did it come to mean to independent India? Bose's vision of free India was realized. His other mission—the communal harmony so distinct but so ephemeral in the INA—was also briefly revived in the 1968 attempt to forge a political party out of the vestiges of the INA. The party, named the *Azad Hind Sangh*, has not really come to life. Again, the reason for this lack of viability is that the goals of the party were partly anachronistic; the chief aim of the INA had already been realized with independence. The communal harmony and unity which so distinctly characterized the INA were achieved in part through resistance, first to British then to Japanese control. One of the fascinating aspects of Bose's appeal and leadership was that, despite his personal religiosity and unlike other Indian nationalist leaders (with the possible exception of Nehru), he did not use religious symbols for political purposes, possibly out of realization that they would have divided Hindu from Muslim and Hindu from Sikh.

The Britsh military model, more than the German or Japanese, provided some continuities in both precedent and legacy for the INA. In the first place, the military experience of most men in the INA was not something new, though the self-confidence they gained in an autonomously officered army was. Nor was the political experience of members of the FIPG innovative, except for certain individuals. British colonial rule in India had already made adjustments to nationalism in gradually admitting Indians to upper echelons of the administration. For both these reasons many of the generalizations about Japanese military occupation in Southeast Asia cannot be applied to the case of the INA. India's pre-war military structure survived nearly intact, a situation unparalleled in the new nations of Southeast Asia. And independent India retains the British tradition of separation between military and civilian spheres; the officer has no political aspirations.[1] This is part of another and more significant story: what happened to the INA officer corps after independence.

The INA leadership has not survived as a cohesive political-military elite, and Bose did not return to become India's man on horseback, as his counterparts elsewhere in Southeast Asia did. The man on horseback—German or otherwise inspired—has not found a real place in the post-war Indian politique. For a variety of historical, sociological, psychological, and cultural reasons he does not conform to the political culture of independent India.

Something else has happened to the INA officer corps. Both professional military men and civilians in the INA and FIPG have been politicized and bureaucratized through their experience. Rather than return to the military careers from which they were purged, they have turned individually to politics.² Some INA veterans have been elected to Parliament, others have received high-level diplomatic appointments, others have become cabinet ministers or vice-ministers, and still others have entered the lower echelons of the bureaucracy. That this politicization has occurred with the INA but not in the same manner with the officer corps of the regular Indian Army suggests that the Japanese interlude acted as a catalyst in the metamorphosis. This is a kind of inversion of what is described elsewhere as an emphasis on the role of the military through Japanese influence.³ It is suggested that this inversion may be in part a function of the pre-war Indian military experience, in contrast to its absence in pre-war Southeast Asia.

The INA experience was revolutionary, then, on more than one level. First, as a direct revolution against British rule the INA was partially successful through the British response to the Indian atmosphere surrounding the court martial. Second, as an indirect revolution within the context of the Japanese co-operation the officer corps was transformed. They were bureaucratized and politicized, and in the process absorbed into the political élite of independent India.

Notes

CHAPTER ONE

1. Fujiwara Iwaichi, *F Kikanchō no Shuki* [Memorandum of the Chief of the F Agency], Jieitai, Tokyo, 1959. Most of the information in this chapter is derived either from Fujiwara's Memorandum, from his more recent (1966) book entitled *F Kikan*, or from interviews with General Fujiwara in Tokyo over a period of four summers, 1964-67.
2. Fujiwara, *F Kikanchō no Shuki*, p. 17.
3. *Harimao* was the Japanese transliteration for "tiger" in Malay.
4. Fujiwara, *F Kikanchō no Shuki*, p. 28.
5. Ibid., pp. 32-33.
6. Ibid., p. 34.
7. Ibid., p. 35.
8. Ibid., pp. 37-38.
9. Ibid., pp. 42-44.
10. *Kikan* means "agency".
11. Maruyama Shizuo, *"Himitsu no Tatakai"* [Secret Struggle], in *Biruma Hen* [Burma Volume], *Hiroku Dai Tōa Senshi* series edited by Ikeda Yū, Tokyo, 1953, p. 89.
12. Ibid., p. 91.
13. Fujiwara, *F Kikanchō no Shuki*, pp. 48-49.
14. Ibid., p. 58.
15. Ibid., pp. 67-68.

CHAPTER TWO

1. Japanese sources and informants uniformly refer to Mohan Singh as "captain". Mohan Singh himself reports he had just been promoted to major at the time.
2. Unpublished manuscript of Mohan Singh, p. 31.
3. Interview with Mohan Singh, 5 March 1966, New Delhi.
4. Interview with Mohan Singh, 15 March 1966, New Delhi.
5. Unpublished statement of Mohan Singh alleged to have been smuggled from prison during the war, now in possession of Ram Singh Rawal, New Delhi.
6. Fujiwara, *F Kikanchō no Shuki*, p. 77.
7. Ibid., p. 85.
8. Ibid., p. 89.
9. Ibid., p. 93.
10. Ibid., p. 97.

11 Mohan Singh smuggled statement, in possession of Ram Singh Rawal, New Delhi.
12 Mohan Singh statement in INA History Committee File, INA Enquiry and Relief Committee, Delhi, pp. 53-54.
13 Unpublished manuscript of Mohan Singh, pp. 82-88. Fujiwara, *F Kikanchō no Shuki*, pp. 110-1.
14 Fujiwara, *F Kikanchō no Shuki*, p. 112.
15 Ibid., pp. 118-9.
16 Ibid., p. 125.
17 Ibid., pp. 134-5.
18 Ibid., p. 137.
19 Ibid., pp. 142-3.
20 Unpublished manuscript of Mohan Singh, pp. 104-7.
21 Fujiwara, *F Kikanchō no Shuki*, p. 175.
22 Unpublished manuscript of Mohan Singh, pp. 108-9.
23 Fujiwara, *F Kikanchō no Shuki*, p. 162.
24 Ibid., pp. 162-3.
25 Ibid., pp. 167-8.
26 Ibid., pp. 169-71.
27 Later known as Sembawang Naval Base.

CHAPTER THREE

1 Tsuji Masanobu, *Singapore, the Japanese Version*, New York, 1960, p. 219.
2 Winston S. Churchill, *The Hinge of Fate*, Boston, 1950, p. 53.
3 Ibid., pp. 53-56.
4 Information derived from an interview with Ishikawa Yoshiaki, former student of Hindi and Urdu at Tokyo University of Foreign Languages who was language officer and interpreter for the *F Kikan;* Tokyo, 13 July 1966.
5 Fujiwara, *F Kikanchō no Shuki*, p. 190.
6 British and Australian prisoners were not turned over to the Japanese together with the Indians at this juncture. This discrimination even in surrender annoyed many Indian officers and in some cases tipped the balance in favour of volunteering for the INA.
7 Fujiwara, *F Kikanchō no Shuki*, pp. 194-5.
8 Mohan Singh unpublished manuscript, p. 124.
9 Figures according to Mohan Singh's unpublished manuscript were 42,000 volunteers, 13,000 non-volunteers, p. 124. Other sources make the division more nearly equal.
10 Shah Nawaz Khan, *My Memories of I.N.A. and its Netaji*, Delhi, 1946, p. i.
11 Statement of Major M.L. Bhagata in the INA History Committee File, p. 11, INA Enquiry and Relief Committee, Delhi.
12 Fujiwara, *F Kikanchō no Shuki*, p. 198.
13 Ibid., pp. 200-1.
14 Information derived from interviews in Bangkok, 26-28 May 1966, with the following Indians active in the *Thai-Bharat* Cultural Lodge and Indian National Council: Ramlal Sachdev, C.R. Narula, S.T. Mahtani, Dr N.T. Joseph, and Raghunath Sharma.

CHAPTER FOUR

1 Fujiwara, *F Kikanchō no Shuki*, pp. 211-2.
2 Fujiwara, *F Kikan*, Tokyo, 1966, p. 288.
3 Fujiwara, *F Kikanchō no Shuki*, p. 215; Fujiwara, *F Kikan*, p. 288.

4   Unpublished manuscript of Mohan Singh, pp. 129-31.
5   Ram Singh Rawal, *The I.N.A. Saga*, Allahabad, 1946, pp. 87-95.
6   N.S. Gill statement in INA History Committee File, INA Enquiry and Relief Committee, p. 7.
7   Correspondence of N.S. Gill, April 1967, with the author. Rawal, *The I.N.A. Saga*, pp. 76-77.
8   Raja Mahendra Pratap, *My Life Story of Fifty-five Years*, Dehra Dun, 1947, pp. 257, 327.
9   Raja Mahendra Pratap, *Reflections of an Exile*, Lahore, 1946, p. 123.
10 Sōma, *Ajiya no Mezame* [The Awakening of Asia], Tokyo, 1953, pp. 17, 24-25.
11 For accounts of Bose's life in Japan see J.G. Ohsawa, *Two Great Indians in Japan—Sri Rash Behari Base and Netaji Subhas Chandra Bose*, Calcutta, 1954; and Sōma, *Ajiya no Mezame* [The Awakening of Asia], Tokyo, 1953.
12 Sōma, *Ajiya no Mezame*, p. 53.
13 Devnath Das in an interview in Calcutta, 7 October 1965, asserts that between 1937 and 1939 the League recruited young Indian volunteers for military training by Japanese military and police advisers in the use of arms, drill, and other military aspects. Certainly during the war some thirty-five Indian students attended the Military Academy in Tokyo. Many of them brought from Southeast Asia by Subhas Chandra Bose: information from interview in Tokyo with A.R. Dutta, August 1967.
14 Sōma, *Ajiya no Mezame*, p. 76.
15 Ibid., p. 77.
16 Ibid., p. 78.
17 Fujiwara, *F Kikanchō no Shuki*, p. 218.
18 Rawal, *The I.N.A. Saga*, pp. 109-10.
19 Unpublished manuscript of Mohan Singh, p. 132.
20 Correspondence of N.S. Gill with the author, April 1967.
21 Unpublished manuscript of Mohan Singh, p. 132.
22 K.C. Ghosh, *The Roll of Honour, Anecdotes of Indian Martyrs*, Calcutta, 1965, p. 57, quotes Prevost Battersby in *The Amrita Bazar Patrika*, 26 February 1906: "The successes of Japan have stirred into something like to flame an ambition which without them would have continued precariously to smoulder."
23 Rabindranath Tagore, *Nationalism*, London, 1950, pp. 49-53.
24 Ibid., pp. 64, 91.
25 Okakura Kakuzō, *The Book of Tea*, New York, 1902, p. 126.
26 Quoted in Krishna Kripalani, *Rabindranath Tagore, a Biography*, London, 1962, p. 385; Edward Thompson, *Rabindranath Tagore, Poet and Dramatist*, London, 1948, p. 284.
27 Rabindranath Tagore, *The Spirit of Japan*, Tokyo, 1916, pp. 12-17.
28 Okakura Kakuzō, *The Ideals of the East with Special Reference to the Art of Japan*, London, 1920, p. 224.
29 *Japan Biographical Encyclopedia and Who's Who*, 3rd ed., 1964-65. In Okakura's other publications, *The Awakening of Japan* and the famous *Book of Tea*, he explicates Japan's spiritual tradition and the philosophy of the tea ceremony.
30 Ōkawa Shūmei, *Ajiya Kensetsusha* [Builders of Asia], Tokyo, 1941, p. 285. Ōkawa's other major works were *Dai Tōa Shin Chitsujo Kensetsu* [Building the New Order in Greater East Asia], Tokyo, 1943, and *Nihon oyobi Nihonjin no Michi* [The Way of Japan and the Japanese], Tokyo, 1926.
31 Richard Storry enumerates the following nationalist organisations with which Ōkawa was associated: *Yūzonsha*, founder; *Jimmukai*, president; *Gyochisha* [The Society of Action], president; *Aikoku Kinrotō* [The Patriotic Labour Party], adviser; *Kokuryūkai* [Black Dragon Society], member; *Kokka Shakaishugi Gakumei* [The National Socialist League], adviser; Storry, *The Double Patriots*, Boston, 1957, pp. 309-13.
32 Quoted in Delmer Brown, *Nationalism in Japan, an Introductory Historical Analysis*, Berkeley, 1955, pp. 183-4.

33 Richard Storry, *The Double Patriots*, p. 72.
34 For an interesting discussion of Japanese pre- and post-war academic interest in India, see Nakamura Keiji, "The Study of Modern Indian Politics in Japan", *Asian Studies in Japan*, published by *Ajiya Seikei Gakkai* [The Society for Asian Political and Economic Studies], Tokyo, 1964, pp. 29-43.

CHAPTER FIVE

1 20 November 1941 Liaison Conference, "Essentials of Policy Regarding the Administration of the Occupied Areas in the Southern Regions"; Ike Nobutaka, *Japan's Decision for War*, Stanford University Press, 1967, pp. 249-53.
2 *Gaimushō Kiroku* [Foreign Ministry Records], *Dai Tōa Sensō Kankei Ikken; Indō Mondai* [Matters Concerning the Greater East Asia War; India Problem], Secret Communiqués from Okazaki to Matsuoka, nos. 11975, 11978, 11979, pp. 30-31, April 1941.
3 Interview with Colonel Ozeki, formerly of the 8th Section, IGHQ, on 15 July 1967, at Hashima, Gifu Prefecture; interview with Lieutenant-General Arisue, former chief, Second Bureau, IGHQ, 19 August 1967, Tokyo.
4 Ike, *Japan's Decision for War*, p. xvi.
5 Correspondence with Lieutenant-General Iemura, 21 August 1967. Colonel Nishiura Susumu, wartime secretary to Tōjō, asserts that this is not true, that he (Nishiura) and Colonel Iwakuro originated the proposal for the Total War Research Institute, and that their model was the French National Defence Institute: correspondence, 7 December 1968.
6 Willard H. Elsbree, *Japan's Role in Southeast Asian Nationalist Movements, 1940-1945*, Cambridge, Massachusetts, 1953, p. 20.
7 Interview with Ishikawa, 13 July 1966, Tokyo.
8 Ike, *Japan's Decision for War*, p. 247.
9 Secret document signed Ott (German Ambassador), Tokyo, 7 January 1942, IMTFE Exhibit 1271.
10 *Gaimushō, Indō Mondai*, p. 1.
11 Tōjō speech in the Diet, early 1942, in the *Bōeichō Bōei Kenshūjo Senshishitsu* [Defence Agency, Defence Training Institute, War History Library]; Tōjō speech on military activities in India, Imperial Conference Decision, 4 April 1942, in the *Bōeichō Senshishitsu*.
12 Instructions from Imperial General Headquarters, Tokyo, to General Kawabe in Burma, 7 January 1944, War History Library, Defence Ministry, Government of India; also quoted in A. J. Barker, *The March on Delhi*, London, 1963, p. 246.
13 Durlab Singh, ed., quotes an extract from Shah Nawaz Khan's diary in *Formation and Growth of the Indian National Army*, Lahore, 1946, p. 46. Shah Nawaz Khan, *My Memories of I.N.A. and its Netaji*, p. 125.
14 17 April 1942 *Renraku Kaigi Kettei* [Liaison Conference Decision] in the *Bōeichō Senshishitsu*.
15 *Bōeichō Senshishitsu, Biruma Kōryaku Sakusen* [Burma Offensive Operation], Tokyo, 1967, pp. 491-2.
16 Kesar Singh Giani, *Indian Independence Movement in East Asia; The Most Authentic Account of the I.N.A. and the Azad Hind Government*, Lahore, 1947, pp. 57-58.
17 Maruyama Shizuo, *Nakano Gakkō*, Tokyo, 1948, p. 114.
18 *Bōeichō, Biruma Kōryaku Sakusen*, pp. 492-3.
19 Kaneko Noboru, *"Pinantō Tokumuhan"* [Penang Island Special Mission Group], in *Nihon no Himitsu Sen* [Japan's Secret War], *Shūkan Yomiuri*, 8 December 1956, p. 129.
20 Ibid., p. 129.
21 Mahmood Khan Durrani, *The Sixth Column*, London, 1955, p. 79.

22 Kaneko, *op. cit.* p. 130.
23 Ibid., p. 130.
24 Ibid., p. 131.
25 Ibid., pp. 132-3.

CHAPTER SIX

1   Kesar Singh Giani, *Indian Independence Movement in East Asia, the Most Authentic Account of the I.N.A. and the Azad Hind Government*, Lahore, 1947, p. 62.
2   Interviews with Mohan Singh, 5 March 1966, New Delhi, and with N. Raghavan, 26 March 1966, Madras.
3   Interview with C.R. Narula, a businessman in Thailand since before the war, on 26 May 1966, Bangkok.
4   Giani, *Indian Independence Movement*, p. 67.
5   Ibid., p. 73.
6   *Gaimushō, Subasu Chandora Bom to Nihon* [Subhas Chandra Bose and Japan], Tokyo, 1956, p. 85.
7   Unpublished manuscript of Mohan Singh, p. 139. One does not question Mohan Singh's capacity to keep an audience enthralled with his personal narrative, having had the privilege of listening to it; interviews in Delhi, spring, 1966, cited above.
8   S.C. Goho secret statement to INA History Committee, INA Enquiry and Relief Committee, quoted in unpublished Ph.D. dissertation by Kalyan Kumar Ghosh, *A Study of the Indian National Army*, Indian School of International Studies, New Delhi, 1965, p. 165. Now published as *The Indian National Army, Second Front of the Indian Independence Movement*, Meerut, 1969.
9   A.C. Chatterji, *India's Struggle for Freedom*, Calcutta, 1947, pp. 20-21; Giani, *Indian Independence Movement*, pp. 80-81.
10 Unpublished manuscript of Mohan Singh, p. 149.
11 Giani, *Indian Independence Movement*, pp. 81-82.
12 Ibid., pp. 83-85. The *Gaimushō* publication, *Subasu Chandora Bosu to Nihon*, p. 86, indicates that the Bangkok Resolution contained sixty articles. With the exception of K.R. Palta in *My Adventures with the I.N.A.*, Lahore, 1946, p. 27, Giani as well as other Indian sources mention only thirty-four articles.
13 Unpublished manuscript of Mohan Singh, p. 148.
14 *Gaimushō, Subasu Chandora Bosu to Nihon*, p. 86.
15 *Bōeichō Bōei Kenshūjo Senshishitsu* [Defence Agency, Defence Training Institute, War History Library], *Biruma Kōryaku Sakusen* [Burma Offensive Operation], Tokyo, 1967, p. 490.
16 Interview with Iwakuro, 4 July 1966, Tokyo.
17 By Iwakuro's own account; interview, 4 July 1966, Tokyo.
18 Iwakuro commented, for example, on Mrs Gandhi's 1966 diplomatic attempts at peaceful mediation: "Open diplomacy can't succeed. Everything must be done in secrecy." Interview, 4 July 1966.
19 Fujiwara used this analogy in a conversation with the author, in July 1966, Tokyo.
20 Iwakuro told the author in July 1966 that he was writing four books. One of them, *Sensō Shiron* [Essays on Military History], was published in 1967.
21 Iwakuro, *"Iwakuro Kikan Shimatsu Ki"* [Record of the Management of the *Iwakuro Kikan*], *Nihon no Himitsu Sen* [Japan's Secret War], *Shūkan Yomiuri*, December 1956, p. 120.
22 Letter from Iwakuro to Rash Behari Bose, IIL Documents File, National Archives, Government of India, New Delhi.

23 Unpublished manuscript of Mohan Singh, p. 151.
24 Ibid., pp. 152-4.
25 Interview with Devnath Das, 7 October 1965, Calcutta.
26 Fujiwara, *F Kikan*, p. 333.
27 Unpublished manuscript of Mohan Singh, p. 155.
28 Secret statement of S.C. Goho to INA History Committee, INA Enquiry and Relief Committee, quoted by K.K. Ghosh in *A Study of the Indian National Army*, p. 165, now published as *The Indian National Army, Second Front of the Indian Independence Movement*, Meerut, 1969.
29 Interview with Ishikawa Yoshiaki, 13 July 1966, Tokyo.
30 Statement of N.S. Gill in the INA History Committee File, INA Enquiry and Relief Committee, Delhi, pp. 7-8.
31 Chatterji, *India's Struggle for Freedom*, p. 46.
32 Gill statement in INA History Committee File, p. 8.
33 Ibid., p. 9.
34 Fujiwara, *F Kikan*, p. 336.
35 Revised unpublished manuscript of Mohan Singh, ch. XV, p. 2.
36 Ibid., pp. 7-8.
37 Ibid., pp. 9-10.
38 Ibid., ch. XVI, p. 1.
39 Ibid., pp. 2-4.
40 Ibid., pp. 5-6.
41 Ibid., p. 7. Giani, *Indian Independence Movement*, p. 100.
42 Revised unpublished manuscript of Mohan Singh, ch. XVI, p. 8. Iwakuro approached Mohan Singh privately, attempting to make a "deal" to give him full support. Under the misapprehension that the civilian members of the Council were primarily concerned with control of civilian property in Burma, Iwakuro thought he could use Mohan Singh against other members of the Council. Ch. XVIII, p. 16.
43 Giani, *Indian Independence Movement*, pp. 100-4.
44 Ibid., p. 103.
45 Ibid., p. 104.
46 Ibid., p. 105.
47 Ibid., p. 105-6.
48 Ibid., p. 106.
49 Revised unpublished manuscript of Mohan Singh, ch. XVI, pp. 9-11.
50 Ibid., p. 13.
51 Ibid., pp. 15-17. Giani, *Indian Independence Movement*, pp. 108-11.
52 Giani, *Indian Independence Movement*, p. 112. Revised unpublished manuscript of Mohan Singh, ch. XVI, pp. 20-21.
53 Ibid., pp. 21-23. Mohan Singh's account here coincides exactly with Giani's, pp. 113-14. Mohan Singh and Giani do not completely agree in their accounts of Mohan Singh's conversations with *Kikan* members, though many of the sentences are identical.

Another version of Iwakuro's reply includes other items as follows: "1) Japan has no territorial, political, military or economic ambitions toward India; 2) India should be an independent country, an 'India of Indians'; 3) as the IIL is an organization of Indians in contact with the national movement within India, Japan has no intention of utilizing it as a Japanese fifth column, but it should not infringe the sovereignty of other countries; 4) the INA is an army belonging to the IIL, not a private army belonging to an individual and Japan has no intention of using it for any purpose other than provided in the resolutions of the Bangkok Conference; 5) Japan's aim of establishing peace in Asia ... is a natural expression of Japanese national sentiment ... respect and love for India." And on other matters: "1) Japan cannot reply to the resolutions of the Bangkok Conference because the IIL is a political organization not a state; 2) Japan has refrained from making a public announcement of the existence of the INA because we thought a greater strategic effect could be gained if this were done simultaneously with the start of the Indian campaign; 3) Japan cannot agree to the proposal to put the Indian prisoners under the supervision of the GOC of the INA. The manners and purposes of using the prisoners shall be solely decided by the Japanese side according to its own discretion; 4) Colonel Gill was arrested because of the defection of Major Dhillon and other subordinates to the British side; 5) the Japanese Army has never attempted the dissolution or disarmament of the INA; 6) "Mr. Mohan Singh, driven by an impulsive sentiment, blinded by a narrow minded subjective idea, has made indiscretely [sic] an error this time of hampering the IIL movement and creating an unfortunate breach between Japan and India. However, considering his distinguished services to the establishment of the INA and his sincere devotion to his mother country, we Japanese will regard him with honour and respect his own will as regards his future movement, as long as he refrains from any conduct that may injure the Japanese Indian relations of the Indian independence movement; 7) regarding the assault and insult inflicted by the Japanese upon the officers and men of the INA, we have already made an arrangement with all those concerned in order to guard against such happenings with full precaution, and therefore in future the situation will be better. Should such things happen again, we shall deal with each case on its merits in good faith." This list, included in a statement to the INA History Committee by Major M.L. Bhagata, in the INA History Committee File, INA Enquiry and Relief Committee, Delhi, does not accord with the statement recorded by Mohan Singh, except for the item about the impossibility of an itemized reply to the Bangkok Resolution.

54 Revised unpublished manuscript of Mohan Singh, ch. XVI, pp. 24-25.
55 Ibid., pp. 26-27. Giani, *Indian Independence Movement*, pp. 115-6.
56 Letter from N. Raghavan to Rash Behari Bose, 4 Dec. 1942, IIL Documents File, National Archives, Government of India, New Delhi.
57 Revised unpublished manuscript of Mohan Singh, ch. XVII, pp. 1-2. Giani, *Indian Independence Movement*, p. 117.
58 Giani, *Indian Independence Movement*, pp. 119-21.
59 Revised unpublished manuscript of Mohan Singh, ch. XVII, pp. 7-8.
60 Ibid., pp. 24-26.
61 Ibid., pp. 26-27.
62 Ibid., pp. 27-29. Letter from Mohan Singh to Rash Behari Bose, 13 December 1942, in IIL Documents File, National Archives, Government of India, New Delhi.
63 Letter from R.B. Bose to M. Singh, 29 December 1942, IIL Documents File, National Archives, Government of India, New Delhi.
64 Radhanath Rath, ed., *Rash Behari Basu, His Struggle for India's Independence*, Calcutta, 1963, p. 231.
65 Iwakuro, *"Iwakuro Kikan Shimatsu Ki"* [Record of the Management of the Iwakuro Kikan], *Nihon no Himitsu Sen* [Japan's Secret War], *Shūkan Yomiuri*, December 1956, p. 121. Mohan Singh, revised unpublished manuscript, ch. XX, p. 15.
66 Fujiwara, *F Kikan*, pp. 338-9. Mohan Singh, revised unpublished manuscript, ch. XX, p. 19.
67 *Bōeichō Senshishitsu, Biruma Kōryaku Sakusen*, p. 492.
68 Jitendra Nath Ghosh, *Netaji Subhas Chandra*, Calcutta, 1946, p. 113. K.R. Palta, *My Adventures with the I.N.A.*, Lahore, 1946, pp. 49-50.
69 M. Sivaram, *The Road to Delhi*, Tokyo, 1967, p. 90.
70 Palta, *My Adventures with the I.N.A.*, pp. 49-57. Chatterji, *India's Struggle for Freedom*, pp. 151-4.
71 Ibid., pp. 60-61. Palta, *My Adventures with the I.N.A.*, pp. 59-61.
72 Mohan Singh, *Leaves from my Diary*, Lahore, 1946, p. 18.
73 Giani, *Indian Independence Movement*, pp. 136-7.

CHAPTER SEVEN

1. Information on Bose's childhood and early life is derived from his autobiography, *An Indian Pilgrim, An Unfinished Autobiography and Collected Letters, 1897-1921*, Asia Publishing House, 1965.
2. Quoted by Bose, ibid., p. 56.
3. Hugh Toye, *Subash Chandra Bose, The Springing Tiger*, Jaico Publishing House, Bombay, 1959, pp. 38-39.
4. Ibid., pp. 29-41.
5. Netaji Research Bureau, *Crossroads, being the Works of Subhas Chandra Bose*, Calcutta, 1962, pp. 140-1.
6. Jawaharlal Nehru, *A Bunch of Old Letters*, Bombay, 1960, pp. 329-49.
7. Subhas Chandra Bose, *The Indian Struggle, 1935-1942*, Calcutta, 1952, pp. 87-93.
8. Ibid., p. 116.
9. Hira Lal Seth, *Personality and Political Ideals of Subhas Chandra Bose: Is He Fascist?* Lahore, 1944, p. 46.
10. Bejon Kumar Sen Gupta, *India's Man of Destiny*, Calcutta, s.d., p. 50. The problem of whether Bose was close to Hilter ideologically, and of how far left or right he was, is still being debated. More than one person offered to collaborate with the author on a book on Bose "to prove that he was not a fascist", and to prove other things about Bose.
11. Sen Gupta, *India's Man of Destiny*, pp. 103-4.
12. Toye, *Subash Chandra Bose*, p. 61.
13. Uttam Chand, *When Bose Was Ziauddin*, Delhi, 1946, pp. 71 ff.
14. Malcolm Muggeridge, ed., *Ciano's Diary*, London, 1947, p. 355.
15. Conversation with Girija Mookerjee, 20 September 1965, New Delhi.
16. Lukasz Hirszowicz, *The Third Reich and the Arab East*, London, 1966, pp. 211-19.
17. Louis P. Lochner, trans. & ed., *The Goebbels Diaries*, London, 1948, p. 67.
18. Ibid., p. 81.
19. Ibid., p. 157.
20. Girija Mookerjee, *This Europe*, Calcutta, 1950, pp. 134-40.
21. Ibid., p. 134. Dr Mookerjee states that Bose was unable to interrupt Hitler and get a chance to speak: conversation, September 1965, New Delhi.
22. Yamamoto Bin, *"Kakumeiji Umi o Wataru—Chandora Bosu Berurin Dasshutsu Ki"* [A Revolutionary Crosses the Ocean—Record of Chandra Bose's Escape from Berlin], in *Nihon no Himitsu Sen* [Japan's Secret War], *Shūkan Yomiuri*, December 1956, p. 123.
23. Maruyama Shizuo, *Nakano Gakkō*, Tokyo, 1948, p. 120.
24. Interviews: Girija Mookerjee, 20 September 1965, New Delhi; former Ambassador Ōshima Hiroshi, 25 July 1966, Chigasaki City, Japan.
25. Yamamoto Bin, *"Kakumeiji Umi o Wataru"*, p. 123.
26. *Gaimushō, Dai Tōa Sensō Kankei Ikken, Indō Mondai, Indō ni taisuru Seisaku Keikaku* [Foreign Ministry, Matters Relating to the Greater East Asia War, India Problem, Plan for Policy toward India], p. 6.
27. *Gaimushō, Ajiya Kyoku* [Foreign Ministry, Asia Office], *Subasu Chandora Bosu to Nihon* [Subhas Chandra Bose and Japan], pp. 90-91.
28. The 10 January decision of the Liaison Conference was: "1) India's sea communications should be intercepted, and 2) to instigate anti-British sentiment in India and to stimulate the anti-British movement, propaganda should be strengthened and the policy should be developed concomitantly. For this purpose we shall invite him to Tokyo and judge his utility value from the standpoint of this policy. At the same time we shall inform him of Japan's national power and the enthusiasm of all Japan for assisting India's independence. The Army section

of IGHQ shall be in charge of his treatment and guidance and the agencies concerned shall co-operate." *Bōeichō Senshishitsu, Renraku Kaigi Kettei* [Liaison Conference Decisions]. *Sambō Hombu* [General Staff Headquarters], *Sugiyama Memo.*
29 Interview with Girija Mookerjee, 29 September 1965, New Delhi.
30 Correspondence with ex-Ambassador Ōshima, 21 July 1967.
31 Interview with ex-Ambassador Ōshima, 25 July 1966, Chigasaki City, Japan; *Bōeichō Senshishitsu, Biruma Kōryaku Sakusen* [Burma Offensive Operation], Tokyo, 1967, p. 582.
32 Repeated invitations by the Indian Government to Mrs Bose have been refused, but her daughter Anita accepted an invitation to visit the homeland of her father.
33 *Bōeichō Senshishitsu, Biruma Kōryaku Sakusen*, pp. 583-4.
34 *Gaimushō, Subasu Chandora Bosu to Nihon*, p. 98.
35 Ibid., p. 99.
36 Generals Fujiwara, Isoda, Ōshima, Katakura, and Iwakuro, of those still alive, regularly assemble annually in Tokyo to pay their respects to the memory of Bose on 18 August, the anniversary of Bose's death in an airplane crash in Taiwan in 1945.
37 *Gaimushō, Subasu Chandora Bosu to Nihon*, p. 100; Yamamoto Bin, "*Kakumeiji Umi o Wataru*", p 126.
38 *Gaimushō, Subasu Chandora Bosu to Nihon*, p. 100.
39 Arun, ed., *Testament of Subhas Bose*, Delhi, 1946, p. 143.
40 Unpublished manuscript by Hayashida Tatsuo, *Biography of Subhas Chandora Bose*, pp. 103-4. Now published as *Higeki no Eiyū* [Hero of Tragedy], Tokyo, 1968.
41 *Gaimushō, Subasu Chandora Bosu to Nihon*, p. 101.
42 Ibid., pp. 108-9.
43 *Hikari* means "light" in Japanese, in this case "light from the East".
44 Indian and Japanese accounts consistently describe Subhas Bose as a huge man over six feet tall. In actuality he was about five feet seven inches. The author was shown a picture of Bose standing with his nephew Sisir K. Bose, a man five feet eight inches in height who resembles his uncle. Subhas Bose was even shorter than his nephew. The illusion of great height was created entirely by Bose's imposing bearing and his commanding, charismatic personality. Perhaps his uniform helped create the illusion.
45 M. Sivaram, *The Road to Delhi*, Tokyo, 1967, pp. 116-7.
46 Giani, *Indian Independence Movement*, part II, pp. 13-14.
47 Ibid., pp. 11-18.
48 A Journalist, *Netaji*, Lahore, 1946, pp. 93-94.
49 Sivaram, *The Road to Delhi*, pp. 122-3.
50 Ibid., pp. 123-4; Das Gupta, *Subhas Chandra*, pp. 217-8.
51 Sivaram, *The Road to Delhi*, p. 125; Chatterji, *India's Struggle for Freedom*, pp. 72-73.
52 Palta, *My Adventures with the I.N.A.*, pp. 73-74; Chatterji, *India's Struggle for Freedom*, p. 75.
53 Ibid., p. 74.
54 Ibid., p. 76.
55 Ibid., pp. 79-80.
56 *Netaji* Oration by Lakshmi Swaminadhan Sahgal, 1964, *Bulletin of the Netaji Research Bureau*, Calcutta, Jan. 1965, pp. 11-12.
57 Sivaram, *The Road to Delhi*, pp. 128-9.
58 Ibid., p. 133.
59 Chatterji, *India's Struggle for Freedom*, p. 83.
60 Units of the *Azad Hind Fauj* were: No. 1 Division, commanded by Major-General M.Z. Kiani, consisting of three guerrilla regiments: 1) Gandhi Regiment, commanded by Colonel I. Kiani; 2) *Azad* Regiment, commanded by Golonel Gulzara Singh; and 3) Nehru Regiment, commanded by Major-General Shah Nawaz Khan; the Field Force, Bahadur Group, Intelligence

Group, and Reinforcement Group remained unchanged; Chatterji, *India's Struggle for Freedom*, pp. 94-97.
61 Ibid., pp. 100-2.
62 Account by Shah Nawaz Khan, who witnessed the meeting of the two commanders, related in Jay Parvesh Chander, *Meet the Heroes*, Lahore, s.d., pp. 104-5. Inada Seijun, *Inada Nikki* [Inada Diary], vol. II, pp. 308-10, *Bōeichō Senshishitsu*, 1943.
63 From interviews with Shah Nawaz Khan, 26 Feb. 1966, and Dr Raju, 2 December 1965, New Delhi.
64 This conversation is as recalled by Mohan Singh during an interview on 5 March 1966, in New Delhi.
65 As recalled by Mohan Singh in an interview on 19 May 1966.
66 This version of the story was related in an interview with Shah Nawaz Khan, 26 February 1966, New Delhi.
67 Correspondence with Ambassador to Mexico, N.S. Gill, 4 April 1967.
68 Interview with N. Raghavan, 26 March 1966, Madras.
69 Fujiwara, *F Kikan*, pp. 347-8.
70 Ibid., pp. 348-9.
71 Ibid., pp. 348-9.

CHAPTER EIGHT

1 Members of the new cabinet were as follows: Subhas Chandra Bose, Head of State, Prime Minister and Minister of War, Minister for Foreign Affairs, and Supreme Commander of the Indian National Army; Captain Lakshmi Swaminadhan, women's organizations; S.A. Ayer, publicity and propaganda; Lieutenant-Colonel A.C. Chatterji, finance; representatives of the Armed Forces: Lieutenant-Colonel Aziz Ahmed Khan, Lieutenant-Colonel N.S. Bhagat, Lieutenant-Colonel J.K. Bhonsle, Lieutenant-Colonel Gulzara Singh, Lieutenant-Colonel M.Z. Kiani, Lieutenant-Colonel A.D. Loganadhan, Lieutenant-Colonel Ehsan Qadir, and Lieutenant-Colonel Shah Nawaz Khan; A.M. Sahay, secretary with ministerial rank; Rash Behari Bose, supreme adviser; advisers: Karim Gani, Devnath Das, D.H. Khan, A. Yellappa, J. Thivy, and Iswar Singh; and A.N. Sircar, legal adviser: Chatterji, *India's Struggle for Freedom*, pp. 133-4; Arun, ed., *Testament of Subhas Bose*, p. 261.
2 Arun, ed., *Testament*, p. 261; Chatterji, *India's Struggle for Freedom*, p. 137.
3 Ibid., pp. 136-7.
4 Hattori Takushirō, *Dai Tōa Sensō Zenshi* [Complete History of the Greater East Asia War], Tokyo, 1953, vol. II, p. 381.
5 Ibid., p. 381.
6 Chatterji, *India's Struggle for Freedom*, pp. 139-40.
7 *Gaimushō, Subasu Chandora Bosu to Nihon*, p. 124.
8 *Azad Hind*, Syōnan (Singapore), 25 October 1943; Sivaram, *The Road to Delhi*, p. 157.
9 Sivaram, *The Road to Delhi*, p. 157.
10 Ibid., p. 158.
11 Hattori Takushirō, *Dai Tōa Sensō Zenshi*, vol. II, pp. 370-1.
12 Robert S. Ward, *Asia for the Asiatics? The Techniques of Japanese Occupation*, Chicago, 1945, pp. 189-90.
13 Hayashida, unpublished biography of Bose, p. 150, now published as *Higeki no Eiyū* [Hero of Tragedy], Tokyo, 1968; Radhanath Rath, ed., *Rash Behari Basu, His Struggle for India's Independence*, Calcutta, 1963, p. 484; Sivaram, *The Road to Delhi*, p. 160.
14 Arun, ed., *Testament*, p. 150.

15 *Gaimushō, Indō Mondai*, Ba Maw of Burma, Speech in Support of the Provisional Government *of Azad Hind*, pp. 1-5.
16 *Gaimushō, Indō Mondai*, Subhas Chandra Bose address, pp. 3-4; Sivaram, *The Road to Delhi*, pp. 161-2.
17 *Gaimushō, Indō Mondai*, Bose address, pp. 5-7.
18 Ibid., pp. 8-10.
19 Robert S. Ward, *Asia for the Asiatics?*, p. 189.
20 Hattori, *Dai Tōa Senso Zenshi*, vol. II, p. 38; Satō Kenryō, *Dai Tōa Senso Kaisōroku* [Recollections of the Greater East Asia War], Tokyo, 1966, p. 316.
21 Sivaram, *The Road to Delhi*, pp. 167-8.
22 Hattori, *Dai Tōa Senso Zenshi*, vol. II, pp. 381-2.
23 Motiram, *Two Historic Trials in Red Fort*, Exhibit UUU, pp. 370-1.
24 Hattori, *Dai Tōa Senso Zenshi*, vol. II, pp. 381-2.
25 This was the explanation given in *Azad Hind*, no. 7/8, 1944, p. 10.
26 Counsel for defence of the INA officers tried for treason in Delhi after the war, in making a case for the FIPG as an independent government, maintained the islands were actually ceded even though not all aspects of the administration of the islands were transferred to the FIPG: K.L. Gaube, *Famous and Historic Trials*, Lahore, 1946, pp. 315-6.
27 Motiram, *Two Historic Trials in Red Fort*, Exhibit EEEEE, Statement to Subhas Chandra Bose by Vice-Admiral Oka Takazumo, Chief of Military Affairs Section, Imperial Japanese Navy, 16 Nov. 1943, pp. 375-6.
28 Ibid., Exhibit EEEEE, Statement to Subhas Chandra Bose by Vice-Admiral Oka Takazumo, Chief of Military Affairs Section, Imperial Japanese Navy, 16 November 1943, pp. 375-6.
29 Ibid., Exhibit LLLLL, Correspondence between Bose and Loganadhan, June-July 1944, pp. 379-81.
30 Interview with Colonel P.K. Sahgal, Kanpur, India, 22 December 1965.
31 Sivaram, *The Road to Delhi*, pp. 168-9; Toye, *The Springing Tiger*, p. 105.
32 Some forty-five Indians from Southeast Asian countries soon after entered the Military Academy: interview with A.R. Dutta, Tokyo, August 1967.
33 Interview with Major-General Nagai Yatsuji, formerly of the 8th Section, Imperial General Headquarters in Tokyo, 10 August 1967.
34 *Kōseishō* [Welfare Ministry], *Hikiage Engokyoku* [Repatriates' Relief Bureau], *Isoda Saburō Chūjō Kaisōroku* [Recollections of Lieutenant-General Isoda Saburō], Tokyo, 1954, pp. 1-6.
35 Ibid., pp. 11-12.
36 S.A. Ayer, *Unto Him a Witness*, pp. 195-6.
37 Ibid., pp. 217-18. Ayer, Minister of Propaganda and Publicity of the FIPG, has recounted in some detail negotiations of Bose and members of his cabinet with staff of the *Kikan. Vide* Appendix.
38 *Isoda Saburō Chūjō Kaisōroku*, pp. 32-33.
39 Interview with Major Ushiro Masaru, former supply officer in the Burma Area Army, Tokyo, 22 July 1967.
40 *Gaimushō, Subasu Chandora Bosu to Nihon*, pp. 88-89.
41 S.A. Ayer, *Unto Him a Witness*, p. 186.
42 Arun, ed., *Testament*, p. 74.
43 *Gaimushō, Subasu Chandora Bosu to Nihon*, p. 176.
44 Chatterji, *India's Struggle for Freedom*, pp. 216-25.
45 *Gaimushō, Indō Mondai*, Plan for Policy toward India, p. 25.
46 *Gaimushō, Subasu Chandora Bosu to Nihon*, pp. 199-200; Hayashida, *op. cit.* p. 188.
47 Ayer, *Unto Him a Witness*, pp. 175-6.
48 Arun, ed., *Testament*, p. 165.
49 *Nippon Times*, 3 November 1944.

50 *Gaimushō, Subasu Chandora Bosu to Nihon*, p. 202.
51 Ibid., p. 203.
52 Ibid., pp. 204-5; *Isoda Saburō Chūjō Kaisōroku*, pp. 23-24.
53 Hayashida, *op. cit.*, p. 193.
54 Subhas Chandra Bose, *India Calling*, Lahore, *s.d.*, p. 78.
55 Sivaram, *The Road to Delhi*, p. 230.
56 *Gaimushō, Subasu Chandora Bosu to Nihon*, p. 207.
57 Ibid., p. 207; *Isoda Saburō Chūjō Kaisōroku*, pp. 26-27.
58 *Gaimushō, Indō Mondai*, Plan for Policy toward India, p. 27.
59 Chatterji, *India's Struggle for Freedom*, p. 251.
60 *Gaimushō, Indō Mondai*, Plan for Policy toward India, pp. 20-21.
61 *Isoda Saburō Chūjō Kaisōroku*, p. 28.
62 Chatterji, *India's Struggle for Freedom*, pp. 249-50.
63 *Gaimushō, Subasu Chandora Bosu to Nihon*, pp. 209-10.
64 Ibid., pp. 212-3.
65 Ibid., pp. 213-4.
66 Ibid., pp. 214-5.
67 Chatterji, *India's Struggle for Freedom*, pp. 253-4.

CHAPTER NINE

1   Field-Marshal Viscount Wavell's Despatch on Operations in the India Command, New Delhi, 1 January-20 June 1943, p. 1; Historical Section, Defence Ministry, Government of India.
2   Ibid., pp. 2-3.
3   A.J. Barker, *The March on Delhi*, London, 1963, p. 61.
4   Wavell's Despatch on Operations in the India Command, p. 6.
5   Air Staff HQ, Air Command, Southeast Asia, The Siege of Imphal: Air Aspects, p. 1; Historical Section, Defence Ministry, Government of India.
6   British military historian Colonel A.J. Barker also accepts the assumption that the Japanese were planning a "march on Delhi". See Barker, *The March on Delhi*.
7   Wavell's Despatch on Operations in the India Command, p. 17.
8   Major-General S. Woodburn Kirby, *The War Against Japan; The Reconquest of Burma*, vol. III, London, 1965, p. 45.
9   Wavell's Despatch on Operations in the India Command, p. 24.
10 These are in general the mountains east of the Imphal plain, the mountains west of the plain, and—more extreme—beyond Dimapur into Assam.
11 *Barker, The March on Delhi*, p. 55.
12 Fourth Despatch from the India Command from 21 June 1943 to 15 November 1943, p. 20.
13 Japanese monograph no. 134, p. 13, File no. 601/13164/H, Burma Operations Record, Historical Section, Defence Ministry, Government of India.
14 Correspondence with the author of former ambassador to Berlin, General Ōshima Hiroshi, 27 July 1967.
15 *Bōeichō, Biruma Kōryaku Sakusen*, p. 547.
16 Ibid., pp. 547-53.
17 Ibid., pp. 554-5. Tanemura, *Dai Hon'ei Kimitsu Nisshi* [Secret Diary of Imperial General Headquarters], Tokyo, 1952, p. 213.
18 *Bōeichō, Biruma Kōryaku Sakusen*, p. 556.
19 Ibid., p. 557.
20 Ibid., pp. 559-61.
21 Ibid., p. 563.
22 Interview with General Katakura, 13 July 1966, Tokyo. Fujio Masayuki, *"Biruma no Ryūko"* [Tiger of Burma], in Ikeda Yū, ed., *Hiroku Dai Tōa Senshi, Biruma-*

Marei Hen [History of the Secret Greater East Asia War, Burma-Malaya volume], Tokyo, 1954, pp. 132-4.
23 *Bōeichō, Biruma Kōryaku Sakusen*, p. 565.
24 Ibid., p. 572.
25 Ibid., p. 566.
26 Interview with General Katakura, 13 July 1966, Tokyo.
27 *Bōeichō, Biruma Kōryaku Sakusen*, pp. 566-70.
28 Ibid., pp. 573-4.
29 Interview with General Ayabe, former vice-chief of staff, Southern Army, 23 July 1966, Tokyo.
30 Hattori Takushirō, *Dai Tōa Sensō Zenshi*, vol. II, pp. 323-4.
31 Ibid., vol. III, p. 198.
32 On 3 April 1943.
33 Japanese monograph no. 134, pp. 25ff., File no. 601/13164/H, Burma Operations Record, Historical Section, Defence Ministry, Government of India.
34 Itō Masanori, *Teikoku Rikugun no Saigō, Shitō Hen* [The End of the Imperial Japanese Army, Death Struggle], vol. IV, Tokyo, 1964, p. 108.
35 Japanese monograph no. 134, pp. 28-29, File no. 601/13164/H, Burma Operations Record.
36 Hattori Takushirō, *Dai Tōa Sensō Zenshi*, vol. III, p. 200.
37 Itō Masanori, *Teikoku Rikugun no Saigō, Shitō Hen*, vol. IV, p. 104.
38 Ibid., p. 104.
39 Interview with General Katakura, 13 July 1966, Tokyo.
40 Japanese monograph no. 134, pp. 30-33, File no. 601/13164/H, Burma Operations Record, Historical Section, Defence Ministry, Government of India. Interview with General Katakura, 13 July 1966, Tokyo.
41 *Gaimushō, Subasu Chandora Bosu to Nihon*, p. 172.
42 Japanese monograph no. 134, pp. 47-49, File no. 601/13164/H, Burma Operations Record, Historical Section, Defence Ministry, Government of India.
43 Ibid., p. 49.
44 General Kawabe Diary, 7 January and 10 January; *Bōeichō Senshishitsu*. Fujiwara, *F Kikan*, p. 358.
45 General Kawabe Diary, 10 January.
46 *Gaimushō, Subasu Chandora Bosu to Nihon*, p. 126. General Katakura's estimate was that 10,000 INA troops saw action in the Imphal fighting; Motiram, *Two Historic Trials*, p. 125; Colonel Fuwa, former Operations Staff Officer, Burma Area Army, confirmed this figure in an interview, 18 July 1967, in Tokyo.
47 Interview with General Katakura, 13 July 1966, Tokyo.
48 Hattori Takushirō, *Dai Tōa Sensō Zenshi*, vol. III, p. 201.
49 Japanese monograph no. 134, p. 37, File no. 601/13164/H, Burma Operations Record, Historical Section, Defence Ministry, Government of India.
50 Interivew with General Ayabe, 23 July 1966, Tokyo.
51 Itō Masanori, *Teikoku Rikugun no Saigō*, vol. II, p. 101.
52 Hattori, *Dai Tōa Sensō Zenshi*, vol. III, p. 209. Itō Masanori, *Teikoku Rikugun no Saigō*, vol. IV, pp. 112-3. Hayashi Saburō and Alvin D. Coox, *Kōgun, the Japanese Army in the Pacific War*, Quantico, Virginia, 1959, p. 95.

CHAPTER TEN

1 Hattori, *Dai Tōa Sensō Zenshi*, vol. III, p. 210. Japanese monograph no. 134, Historical Section, Defence Ministry, Government of India. A.J. Barker, *The March on Delhi*, p. 92.
2 This was a classical *hiyodorigoe* stratagem. The *hiyodorigoe* manoeuvre takes its name from a battlefield near Kobe where an historic battle was fought in 1184

during the Gempei Wars between the Taira and Minamoto clans. The Taira armies, defending the reputedly impregnable fortress of Ichinotani, were overcome by a surprise attack launched by Minamoto Yoshitsune, converging on the Ichinotani plain from ridges both east and west of the plain.

3. Shah Nawaz Khan, *My Memories of I.N.A. and its Netaji*, pp. 111-3.
4. Ibid., pp. 111-3.
5. Ibid., pp. 121-3.
6. Ibid., p. 126. Fujiwara, *F Kikan*, p. 239.
7. Fujiwara, *F Kikan*, p. 353.
8. Ibid., pp. 353-4.
9. Shah Nawaz Khan, *My Memories of I.N.A.*, p. 125, Colonel P.K. Sahgal disagreed with Shah Nawaz's diagnosis of Japanese motives, emphasizing the severe strain on the Japanese supply situation and stating that he, unlike Shah Nawaz, had received excellent cooperation: interview, Kanpur, India, 21-22 December 1966.
10. Fujiwara, *F Kikan*, p. 361.
11. Shah Nawaz Khan, *My Memories of I.N.A.*, pp. 129-39.
12. Interview with Lieutenant-Colonel Ozeki at Kawashima cho, Hashima gun, Gifu prefecture, 15 July 1967.
13. Shah Nawaz Khan, *My Memories of I.N.A.*, pp. 138-46, 161, 223-4.
14. Fujiwara, *F Kikan*, pp. 359-60.
15. Ibid., p. 360.
16. Sivaram, *The Road to Delhi*, p. 142.
17. Unpublished summary of General Kawabe Diary, *Bōeichō Senshishitsu*, covering 1944 and part of 1943: 18 March, 6-7 April 1944.
18. Ibid., 10 May 1944.
19. Ibid., 22 June 1944.
20. Shah Nawaz Khan, *My Memories of I.N.A.*, pp. 162-5.
21. *Gaimushō, Subasu Chandora Bosu to Nihon*, p. 201.
22. Takagi Shirō, *Kōmei* [Insubordination], Tokyo, 1966, p. 27.
23. Kojima Noboru, *Taiheiyō Sensō* [Pacific War], 2 vols., Tokyo, 1967, vol. II, pp. 139-40.
24. Fujiwara, *F Kikan*, pp. 357-8. Hattori, *Dai Tōa Sensō Zenshi*, vol. III, p. 222.
25. Kojima, *Taiheiyō Sensō*, vol. II, p. 147.
26. Ibid., vol. II, p. 147.
27. Ibid., vol. II, p. 147.
28. Takagi, *Kōmei*, pp. 261-4.
29. Hattori, *Dai Tōa Sensō Zenshi*, vol. III, p. 224.
30. Takagi, *Kōmei*, p. 242.
31. Ibid., p. 246.
32. Takagi, *Kōmei*, pp. 246-7, quotes from Satō's memoirs.
33. *Gaimushō, Subasu Chandora Bosu to Nihon*, p. 192. Kojima, *Taiheiyō Sensō*, vol. II, p. 167, quotes from Ushiro Masaru, *Biruma Sensenki* [Burma Battle Record], Tokyo. 1953.
34. Ushiro Masaru, *Biruma Sensenki* [Burma Battle Record], p. 34. Interview with Ushiro Masaru, 29 July 1967, Tokyo.
35. Interviews with: Major Ushiro, 29 July 1967, General Inada, 12 July 1966, and General Sugita, 6 August 1966, all in Tokyo.
36. Ushiro, *Biruma Sensenki*, p. 36. Kojima, *Taiheiyō Sensō*, vol. II, p. 157. Interview with General Sugita, former chief of staff, Ground Self Defence Forces, 6 August 1966.
37. Interview with General Sugita, 9 August 1966, Tokyo. Takagi, *Kōmei*, p. 171.
38. Unpublished summary of General Kawabe Diary, 7 June 1944.
39. Kojima, *Taiheiyō Sensō*, vol. II, p. 167.
40. Hattori, *Dai Tōa Sensō Zenshi*, vol. III, p. 224.
41. Ushiro, *Biruma Sensenki*, pp. 43-44.

42 Fujiwara written and oral statement, 27 July 1967.
43 The following account of the same event was related by Lieutenant Nakai Goshirō and is the basis for the Takagi version: "Fujiwara was at 15th Array Headquarters when Operation U collapsed. He sat at his desk in staff headquarters, drafting an operation order. Apart from Mutaguchi, four other staff officers were in the room. Fujiwara was suddenly aware that someone was standing before his desk. It was General Mutaguchi's voice: 'So many subordinates have been killed and so much equipment lost. Now, as commanding general, I must commit suicide. I am responsible to the Emperor and to the souls of the dead men. What do you think of my position, Fujiwara?' Fujiwara was aware that the other staff officers had stopped work and were listening. He still did not look up or stop writing. There was no perceptible change in his expression as he replied loudly: 'It has always been since ancient times that those who say they want to die don't die. Now you, a general, are asking me whether or not you should commit suicide. I must ask you not to commit suicide. I can do nothing else. If you feel responsible yourself, please commit suicide in silence. No one will interrupt you. And please go on to paradise. The failure of this operation is worthy of more than your suicide.' Mutaguchi replied only, 'I see. I understand.'" Nakai Goshirō, *"Junketsu no Otakebi"* [War Cry of Thoroughbreds], in Rokunanakai, pub., *Hōhei Rokujūnana Rentai Bunshū* [Collected Record of the Sixty-seventh Artillery Regiment], Tokyo, 1962, p. 88. Takagi, *Kōmei*, p. 284. Fujiwara asserts this account is apocryphal. "I am a soldier. I would never say such a thing to my commander. And I am not such an unmilitary man as to neglect to stand up and salute or answer squarely if my commander should come to my room. Furthermore, the general was not a person to come to a room where his own subordinate was working to consult about his suicide." Fujiwara interview and statement, 27 July 1967, Tokyo.
44 Hattori, *Dai Tōa Sensō Zenshi*, vol. III, p. 226. Fujiwara, *F Kikan*, p. 364. Kojima, *Taiheiyō Sensō*, vol. II, p. 169.
45 Nakai, *"Junketsu no Otakebi"*, p. 63. Takagi, *Kōmei*, pp. 248-9. Maruyama Shizuo states that he heard several similar accounts of this speech at the time from Mutaguchi's staff officers: interview, 2 August 1967, Tokyo.
46 Maruyama Shizuo, a war correspondent in Burma, poignantly describes the retreat in *"Imparu shi no Haisō"* [Imphal Death Flight], in *Chūō Kōron*, August 1964, pp. 225-31. Hattori, *Dai Tōa Sensō Zenshi*, vol. III, p. 227. A.J. Barker in *The March on Delhi*, p. 226, puts the casualties this way: "... of the 6,000 INA members who had set out for Imphal only 2,600 returned. Of these, 2,000 had to go straight into the hospital. During their campaign approximately 1,500 had died of disease and starvation, 400 were killed in action, 800 surrendered and 715 others deserted and could not be accounted for."
47 Fujiwara, *F Kikan*, p. 364. Unpublished summary of General Kawabe Diary, 22 June 1944, p. 108 and 12 July, p. 118.
48 Major-General Nagai Yatsuji, former chief of the 8th Section, IGHQ, asserts, that Bose in November 1944 in Tokyo complained that the INA units received the order to retreat several days after Japanese forces did: interview, 10 August 1967 Tokyo.
49 Fujiwara, *F Kikan*, pp. 364-6.
50 *Azad Hind*, Singapore, no. 11/12, 6 November 1944.
51 S.A. Ayer, Propaganda and Information Minister of the FIPG, when questioned about Bose's September 1943 statement that he would be on Indian soil before the end of the year, replied: "I found it difficult to fathom his mind on this point. He was a tremendous optimist. He may have done if for morale-building purposes. He may have believed with a lot of luck it would happen. He always talked in terms of symbolic achievements. But he was not under any illusion": interview, 2 May 1966, Bombay. Lieutenant-General Arisue, wartime chief of the Second Bureau, IGHQ, reported that Bose in a secret conversation with him even before the start of

the Imphal campaign had expressed a desire to go to the Soviet Union: interview 19 July 1966, Tokyo. There was also the evidence of Bose's attempt to contact the Soviet Ambassador in Tokyo. This suggests that Bose had already contemplated where to turn to in the event of a Japanese defeat.
52 Shah Nawaz Khan, *My Memories of I.N.A.*, p. 243. Interview with former Ambassador Hachiya, July 1965, Tokyo. Interview with Lieutenant-General Isoda, 11 July 1966, Tokyo.
53 Shah Nawaz Khan, *My Memories of I.N.A.*, p. 173.
54 Fujiwara in Hayashida, unpublished biography of Bose, pp. 229-31. Now published as *Higeki no Eiyū* [Hero of Tragedy], Tokyo, 1968.
55 This evaluation is reflected in *Subasu Chandora Bosu (Gaimushō)*, to which General Kawabe contributed significantly. See p. 198.
56 Interview, 12 July 1966, Tokyo.
57 This is suggested by Colonel Hattori, wartime chief, 2nd Section, First Bureau, IGHQ: Hattori, *Dai Tōa Sensō Zenshi*, vol. III, p. 231.

CHAPTER ELEVEN

1 *Isoda Saburō Chūjō Kaisōroku* [Recollections of Lieutenant-General Isoda Saburō], pp. 36-38.
2 Chatterji, *India's Struggle for Freedom*, p. 272.
3 *Gaimushō, Subasu Chandora Bosu to Nihon*, pp. 221-2; *Isoda Saburō Chūjō Kaisōroku*, pp. 38-41.
4 *Gaimushō, Subasu Chandora Bosu to Nihon*, pp. 227-8.
5 Suresh Chandra Bose, *Dissentient Report*, Calcutta, 1961, pp. 65-66.
6 Ibid., p. 67. The official report of the Enquiry Committee, however, cites, evidence by General Isoda that the plane was bound direct for Tokyo, where the Japanese Government was to arrange the details of Bose's transport to Soviet Russia via Manchuria. But since the Soviet Union was already at war with Japan, it seems more likely that Bose was hoping to go direct from Taihoku to Dairen and then on to Russia. Other officers gave Dairen as the regular stop-off en route from Taihoku to Tokyo. General Shidei, whom Bose met by accident at Saigon airport, was at any rate en route to Dairen as chief of staff of the Kwantung Army: Government of India, Ministry of Information and Broadcasting, Publications Division, *Sadachar Movement for Purity in National Life*, 1956, pp. 7-10.
7 Suresh Chandra Bose, *Dissentient Report*, p. 103.
8 Calcutta, 1961.
9 Suresh Chandra Bose, *Dissentient Report*, p. 6.
10 Ministry of Information and Broadcasting, *Sadachar*, p. 31.

CHAPTER TWELVE

1 Hugh Toye, *Subash Chandra Bose*, p. 186.
2 Ibid., p. 187.
3 Nirad Chaudhuri, "Subhas Chandra Bose—His Legacy and Legend", *Pacific Affairs*, vol. 26, 1953, p. 350.
4 Report of Field-Marshal Sir Claude Auchinleck, Commander-in-Chief in India, covering the period 1 January to 31 December 1945: Historical Section, Defence Ministry, Government of India, New Delhi, p. 20.
5 Ibid., p. 20.
6 Ibid., pp. 20-21.
7 Chaudhuri, "Subhas Chandra Bose", p. 350.

8 Foreword by Jawaharlal Nehru in Motiram, *Two Historic Trials in Red Fort*, p. iii.
9 Toye, *Subash Chandra Bose*, pp. x-xi.
10 Gaube, *Famous and Historic Trials*, pp. 271-2.
11 Ibid., p. 272.
12 Ibid., p. 306; K.N. Katju in Shri Ram Sharma, ed., *Netaji, His Life and Work*, Agra, 1948, p. 216.
13 Motiram, *Two Historic Trials in Red Fort*, pp. 111-2, 119.
14 Gaube, *Famous and Historic Trials*, pp. 315-6.
15 Motiram, *Two Historic Trials in Red Fort*, p. 271.
16 Ibid., p. 141.
17 Gaube, *Famous and Historic Trials*, p. 331.
18 Testimony in Motiram, *Two Historic Trials in Red Fort*, p. 128.
19 Ibid., pp. 129-30.
20 Shah Nawaz Preliminary Statement to Counsel, pp. 14-19, INA Committee File, INA Enquiry and Relief Committee, Delhi.
21 Kusum Nair, *The Story of I.N.A.*, Bombay, 1946, p. 16.
22 Jay Parvesh Chander, *Meet the Heroes*, Lahore, s.d., pp. 78-79.
23 P.K. Sahgal Preliminary Statement to Counsel, INA Committee File, p. 40, INA Enquiry and Relief Committee, Delhi.
24 Dhillon Preliminary Statement to Counsel, pp. 6-16, INA Committee File, INA Enquiry and Relief Committee, Delhi.
25 *Gaimushō, Subasu Chandora Bosu to Nihon*, pp. 226-7.
26 Motiram, *Two Historic Trials in Red Fort*, p. 122.
27 Ibid., p. 123.
28 Ibid., pp. 124-6.
29 Ibid., pp. 120-6.
30 Fujiwara, *F Kikan*, pp. 368-9.
31 Ibid., p. 369.
32 Ibid., pp. 370-1.
33 Ibid., pp. 374-5.
34 Ibid., p. 375.
35 Ibid., p. 376.
36 Ibid., pp. 377-80.
37 Ibid., pp. 381-2.
38 Ibid., p. 384.
39 Ibid., p. 384.
40 Interview with Mrs Kusum Nair, 25 January 1966, New Delhi.
41 For a discussion of this issue, see K.K. Ghosh, *The Indian National Army*.
42 Chaudhuri, "Subhas Chandra Bose", p. 352.

CHAPTER THIRTEEN

1 Edward Shils, "The Military in the Political Development of the New States", in John Johnson, *The Role of the Military in the Underdeveloped Countries*, Princeton University Press, 1962, pp. 39-40; Humphrey Evans, *Thimayya of India: a Soldier's Life*, pp. 283-4.
2 See discussion on transference of military skills to civilian administration in new nations in Morris Janowitz, *The Military in the Political Development, of New Nations*, The University of Chicago Press, 1964, pp. 41-44.
3 Josef Silverstein, "The Importance of the Japanese Occupation of Southeast Asia to the Political Scientist", Josef Silverstein, ed., *Southeast Asia in World War II: Four Essays*, Yale Southeast Asia Studies Monograph Series, no. 7, 1966, p. 8.

Bibliographical Note

RESEARCH for this volume was conducted in both Japan and India. In both countries unpublished official documents, published primary and secondary sources, wartime newspapers, private collections and general collections in university libraries were consulted and used. In addition interviews were conducted with individuals, both civilian and military, who were involved in the wartime Japanese-INA cooperation. Some of the individuals who played signal roles had already passed away. Access to some materials on occasion proved capricious.

In Japan the War History Library of the Defence Agency was of major significance in the availability of unpublished official documents such as IGHQ-Government Liaison Conference policy pronouncements, excerpts from diaries of individuals such as Generals Kawabe Masakazu and Inada Seijun; other classified documents were similarly useful. Some wartime memoirs of generals are available in government report form, for example those of Generals Fujiwara Iwaichi and Isoda Saburō. In the case of another general, Katakura Tadasu, excerpts of his wartime diary were read to the author. In the Foreign Ministry archives a file concerning the "Greater East Asia War: the India Problem" proved helpful. This file also includes secret correspondence between the Japanese consul-general in India and the Japanese foreign minister. Of special importance was a Foreign Ministry publication compiled by a group of generals and entitled *Subhas Chandora Bosu to Nihon* (Subhas Chandra Bose and Japan). Also invaluable were such semi-official accounts as Hattori Takushirō's *Taiheiyō Sensō Zenshi* (Complete History of the Pacific War, Hara Shobo 1965) and the two-volume *Sugiyama Memo* by Chief of General Staff Sugiyama (Hara Shobo 1967). Materials in the Diet Library were also consulted. Interviews with some thirty wartime generals and colonels were illuminating. The official history of the Pacific War currently being compiled by the War History Library of the Defence Agency is expected to include one hundred volumes when completed; the volumes on Burma and Malaya were consulted. In addition, some of the plethora of volumes on battles and aspects of the war by officers who participated and by journalists were read.

In India official military reports in the Defence Ministry Historical Section were consulted, including: the Report of General Terauchi, commander of the Southern Army, on Japanese Operations in Burma (in English); General Wavell's Despatch on Operations in the India Command; Admiral Mountbatten's Despatch from the India Command and his Report of the Combined Chiefs of Staff of the Southeast Asia Theatre; General Auchinleck's Report as Commander-in-Chief in India; Lieutenant-General Slim's Report on the Campaign of the Fourteenth Army; the Report of the Siege of Imphal, Air Aspects, by the Air Command in Southeast Asia; a Short History of the 18th Division (Japanese); the Payagi Interrogation Report; Translations of Japanese Documents including Army Orders and Directives of Japanese Operations in Burma, 15th Army Operations in the Imphal Area and the Burma Operations Record. The Indian Independence League Documents in the National Archives proved valuable.

The *Netaji* Research Bureau collection in Calcutta included useful volumes and papers. The INA Enquiry and Relief Committee in Delhi preserves the INA History Committee File with statements by several INA officers, for example statements to counsel by INA officers Dhillon and P.K. Sahgal. This office also has evidences of the witnesses for the defence and prosecution of the first INA court martial and proceedings, exhibits and evidences of the same court martial in 1945-46. In addition the author had access to an unpublished manuscript by General Mohan Singh, first commander of the INA, and a statement by Mohan Singh allegedly smuggled from prison by Ram Singh Rawal. Correspondence with N.S. Gill also proved valuable. Secondary materials in the library of the Indian School of International Affairs were consulted. Interviews were conducted with some twenty individuals, civilian and military, including two of the officers tried in the Red Fort court martial.

Wartime newspapers in Japan, India, Bangkok and Singapore were used. In Bangkok the author interviewed six Indians who were active in the independence movement.

Bibliography

Official Documents in India

MILITARY REPORTS IN DEFENCE MINISTRY, HISTORICAL SECTION
Report of General Terauchi on Japanese Operations in Burma
General Wavell's Despatch on Operations in the India Command
Admiral Mountbatten's Despatch from the India Command
General Auchinleck's Report as Commander-in-Chief in India
Lieutenant-General Slim's Report on the Campaign of the Fourteenth Army as GOC
Vice-Admiral Mountbatten's Report of the Combined Chiefs of Staff by Allied Commander in Southeast Asia
Report on the Siege of Imphal, Air Aspects, by Air Command, Southeast Asia
A Short History of the 18th Division (Japanese), Twelfth Army, Weekly Intelligence Summary no. 9
Payagi Interrogation Report no. 3

TRANSLATIONS OF JAPANESE DOCUMENTS
Army orders and directives:
Japanese Operations in Burma
15th Army Operations in the Imphal Area
Burma Operations Record

OTHER UNPUBLISHED DOCUMENTS

Indian Independence League Documents in the National Archives
Unpublished Manuscript of General Mohan Singh
Mohan Singh Statement allegedly smuggled from prison by Ram Singh Rawal
Correspondence with Colonel N.S. Gill

INA ENQUIRY AND RELIEF COMMITTEE, DELHI
Mohan Singh Statement to INA History Committee
Major M.L. Bhagata Statement to INA History Committee
Statements to Counsel of Dhillon and P.K. Sahgal
N.S. Gill Statement to INA History Committee
Testimony by Lieutenant-General Katakura Tadasu, Sawada Renzō and Matsumoto Shun'ichi in Proceedings and Testimony of the Court Martial

Official Documents in Japan

WAR HISTORY LIBRARY, DEFENCE AGENCY

Daihon'ei Seifu Renraku Kaigi Gijiroku [Records of Proceedings of IGHQ-Government Liaison Conferences], 1941-45.
Daihon'ei Kimitsu Sensō Nisshi [IGHQ Secret Diary], October 1941-December 1943.
Inada Seijun, *Inada Nikki* [Inada Diary], 4 vols. and *Shōnan Nikki* [Singapore Diary], summary in 3 vols.
Kawabe Masakazu, *Biruma Nikki Shōroku* [Summary of the Burma Diary], 1943 and 1944.

FOREIGN MINISTRY

Gaimushō Kiroku [Foreign Ministry Records], *Dai Tōa Sensō Kankei Ikken: Indō Mondai* [Matters Relating to the Greater East Asia War: the India Problem].

Interviews

IN BANGKOK

Ramlal Sachdev
C.R. Narula
S.T. Mahtani

Dr N.T. Joseph
Walter L. Meyer
Pandit Raghunath Sharma

IN INDIA

Dr Girija Mookerjee
General Mohan Singh
Colonel P.K. Sahgal
Major Shah Nawaz Khan
N. Raghavan
S.A. Ayer

Ram Singh Rawal
P.N. Oak
Dr Raju
Devnath Das
S.S. Yadava
R.M. Arshad

IN JAPAN

Lieutenant-General Fujiwara Iwaichi
Lieutenant-General Isoda Saburō
Lieutenant-General Arisue Seizō
Lieutenant-General Katakura Tadasu
Major-General Iwakuro Hideo
Lieutenant-General Satō Kenryō
General Sugita Ichiji
Lieutenant-General Ayabe Kitsuju
Lieutenant-General Inada Seijun
Lieutenant-General Ōshima Hiroshi
Colonel Nishiura Susumu
Lieutenant-Colonel Ozeki Masaji
Major Horie Yoshitaka

Lieutenant Itō Keisuke
Ishikawa Yoshiaki
Colonel Fuwa Masao
Colonel Kaneko Seigō
Lieutenant-Colonel Kanadomi Yoshiji
Major Ushiro Masaru
Maruyama Shizuo
Lieutenant Kunizuka Kazunori
Major Kaetsu, alias Maeda Hiroshi
Major-General Nagai Yatsuji

Published Works in English

Aiyer, K.A. Neelakandha, *Indian Problems in Malaya, a Brief Survey in Relation to Emigration,* Kuala Lumpur, 1938.
Arun, ed., *Testament of Subhas Bose,* Delhi, 1946.
Ayer, S.A., *Unto Him a Witness, The Story of Netaji Subhas Chandra Bose in East Asia,* Bombay, 1951.
Aziz, M.A., *Japan's Colonialism and Indonesia,* The Hague, 1955.
Barker, A.J., *The March on Delhi,* London, 1963.
Benda, Harry, *The Crescent and the Chrysanthemum,* The Hague, 1958.
Bhagat, K.P., *A Decade of Indo-British Relations, 1937-47,* Bombay, 1959.
Bose, Subhas Chandra, *Crossroads, being the works of Subhas Chandra Bose,* Netaji Research Bureau, Calcutta, 1962.
Bose, Subhas Chandra, *Important Speeches and Writings,* ed. J.S. Bright, Lahore, 1946.
Bose, Subhas Chandra, *Impressions in Life,* Lahore, 1947.
Bose, Subhas Chandra, *The Indian Struggle, 1920-1934,* Lahore, 1935.
Bose, Subhas Chandra, *Netaji's Life and Writings,* Calcutta, 1948.
Bose, Subhas Chandra, *Blood Bath,* Lahore, 1947.
Bose, Subhas Chandra, *Through Congress Eyes,* Allahabad, 1938.
Bose, Subhas Chandra, *On to Delhi,* Bombay, 1946.
Bose, Subhas Chandra, *An Indian Pilgrim, an Unfinished Autobiography and Collected Letters, 1897-1921,* Asia Publishing House, 1965.
Bose, Subhas Chandra, *India Calling,* ed. R.I. Paul, Lahore, s.d.
Bose, Subhas Chandra, *The Mission of Life,* Calcutta, 1953.
Bose, Suresh Chandra, *Dissentient Report,* Calcutta, 1961.
Brown, Delmer, *Nationalism in Japan, an Introductory Historical Analysis,* Berkeley, 1955.
Chand, Uttam, *When Bose was Ziauddin,* Delhi, 1946.
Chander, Jay Parvesh, *Meet the Heroes,* Lahore, s.d.
Chatterji, Major-General A.C., *India's Struggle for Freedom,* Calcutta, 1947.
Chaudhuri, Nirad, "Subhas Chandra Bose—His Legacy and Legend", *Pacific Affairs,* vol. 26, 1953.
Churchill, Winston S., *The Hinge of Fate,* Boston, 1950.
Cohen, Stephen P., "Subhas Chandra Bose and the Indian National Army", *Pacific Affairs,* vol. 35, 1963-64.
Coox, Alvin and Hayashi Saburō, *Kōgun: the Japanese Army in the Pacific War,* Quantico, Virginia, 1959.
Das Gupta, Hemendranath, *Subhas Chandra,* Calcutta, 1946.
Desai, Bhulabhai J., *I.N.A. Defence,* Bombay, 1945.
Durrani, Mahmood Khan, *The Sixth Column,* London, 1955.
Elenjimittam, Anthony, *The Hero of Hindustan,* Calcutta, 1947.
Elsbree, Willard H., *Japan's Role in Southeast Asian Nationalist Movements, 1940-1945,* Cambridge, 1953.
Evans, Humphrey, *Thimayya of India: A Soldier's Life,* N.Y., 1960.
Ganpuley, N.G., *Netaji in Germany, a Little-known Chapter,* Bombay, 1959.
Gaube, K.L., *Famous and Historic Trials,* Lahore, 1946.
Ghosh, Jitendra Nath, *Netaji Subhas Chandra, Political Philosophy of Netaji, History of Azad Hind Government, I.N.A. and International Law,* Calcutta, 1946.
Ghosh, K.C., *The Roll of Honour, Anecdotes of Indian Martyrs,* Calcutta, 1965.
Ghosh, K.K., *The Indian National Army, Second Front of the Indian Independence Movement,* Meerut, 1969.
Ghosh, K.K., *A Study of the Indian National Army,* Ph.D. thesis, Indian School of International Studies, New Delhi, 1965.
Giani, Kesar Singh, *Indian Independence Movement in East Asia, The Most Authentic Account of the I.N.A. and the Azad Hind Government,* Lahore, 1947.
Gibson, Hugh, ed., *The Ciano Diaries, 1939-1943,* New York, 1946.
Goette, John, *Japan Fights for Asia,* London, s.d.

Government of India, Ministry of Information and Broadcasting, Publications Division, *Sadachar, Movement for Purity in National Life*, New Delhi, 1956.
Government of India, Ministry of Information and Broadcasting, Publications Division, *Selected Speeches of Subhas Chandra Bose*, Delhi, 1962.
Government of India, *Netaji Enquiry Committee Report*, Delhi, 1956.
Hardas, Shr. Balshastri, *Armed Struggle for Freedom, Ninety Years War of Indian Independence, 1857 to Subhash*, Poona, 1958.
Hirszowicz, Lukasz, *The Third Reich and the Arab East*, London, 1966.
Ike Nobutaka, *Japan's Decision for War, Records of the 1941 Policy Conferences*, Stanford, 1967.
James, David, *The Rise and Fall of the Japanese Empire*, London, 1951.
Janowitz, Morris, *The Military in the Political Development of New Nations*, Chicago, 1964.
Japan Biographical Encyclopedia and Who's Who, 3rd ed., Tokyo, 1964-65.
Jhaveri, Vithalbhai K., ed., *Jai-Hind, the Diary of a Rebel Daughter of India with the Rani of Jhansi Regiment*, Bombay, 1945.
Johnson, John, *The Role of the Military in the Underdeveloped Countries*, Princeton, 1962.
Jones, F.C., *Japan's New Order in East Asia*, New York, 1954.
A Journalist, *Netaji*, Lahore, 1946.
Kahin, George McT., ed., *Governments and Politics in Southeast Asia*, Ithaca, 1959.
Kahin, George McT., *Nationalism and Revolution in Indonesia*, Ithaca, 1966.
Khan, Shah Nawaz, *My Memories of I.N.A. and Its Netaji*, Delhi, 1946.
Khan, Shah Nawaz, *The I.N.A. Heroes, Autobiographies of Col. Prem K. Sahgal, Col. Gurbax Singh Dhillon, Maj. Gen. Shahnawaz*, Lahore, 1947.
King, John Kerry, *Southeast Asia in Perspective*, New York, 1956.
Kirby, Major-General S. Woodburn, *The War Against Japan*, vol. IV, *The Re-conquest of Burma*, Sir J. Butler, ed., History of the Second World War, United Kingdom Military Series, London, 1965.
Kirby, Major-General S. Woodburn, *The War Against Japan*, vol. III, *The Decisive Battles*, Sir J. Butler, ed., History of the Second World War, United Kingdom Military Series, London, 1961.
Kripalani, Krishna, *Rabindranath Tagore, a Biography*, London, 1962.
Lahiri, Amar, *Said Subhas Bose*, Calcutta, 1947.
Lal, Chaman, ed., *India and Japan, Friends of Fourteen Centuries*, Punjab, 1959.
Lochner, Louis P., ed., *The Goebbels Diaries*, London, 1948.
Lu, David, *From the Marco Polo Bridge to Pearl Harbor, Japan's Entry into World War II*, Washington, 1961.
Majumdar, R.C., *History of the Freedom Movement in India*, vol. 3, Calcutta, 1962-63.
Menon, Narayana, *On to Delhi, or Speeches and Writings of Subhas Chandra Bose*, Bangkok, 1944, vol. 1.
Meskill, Johanna M. Menzel, *Hitler and Japan: the Hollow Alliance*, New York, 1966.
Mookerjee, Girija, *This Europe*, Calcutta, 1950.
Morris, Ivan, *Nationalism and the Right Wing in Japan, A Study of Postwar Trends*, London, 1960.
Motiram, *Two Historic Trials in Red Fort, An Authentic Account of the Trial by a General Court Martial of Captain Shah Nawaz Khan, Captain P.K. Sahgal, Lieutenant G.S. Dhillon and the Trial by a European Military Commission of Emperor Bahadur Shah*, New Delhi, 1946.
Muggeridge, Malcolm, ed., *Ciano's Diary*, London, 1947.
Mulkar, Lieutenant M.G., *I.N.A. Soldier's Diary*, Calcutta, s.d.
Nadkarni, Mohan, "Japan's Pose as Asia's Saviour", *Modern Review*, vol. LXXI, 1942.
Nair, Kusum, *The Story of I.N.A.*, Bombay, 1946.
Nakamura Keiji, "The Study of Modern Indian Politics in Japan", pp. 29-43 in The Society for Asian Political and Economic Studies, ed., *Asian Studies in Japan*, Tokyo, 1964.

Nehru, Jawaharlal, *A Bunch of Old Letters*, Bombay, 1960.
Noguchi Yone, *Japan and America*, Tokyo, 1921.
Nu, Thakin, *Burma under the Japanese, Pictures and Portraits*, London, 1954.
ŌgataTaketora, "Mitsuru Tōyama", *Contemporary Japan*, vol. 9, no. 7, 1940.
Ohsawa J.G., *Two Great Indians in Japan — Shri Rash Behari Bose and Netaji Subhas Chandra Bose*, Calcutta, 1954.
Okakura Kakuzō, *The Book of Tea*, New York, 1902.
Okakura Kakuzō, *The Ideals of the East with Special Reference to the Art of Japan*, London, 1920.
Ōkuma Memorial Social Sciences Research Institute, Tokyo, *Japanese Military Administration in Indonesia*, US Dept. of Commerce, Office of Technical Services, 1963.
Palta, K.R., *My Adventures with the I.N.A.*, Lahore, 1946.
Park, Richard L. and Irene Tinker, eds., *Leadership and Political Institutions in India*, Princeton, 1959.
Percival, Lieutenant-General A.E., *The War in Malaya*, London, 1949.
Prasad, Rajendra, *India Divided*, Bombay, 1947.
Pratap, Raja Mahendra, *My Life Story of Fifty-five Years*, Dehra Dun, 1947.
Pratap, Raja Mahendra, *Reflections of an Exile*, Lahore, 1946.
Raghavan, Nedyam, *India and Malaya*, Bombay, 1954.
Rath, Radhanath, ed., *Rash Behari Basu, His Struggle for India's Independence*, Calcutta, 1963.
Rawal, R.S., *The I.N.A. Saga*, Allahabad, 1946.
Roy, Provash Chandra, *Subhas Chandra*, Rajshahi, 1949.
Roy, Dilip Kumar, *Subhash I knew: An Account of Subhash Bose*, Bombay, 1946.
Saggi, P.D., ed., *A Nation's Homage, Life and Work of Netaji Subhas Chandra Bose*, Bombay, s.d.
Sahgal, Lakshmi, "The Role of Women in the Azad Hind Movement", Netaji Oration: 1964, *Bulletin of the Netaji Research Bureau*, Calcutta, 1965.
Sen Gupta, Bejon Kumar, *India's Man of Destiny*, Calcutta, s.d.
Seth, Hira Lal, *Personality and Political Ideals of Subhas Chandra Bose: Is He Fascist?* Lahore, 1944.
Sharma, Shri Ram, ed., *Netaji, His Life and Work*, Agra, 1948.
Shils, Edward, "The Military in the Political Development of the New States", in John Johnson, ed., *The Role of the Military in the Underdeveloped Countries*, Princeton, 1962.
Silcock, T.H. and Ungku Abdul Aziz, "Nationalism in Malaya: The Impact of the Japanese Occupation", in *Asian Nationalism and the West, A Symposium Based on Documents and Reports of the Eleventh Conference*, ed. W.L. Holland, Institute of Pacific Relations, New York, 1953.
Silverstein, Josef, "The Importance of the Japanese Occupation of Southeast Asia to the Political Scientist", in *Southeast Asia in World War II: Four Essays*, ed. J. Silverstein, New Haven, 1966.
Singh, Durlab, ed., *Formation and Growth of the Indian National Army*, Lahore, 1946.
Singh, Durlab, *The Rebel President*, Lahore, 1946.
Singh, General Mohan, *Leaves from my Diary*, Lahore, 1946.
Singh, Mohan, "I.N.A. Arrears", *Rajya Sabha Debates*, vol. 46, part 1, 18 February 1964.
Singh Rajendra, Brigadier, *Far East in Ferment*, Delhi, 1961.
Sivaram, M., *The Road to Delhi*, Tokyo, 1967.
Slim, Field-Marshal Sir William, *Defeat into Victory*, London, 1956.
Sopan, *Netaji Subhash Chandra Bose, His Life and Work*, Bombay, 1946.
Storry, Richard, *The Double Patriots*, Boston, 1957.
Tagore, Rabindranath, *The Message of India to Japan*, Tokyo, 1916.
Tagore, Rabindranath, *Nationalism*, London, 1950.
Tagore, Rabindranath, *The Spirit of Japan*, Tokyo, 1916.
Thompson, Edward, *Rabindranath Tagore, Poet and Dramatist*, London, 1948.

Toye, Hugh, *Subash Chandra Bose, The Springing Tiger*, Jaico Publishing House, Bombay, 1959.
Tsuji Masanobu, *Singapore, the Japanese Version*, Sydney, 1960.
Tuker, Francis, *While Memory Serves*, London, 1950.
Ward, Robert S., *Asia for the Asiatics? The Techniques of Japanese Occupation*, Chicago, 1945.
Wofford, Clare and Harris, Jr, *India Afire*, New York, 1951.
Yoshihashi, Takehiko, *Conspiracy at Mukden, The Rise of the Japanese Military*, New Haven, 1963.

Newspapers

Azad Hind, Singapore, 1945.
Azad Hind, Zeitschrift für ein Freies Inden, Berlin, 1943-44.
Bangkok Chronicle, Bangkok, December 1942-January 1945.
Hindustan Times, New Delhi, 1943-45.
Nippon Times, Tokyo, 1941-45.
Syonan Times, Singapore, 1943-44.

Published Works In Japanese

Asahi Shimbunsha, *Taiheiyō Sensō e no Michi* [The Road to the Pacific War], 7 vols. and supplement, Tokyo, 1963.
Bōeichō Bōei Kenshūjo Senshishitsu [Defence Agency, Defence Training Institute, War History Library], *Biruma Kōryaku Sakusen* [Burma Offensive Operation], Tokyo, 1967.
Bōeichō Bōei Kenshūjo Senshishitsu, *Marei Shinkō Sakusen* [Malaya Operation], Tokyo, 1966.
Bose, Rash Behari, *Indō no Kakumei* [The Indian Revolution], Tokyo, 1932.
Fujio Masayuki, "*Biruma no Ryūko*" [Tiger of Burma], in *Hiroku Dai Tōa Senshi, Biruma-Marei Hen* [Secret History of the Greater East Asia War, Burma-Malaya Volume], ed. Ikeda Yū, Tokyo, 1954.
Fujiwara Iwaichi, *F Kikan* [F Agency], Tokyo, 1966.
Fujiwara Iwaichi, *F Kikanchō no Shuki* [Memorandum of the Chief of the F Agency], Tokyo, 1959.
Gaimushō, *Ajiya Kyoku* [Foreign Ministry, Asia Office], *Subasu Chandora Bosu to Nihon* [Subhas Chandra Bose and Japan], Tokyo, 1956.
Hattori Takushirō, *Dai Tōa Sensō Zenshi* [Complete History of the Greater East Asia War], Tokyo, 4 vols. 1953. (Also a 1965 ed. in 1 vol.)
Hayashida Tatsuo, *Higeki no Eiyū—Chandora Bosu no Shōgai* [Hero of Tragedy —the Life of Chandra Bose], Tokyo, 1968.
Isoda Saburō, *Isoda Saburō Chūjō Kaisōroku* [Recollections of Lieutenant-General Isoda Saburō], Tokyo, 1954.
Itō Masanori, *Teikoku Rikugun no Saigō* [The End of the Imperial Japanese Army], 4 vols., 1959-65.
Iwakuro Hideo, "*Iwakuro Kikan Shimatsuki*" [Record of the Management of the Iwakuro Agency], in *Shūkan Yomiuri*, "*Nihon no Himitsu Sen*" [Yomiuri Weekly, Japan's Secret War], 8 December 1956, Tokyo.
Izumiya Tatsurō, *Biruma Dokuritsu Hishi—Sono na wa Minami Bōryaku Kikan* [The Secret History of Burmese Independence—its Name: the Southern Stratagem Agency], Tokyo, 1967.

Kaneko Noboru, "*Pinantō Tokumuhan*" [The Penang Island Special Mission Group], in *Shūkan Yomiuri*, "*Nihon no Himitsu Sen*", [Japan's Secret War], 8 December 1956.
Kan'in Sumihito, *Watakushi no Jijoden* [My Autobiography], Tokyo, 1966.
Kojima Noboru, *Taiheiyō Sensō* [Pacific War], 2 vols., Tokyo, 1967.
Kunizuka Kazunori, *Indōyō ni Kakeru Niji* [Rainbow over the Indian Ocean], Tokyo, 1959.
Kuzuu, *Tōa Senkakushashi Den* [Biographies of Pioneers of East Asia], vol. 2, Tokyo, 1935.
Maruyama Shizuo, "*Arakan Kōsakusen*" [Arakan Manoeuvre], in *Hiroku Dai Tōa Senshi, Biruma Hen*, ed. Ikeda Yū, Tokyo, 1953.
Maruyama Shizuo, "*Biruma Sakusen no Zembō*" [Whole Picture of the Burma Campaign], in *Hiroku Dai Tōa Senshi, Biruma Hen*, ed. Ikeda Yū, Tokyo, 1953.
Maruyama Shizuo, "*Dai Tōa Kyōeiken no Kyōkun*" [Precepts of the Greater East Asia Co-Prosperity Sphere], in *Chūō Kōron*, April 1965, pp. 113-27.
Maruyama Shizuo, "*Haisō Senri*" [Twenty-five-hundred-mile Flight], in *Hiroku Dai Tōa Senshi*, ed. Ikeda Yū, Tokyo, 1953.
Maruyama Shizuo, "*Himitsu no Tatakai*" [Secret Struggle], in *Hiroku Dai Tōa Senshi*, ed. Ikeda Yū, Tokyo, 1953.
Maruyama Shizuo, "*Imparu Shi no Haisō*" [Imphal Death Flight], in *Chūō Kōron*, August 1964, pp. 225-31.
Maruyama Shizuo, *Nakano Gakkō Tokumu Kikan in no Shuki* [Memorandum of a Member of the Nakano School Special Agency], Tokyo, 1948.
Murata Heiji, *Imparu Sakusen—Retsu Heidan Kohima no Shitō* [The Imphal Operation—Death Struggle at Kohima of the *Retsu* group], Tokyo, 1967.
Nakai Goshirō, *Junketsu no Otakebi—Biruma Haisenshi* [War Cry of Thoroughbreds—History of the Lost Battle for Burma], Tokyo, 1962.
Ōkawa Shūmei, *Ajiya Kensetsusha* [Builders of Asia], Tokyo, 1941.
Ōkawa Shūmei, *Dai Tōa Shin Chitsujo Kensetsu* [Building the New Order in Greater East Asia], Tokyo, 1943.
Ōkawa Shūmei, *Nihon oyobi Nihonjin no Michi* [The Way of Japan and the Japanese], Tokyo, 1926.
Sambō Hombu [General Staff Headquarters], *Sugiyama Memo—Dai Hon'ei Seifu Renraku Kaigi Tō Hikki* [Sugiyama Memo—Records of the IGHQ-Government Liaison Conferences], 2 vols., Tokyo, 1967.
Satō Kenryō, *Dai Tōa Sensō, Kaisōroku* [Recollections of the Greater East Asia War], Tokyo, 1966.
Sōma Kurohika and Sōma Yasuo, *Ajiya no Mezame—Indo Shishi Bihari Bosu to Nihon* [The Awakening of Asia—the Indian Patriot Behari Bose], Tokyo, 1953.
Takagi Shirō, *Kōmei* [Insubordination], Tokyo, 1966.
Tanemura Suketaka, *Dai Hon'ei Kimitsu Nisshi* [Secret Diary of IGHQ], Tokyo, 1952.
Tsuji Masanobu, *Jūgo Taiichi—Biruma no Shitō* [Fifteen versus One—Death Struggle of Burma], Tokyo, 1950.
Ushiro Masaru, *Biruma Sensenki* [Burma Battle Record], Tokyo, 1953.
Yamamoto Bin, "*Kakumeiji Umi o Wataru—Chandora Bosu Berurin Dasshutsu Ki*" [A Revolutionary Crosses the Ocean—Record of Chandra Bose's Escape from Berlin], in *Shūkan Yomiuri, Nihon no Himitsu Sen*, December 1956, Tokyo.

Index

Afghanistan, 47-48, 108, 197
Africa, 109, 114, 159
Aguinaldo, 54
Ahmed, Aziz (Col.), 146
Akram, Mohammed (Capt.), 23, 42-44
Akyab (sector), 66, 86, 162, 170-1
Alagoppan, S.A. (Col.), 146
Ali, Asaf, 202
All-India Congress Committee, 106, 201
Allah Ditta (Capt.), 29, 36
Allied forces, 159, 163, 170, 172-3, 192, 201, 206, 213
Alor Star, 14-20, 23, 44; Japanese occupation of, 18-21
Amar Singh, 6, 12
Americans, *see* United States
Amritsar massacre, 104
Andaman Islands, 6, 66, 82, 89, 132-4, 145, 191, 203, 214-6
Annaburg Camp, 109
Anti-British: countries, 76; movement in India, 3, 5, 53, 64-65, 207, 210, 214, 217; movement in Southeast Asia, 67; Malay organizations, 7; sentiment in Burma, 29
Anglo-Japanese War, 3
Aoki, 130, 143
Arakan mountains, 153-4, 158, 171, 176
Arisue (Lt.-Gen.), 63, 112, 143, 169, 217
Army Intelligence School, *see* Rikugun Nakanō Gakkō
Asia, 2, 6, 22, 24, 27, 31, 34, 40, 48-51, 53-57, 59-60, 62, 67, 75-77, 91, 109, 111-3, 117-20, 122, 131-2, 141, 150, 157, 192, 212-4; Indians in, 7, 22, 40, 50, 119, 164; "New Asia" concept, 3, 6; "Asia for the Asiatics", 55, 60, 69, 132, 212

Asian(s): revolutionaries, 54, 58, 63, 117; liberation of, 37, 48, 54-56, 118, 208, 212; Pan-Asianism, 48, 54-55, 58, 63, 132
Asiatic Army, 48
Assam, 81, 154, 157, 159, 164, 171-2, 176-7, 182, 198; Assam-Burma border, 72
Auchinleck, Sir Claude (Gen.), 151, 202
Aung San, 28-29, 69, 147, 178
Aurobindo Ghosh, 103
Australia, 32, 64, 150
Axis (powers), 107-8, 112, 117, 119, 121, 128, 140, 150, 159
Ayabe (Lt.-Gen.), 171, 173
Ayer, K.A.N., 42
Ayer, S.A., 100, 121, 139, 180, 195, 204
Azad Brigade, 83
Azad Regiment, 179
Azad Hind (Free India), 128, 132, 135, 137, 203-4, 206, 214-5
Azad Hind (magazine), 109, 191
Azad Hind (Free India) Radio, 109, 180
Azad Hind Fauj (Free India Army), 119-20, 122
Azad Hind Sangh, 218

Ba Maw, Dr, 122
Bahadur Shah (Emperor), 122
Bangkok, 1, 2, 4, 6-8, 11-12, 14, 41, 43, 46, 50-51, 65, 68, 75-76, 78, 85, 95, 138, 147, 194-5, 200, 211
Bangkok Conference, 75-77, 79, 85, 88, 91, 100
Bangkok Resolution, 78-84, 88, 90-91, 93-95, 115
Bannerji, Surendra Nath, 103
Bengal, 60, 102-4, 106, 115, 122, 129,

246

140, 145, 147, 154, 170, 176, 211; Bay of, 133, 150-1, 173; partition of, 53
Bengali (language), 102-3
Bengali (population), 53, 73; students, 48
Berlin, 22, 41, 61, 66-67, 98, 100, 105, 108-15, 117, 121, 126, 157, 169, 176, 191, 211, 213-4
Bhagat, N.S. (Lt.-Col.), 122
Bharat Mandir, 46
Bhonsle, J.K. (Lt.-Col., Maj.-Gen.), 98, 122, 146, 195
Bidadari (Camp), 38
Bokhara, 108
Bombay, 53, 105, 202, 208-9
Book of Tea, 55
Borneo, 75
Bose, Janakinath, 102
Bose, Prabhavati, 102
Bose, Rash Behari, 40, 45-52, 54, 66, 70, 75-77, 81-84, 90, 94-100, 112, 115, 117-9, 125, 142, 144, 213
Bose, Sisir Kumar, 107
Bose, Subhas Chandra, 22-24, 27, 42, 61, 63, 65-67, 70-71, 82, 97, 100, 102-47, 149, 156, 169-70, 174-6, 178-81, 186, 191-2, 194-200, 205-6, 208-9, 211-8; in Berlin, 22, 41, 61, 66-67, 76, 98, 105, 108-9, 111-2, 117, 126, 169, 211, 213; differences with Gandhi and Nehru, 105-6; escape from India, 107-8; and Forward Bloc, 106; in East Asia, 27, 31, 42, 61, 67, 111-2, 119; meeting with Fujiwara, 126-7; meeting with Mohan Singh, 124-5; in Southeast Asia, 41, 70, 117, 119, 125, 128, 163, 192, 194, 213-14; in Tokyo, 66, 71, 114, 131-2, 141-4, 162, 164, 169, 181
Bose, Suresh Chandra, 198-9
Boston Museum, 57
Brahmaputra River, 168, 175
Britain, 6, 11, 23, 26, 32, 34, 56, 60-62, 107, 109, 111, 117-8, 130, 150, 159, 162, 194, 210, 217
British, 65-66, 72, 86, 92, 103, 108-9, 112, 118-9, 121, 132, 136, 146-7, 149-51, 153, 156-8, 161, 175, 180, 194-5, 198, 200, 206, 210, 216, 218; in Bangkok, 2; in Burma, 150-1, 153, 157-8, 163; in Hong Kong, 2; in Singapore, 34, 36, 149; colonial history, 59; East India Company, 34; advance into Thailand, 17; relations with Thai Government, 4; rule in India, 4, 6, 18, 20, 46, 48-49, 51, 53, 56, 60, 69, 92-93, 98, 102, 104-5, 107, 116-7, 120-1, 128-9, 131, 150-1, 157, 159, 162, 173, 177, 201, 207-9, 211, 216, 219; strategy, 16, 34, 151, 153; warships, sinking of, 12
British Air Force, 36
British-American-Dutch economic blockade, 2, 210
British Army, 1, 12, 21, 26, 36-37, 72, 83, 85, 104, 120, 153-5, 163, 182-3, 208, 214; attack on Singora, 12; in Malaya, 9, 25, 27-28; retreat in Malaya, 14, 32; in Singapore, 29, 32
British-Indian Army, 3, 7, 14, 16-21, 24-28, 36-39, 67, 72, 84-86, 120, 125, 150, 155, 157-8, 173, 176-7, 201, 207, 209, 217; surrender, 20, 28, 36-39; in Malaya, 3, 10, 16-19
Buddhists, 56, 73, 132, 213
Burma, 3, 10, 27-28, 40, 46, 65-67, 69-70, 75, 79, 81, 85, 88-89, 91, 92, 100, 111, 119, 122, 127, 129, 133, 137, 139-41, 144, 147, 149-51, 153-4, 156-7, 159-61, 163-6, 170, 173, 177, 179, 182, 185, 187, 192, 203, 205, 207, 213-4; under Japanese military administrations, 69; anti-British sentiment in, 29; independence movement, 2, 28, 69-70, 122; and Japanese, 29, 50, 69, 93, 111, 119; Slim battleline, 26-27; Thakin Party, 28
Burma Area Army (BAA), 136-7, 140, 147, 157, 160, 164-71, 174, 178, 181-2, 184, 186, 188-9, 194, 205-6
Burma Independence Army (BIA), 29, 147, 178-9
Burma Road, 35, 150, 153, 172
Bushi ideal, 81

Cairo, 163
Calcutta, 48, 53, 55, 60, 65, 103-7, 113-4, 118, 158, 173-4, 208-11; Black Hole of, 107
Cambridge, 103
Canton, 75
Casablanca, 163
Celebes Islands, 29
Central Indian Association of Malaya, 39
Ceylon, 65, 71, 73
Chand, Tek, 202
Chander, J.P., 204
Chang Ching-hui, 130
Chatterji, A.C. (Lt.-Col., Gen.), 39, 98, 100, 121, 140-1, 145-6, 181

247

Chatterji, Bankim Chandra, 102
Chennault, Claire (Maj.-Gen.), 150
Chiang Kai-shek, 81, 150, 153, 156, 159, 163
Chin Hills, 153-4, 170-1, 175, 177, 179, 189
China, 3, 6, 63, 118, 150, 153, 156-8, 162, 165, 172, 192, 194, 211; and Burma, 150, 154; Japanese in, 6, 21, 196
Chindits, 150, 164
Chindwin River, 73, 150, 153, 164-5, 167, 171, 173, 178, 184, 188-90, 192
Chinese (language), 56
Chinese: in Bangkok, 2; in Tokyo, 48; in Malaya, 3, 8, 19-20; in Singapore, 120; organizations, 14, 211; overseas markets, 4, 7; troops, 35, 156-7, 170-3, 199
Chittagong, 115, 140, 142, 158-9, 162, 168, 173
Chou Fu-hai, 130
Chungking, 65, 118, 157, 159, 213
Churchill (Prime Minister), 34-35
Ciano, 108
Communism, 107
Congress Socialist Party, 106
Co-Prosperity Sphere, *see* Greater East Asia Co-Prosperity Sphere
Council of Action (of IIL), 46, 51-52, 77-79, 81-82, 84-97, 99
Croatia, 129
Curzon, Lord (Viceroy), 53
Cuttack, 102-3

Dairen, 195-6, 198
Das, C.R., 104
Das, Devnath, 5, 46, 83, 195, 198
Das Rai Bahadur Badri, 202
De Valera, Eamon (President), 129
Delhi, 48, 79, 83, 125, 206-8, 216
Desai, Bhulabhai, 202, 208
Deshpande, 100
Dhillon, Gurbaksh Singh (Lt.), 203-5, 207
Diet (Japanese), 61, 64, 68, 76, 91, 110, 116-7, 151, 211-2, 214
Dimapur, 153-4, 168, 175, 182, 192
Dōmei (Japanese news agency), 180, 197
Dresden, 109
Durrani, Mahmood Khan (Lt.-Col.), 72
Dutch, 206

East Asia, 130-2, 140
East Indies, 98
Eastern Europe, 105

Egypt, 150
Engineer, N.P., 202
Europe, 5, 56-57, 105, 107, 113, 119, 197

F Kikan, see Fujiwara Kikan
Farrer Park, 36-37, 39-40, 209
Fascism, 107
Fifteenth Army, 12, 40, 70, 73, 126-7, 136-7, 146, 151, 158-61, 164, 166-7, 170-3, 175, 181, 184-5, 188-9
Fitzpatrick (Col.), 17-20
Forward Bloc, 60, 106
Free India, 106
Free India Provisional Government (FIPG), 47, 66, 119, 121, 125, 128-36, 138-41, 143-5, 147, 149, 169, 176, 180-1, 191, 194, 203-5, 216
French Revolution, 25
Fuehrer, 107, 122
Fujiwara, Iwaichi (Maj., Lt.-Gen.), 1-2, 19-21, 24, 26-31, 36-46, 48, 50-51, 63, 65, 67-70, 72, 80-81, 83, 87-88, 93-95, 97, 126-7, 167, 169, 175, 179, 188, 190, 192, 206-9, 211-3, 215-6; and Indian independence movement, 3-5, 20, 67-68, 81, 137, 176; and formation of INA, 24-25, 81, 211; operations in Burma, 3, 29; operations in Thailand, 3, 5-6, 11, 65; operations in Malaya, 3, 8-9, 19-20, 27; operations in Sumatra, 7; and Mohan Singh, 20, 22-26, 81, 84, 87, 93-95, 97, 126; and Pritam Singh, 4-7, 10, 12, 14-15, 19-20, 22, 126; and Tamura (Col.), 4, 6, 10; and Tanaka (Gen.), 31-32; and Tani Yutaka, 9-10; and Subhas Chandra Bose, 126-7
Fujiwara Kikan (F Kikan), 7-10, 14-15, 18-22, 29, 31, 36-41, 43, 45, 50, 63, 67, 72, 84, 87, 157, 164, 207, 215
Fukuoka, 206
Fukutome (Vice-Admiral), 146
Fuwa (Lt.-Col.), 188

Gaimushō (Japanese Foreign Ministry), 60-61, 64, 66, 80, 111, 129, 142, 144, 181, 205, 211
Gandhi, Mahatma, 21, 23, 48, 56, 59, 86, 101, 105-6, 121, 140, 162, 212, 216
Gandhi Brigade, 83
Gandhi Regiment, 179
Ganges River, 160
Gani, Karim, 100
Germany, 61, 76, 97, 107, 109-14, 129, 146, 150, 157, 163, 191, 218; army, 110; Foreign Ministry, 66, 110-2,

114; Press, 109; Japanese alliance with, 2
Gilani, G.Q. (Lt.-Col.), 72, 77, 94-95
Gilbert Islands, 173
Gill, N.S. (Lt.-Col.), 37-38, 40, 45, 47, 52, 84-85, 125; arrest of, 86-87, 95
Goebbels, 109
Goho, S.C., 39-43, 77, 85
Government of India Act (1935), 105
Greater East Asia, 130-1, 158
Greater East Asia Co-Prosperity Sphere, 3, 30-31, 37, 60, 62, 64-65, 67, 80, 91, 116, 130-2, 156, 210-1, 214, 217
Greater East Asia Conference, 130-1, 133
Gulzara Singh (Col.), 146, 195
Gurkhas, 72-73, 175

Hachiya Teruo, 143-5, 203, 205
Hainan Island, 28, 43
Hani Gorō, 59
Hanoi, 195
Hardinge (Viceroy), 48
Harimao project, 4, 7-8, 72
Haripura, 105
Hashimoto Kingorō, 63
Hassan, Abid (Maj.), 195
Hata Hikosaburō (Lt.-Gen.), 185-7
Hattori (Col.), 159, 192
Hayashi Akira (Lt.-Gen.), 158-60, 167
Hikari Kikan, 63, 118, 129, 135-8, 140-1, 144-5, 157, 169, 181, 191, 203, 205
Himalayas, 157, 199
Hinduism/Hindus, 53, 56, 106, 122, 212, 218
Hindustani (Hindi), 26, 59, 131
Hirohito (Emperor), 142
Hitler, 105, 108-10, 113
Hokkaido, 185
Hong Kong, 43, 68, 75
Honshu, 43-44
Hukawng Valley, 153, 170-2
Hull-Nomura peace negotiations, 7, 43
Hunt (Lt.-Col.), 37

Iemura Minoru (Lt.-Gen.), 62
Iida Shōjirō (Lt.-Gen.), 12, 70, 158-61, 169
Imperial Conferences, 61-62, 64, 130
Imperial General Headquarters (IGHQ), 1-3, 7, 11, 22, 26-27, 29-30, 40-41, 43-45, 50-51, 61-63, 66-68, 70, 79-82, 86, 110-2, 115, 117, 129, 138, 143-5, 149, 156, 159-69, 173, 178, 181-2, 185, 187, 195, 211, 215-6
Imperial Rule Assistance Association, 143

Imperial War Edict, 12
Imphal, 65, 73, 86, 130, 137, 139, 143, 149-50, 153-4, 165-8, 171, 173-5, 178-9, 181-3, 186, 190, 192, 200, 205, 208; campaign, 65, 67, 113, 123, 126, 137-8, 141-2, 149, 151, 155-6, 158, 161-4, 167-9, 172, 179, 181, 183, 189-91, 204, 206, 213-5
Inada Seijun (Maj.-Gen.), 167-8, 192
India, 3, 14, 24-25, 27-28, 38, 42-43, 45, 47, 50, 53, 55-76, 79-81, 85-86, 88-93, 97-99, 101-9, 131-3, 136-8, 141-2, 149-51, 153-4, 156-63, 166, 168, 174-5, 177-8, 180, 186, 190-5, 197-8, 200-5, 207, 209-15, 219; anti-British sentiment in, 64, 128, 157, 161, 169; "India Policy Project", 45, 50-51, 70-71, 80; "Quit India" resolution, 101, 162; civil service, 103-4
India Club, 46
India Lodge, 47
Indian Association, 50; of Malaya, 39
Indian Chamber of Commerce, 39, 46
Indian Congress Party, 21-23, 162
Indian Friendship Association, 50
Indian Independence League (IIL), 3, 5, 7, 14-15, 18, 21, 24-25, 27, 30, 37-41, 46, 50-52, 68-71, 75, 77-78, 82, 84-86, 88-90, 93, 98-100, 125, 128, 136-7, 141, 144, 157, 165, 197, 214; Council of Action, 77, 81-82, 84-99; in Malaya, 5, 25, 40, 123; branch in Rangoon, 15; in south Thailand, 5, 14
Indian independence movement, 2-5, 7, 10, 18, 23, 27, 30-31, 37, 46-51, 59, 63-64, 69-72, 76, 78, 82, 85, 91-92, 97-98, 100, 104-6, 108-13, 116-23, 125, 131-3, 136, 139-42, 149, 159, 162, 164, 169, 179, 181, 186, 191, 200-1, 205-19; Japanese aid in, 10, 18, 22-23, 27, 31, 37-38, 42-43, 45, 50-52, 69-70, 79, 82, 85, 88-90, 92, 110, 116, 118, 120, 125, 131, 149, 162, 170, 192, 195, 208, 210, 216-7; in East Asia, 77, 90, 121; in Southeast Asia, 2, 63, 125, 157, 213-4
Indian Legion, 109-10
Indian Mutiny, 200, 207
Indian National Army (INA), 24-31, 36-42, 44, 51, 63, 65, 67-72, 76-79, 81-101, 109, 112-3, 115-27, 128-30, 134-41, 143-7, 149, 153, 156-7, 161-2, 164, 167-70, 174-82, 189-94, 196, 200-8, 210-2, 214-9; and Indian Independence

249

League (IIL), 24-25, 70, 77, 79, 82, 89, 96, 98, 104, 117, 119, 121, 144, 157; and Burma Independence Army (BIA), 29; postwar trial in Delhi, 79, 200-9, 216; differences with Japanese, 84, 89, 95, 97-98; History Committee, 77, 86
Indian National Association, 46
Indian National Committee of Japan, 46-47
Indian National Congress, 46-48, 50, 53, 59, 64, 77, 82, 93, 100-1, 103-6, 118, 207-9
Indian National Council, 41-42
Indian nationalism, 53-54, 59-60
Indian Ocean, 113, 132, 146, 157
Indian Pan-Asianism, 54
Indian Social Association, 46
Indian Universities Act (1904), 53
Indian Youth Movement, 99-100
Indian(s), 82, 85, 91, 93, 98-99, 103-5, 107-10, 117-8, 129-30, 138-9, 141-2, 176, 186, 194-7, 202, 207-8, 210-2, 215, 218; in Africa, 109; in Asia, 7, 27, 39-40, 75, 119, 122; in Bangkok, 5, 12, 41, 75-76; in Burma, 89, 122; in East Asia, 91, 98, 140, 142; in Hong Kong, 2, 4, 89; in Japan, 46-49; in Malaya, 19-20, 25, 39, 45, 51-52, 69-70, 74, 98; POWs, 38-39, 42, 49, 51, 68, 79, 83, 91, 93-94, 97, 109-10, 124, 136-8, 143, 156, 169, 174, 200, 204, 207, 209, 211; in the Middle East, 108; in Rangoon, 145, 147; in Shanghai, 5, 89; in Singapore, 39-40, 45, 120, 128, 130; in Southeast Asia, 49, 51-52, 69-70, 75, 77, 79, 82, 112, 119, 128, 162, 191, 212-4; in Thailand, 12, 42, 45; in Tokyo, 5, 42, 44-46, 50, 70, 75, 77, 82, 141-2, 144, 214
Indo-Burmese border, 24, 60, 85, 87, 99, 101, 136, 142, 158
Indochina, 2, 11, 50, 196; Thai-Indochinese boundary dispute, 4
Indo-Japanese Association, 47
Indo-Japanese relations, 3, 5-6, 10, 20-24, 26-27, 31, 37-40, 42-44, 46-47, 50, 52-53, 55-59, 69-70, 78, 91, 93, 97-100, 118 123, 127, 138-9, 149, 204-5, 212, *see* Japan
Indo-Japanese War Co-operation Council, 137
Indonesia, 131, 156
Indo-Thai cultural organization, 5
International Military Tribunal (for the Far East), 58

Inukai Tsuyoshi (Premier), 57-58
Ipoh, 9, 16, 25-27, 50
Irish Free State, 129
Irrawaddy, 133, 146-7, 153, 178
Isayama Haruki (Maj.-Gen.), 160-1
Ise Bay, 44
Ishii (Col.), 70
Ishikawa Yoshiaki, 63, 69
Ishiwara Kanji, 63
Islam, 132
Ismay (Gen.), 35
Isoda Saburō (Lt.-Gen.), 136-9, 141, 143, 146, 169, 191, 194-6, 207, 213, 215
Italy, 76, 108, 110, 114; Japanese alliance with, 2
Itō Keisuke, 21
Iwakuro (Col.), 40-41, 43, 45, 51, 68-71, 79-82, 84-86, 88, 90-95, 97, 117, 126, 161, 204, 212-3
Iwakuro Kikan, 45, 63, 65, 68-74, 79, 82-87, 89-91, 93-97, 99-100, 117-8, 126, 137, 157

Jahangir, A.D. (Maj.), 98, 123, 127
Jai Hind, 122
Japan, 47, 52, 54-57, 60-63, 65-67, 69, 71, 75-76, 78-79, 81, 84, 87, 89-90, 92-93, 97, 110-9, 121, 124, 129, 131-4, 136-7, 139-42, 145, 149-51, 156-9, 161, 163, 165-6, 169, 172, 176, 181, 186-7, 191-2, 195, 198, 203, 205-6, 208, 210, 212-4, 217; and China, 3, 6, 35, 55, 57, 83; alliance with Germany, 2; and Indochina, 2, 50; relations with India, 20, 26, 40-42, 45, 53-58, 89, 93, 117, 143, 169, 195, 212, 214-5; policy toward India, 27, 29-31, 37, 41, 43, 45, 60-71, 79-81, 92-93, 99, 110-3, 129, 131, 139-40, 144, 149-51, 157, 163, 178, 205, 212-7; policy toward Indian National Army (INA), 65-67, 88-90, 92, 138, 141, 149, 153, 161-2, 169, 192, 205, 212, 214-9; alliance with Italy, 2; in Korea, 21; and Manchuria, 3, 21; military strategy, 3, 35, 61, 215; policy in Asia, 62, 91, 116; policy in Southeast Asia, 2, 19, 37, 60, 218; relations with Thailand, 4; victory over Russia, 48, 52-53, 56; War Ministry, 66; Foreign Ministry, *see Gaimushō*
Japan Fine Arts Institute, 57
Japan-India Society, 142
Japanese (language), 56, 59
Japanese, 56-58, 72, 75, 79, 82-84, 86,

250

89-91, 93, 97-98, 100-1, 108, 121, 125, 128, 130-1, 138-9, 154, 179, 211
Japanese Army (Imperial), 1, 3, 6, 8-10, 12, 15, 17, 19-20, 23, 26-29, 32, 34-35, 37-38, 49-50, 53, 59, 61-63, 65-66, 78-80, 83-84, 87, 95, 98, 116, 122, 137-8, 140, 146-7, 149-51, 153-6, 159, 162-4, 169-70, 172-9, 182-4, 189-92, 194, 204-7, 211, 214, 218; occupation of Malaya, 12, 16-20, 25, 27-28, 32, 34, 149; attack on Singapore, 36, 149; occupation of Thailand, 11-12, 149; *see also* Burma Area Army, Fifteenth Army, Southern Army, Twenty-fifth Army, Twenty-eighth Army
Japanese Government, 27, 43, 45, 49, 59, 91, 131, 181
Japanese Navy, 53, 61-62, 66, 80, 133-4, 145-6, 150, 157
Japanese-Indian cooperation, 3, 40, 42-44, 69, 83-84, 98-100, 164, 204, 212, 215, 217-9
Java, 50, 75, 98
Jimmu (Emperor), 32, 57
Jimmukai, 57
Jitra, 9, 16-18, 21
Johore Bahru, 9, 35; fall of, 32, 34-35
Johore Strait, 32, 35, 97

Kabaw Valley, 166, 168, 177, 179, 182, 189
Kabul, 107-8
Kachin (tribes), 172
Kadomatsu (Lt.-Col.), 50
Kaizaki (Maj.), 186
Kalewa, 86, 171, 178
Kamimoto, 8, 72
Kaneko Noboru (Capt.), 71
Kanglatongbi, 184
Katakura Tadasu (Col., Lt.-Gen.), 160-1, 164, 168-9, 174, 188, 192, 205-6
Katju, K.N., Dr, 202
Katō Nagao, 59, 185
Kawabe, Masakazu (Lt.-Gen.), 137, 140, 164-5, 167, 169-70, 180-3, 185-90, 192-3, 206, 215
Kedah, Sultan of, 21
Kemawari (Maj.), 179
Kempeitai (Military Police), 86
Kerin, F.C.A. (Col.), 202
Khan, D.M., 100
Kiani, M.Z. (Lt.-Col., Gen.), 98, 141, 146, 179, 190
Kiani (Col.), 179
Kikan, Penang branch of, 71, 73; *see also* Fujiwara Kikan; Hikari Kikan;
Iwakuro Kikan; Minami Kikan
Kim Ok-kiun, 54
Kimura Heitarō (Gen.), 147, 189, 194
Kinoshita (Col.), 185
Kitabe Kunio (Lt.-Col.), 69-70, 85, 88-89, 100
Kitamura Shihachi (Gen.), 189
Kluang, 29, 32
Kobe, 46-47
Kohima, 73, 153-4, 170-1, 174, 177, 182, 184-5, 189, 192
Koiso (Gen.), 142; Cabinet, 141
Kokuryūkai, (Black Dragon Society), 49-50
Kondo (Maj.), 167
Konoe, 62; Cabinet, 7
Konoe Imperial Guards Division, 11-12, 29, 35-36, 40, 43, 80, 212
Korea, 21
Kota Bahru, 8-9, 12, 14
Koyama Ryō, 68, 91
Kuala Lumpur, 26-28, 30, 40, 123
Kunizuka (2nd Lt.), 21, 37, 90, 92
Kunming, 81, 150, 153
Kunomura Homoyo (Maj.-Gen.), 126-7, 165-7, 185
Kurahashi (Lt.-Col.), 186
Kuroda Shigetoku (Lt.-Gen.), 82, 158
Kuromaku, 58
Kurusu, 80
Kwantung Army, 62-63, 160, 165
Khyber Pass, 108
Kyushu, 44

Lahore, 48, 208
Lashio, 150
Laurel, José (President), 130
Ledo, 153, 163, 165, 172
Liaison Conferences, 61-62, 64, 133
Loganadhan, A.D. (Lt.-Col., Maj.-Gen.), 122, 134-5, 146-7
London, 62, 102-3
Lucknow, 208

Madagascar, 114
Madras, 71, 121, 133, 208
Maki Tatsuo (Lt.-Col.), 68
Maimyo, 171, 175, 184
Maitra, S.N., 198
Malaya, 3-4, 8, 14, 16-17, 27, 39-43, 45-46, 51-52, 72, 74-76, 80, 93-94, 97-99, 111, 130, 144, 149, 156, 200, 212, 217; anti-Japanese feeling in; 8; Japanese advance through; 7, 10, 12, 25-27, 32, 50, 65, 149, 155, 211

251

Malayan(s), 3; independence movement, 2
Malay(s), 3, 8, 18-19, 21, 120; sultans, 4, 11, 14, 19; organizations, 4, 7, 211
Malay Volunteer Army, 9
Malay Youth League, 7, 11, 21
Malik (Soviet Ambassador), 144
Manchuria (Manchukuo), 3, 57, 62-63, 75, 92, 129-30, 139, 160, 195, 205; Japanese takeover of, 8, 21, 57, 196
Mandalay, 104, 146, 150-1, 181
Manila, 114, 120, 187-8
Manipur, 154, 203
March Affair (1931), 57
Marco Polo Brigade (incident), 165
Matsumoto Shun'ichi, 205
Matsuoka, 60, 211
Meiji (Emperor), 3; Restoration, 2, 6
Meiktila, 146
Menon, K.P.K., 39, 42-43, 77-79, 89, 91, 95, 98
Mexican revolution, 72
Middle East, 72
Mikasa (Prince), 187
Minami Kikan, 28-29, 85
Mintani mountains, 154
Mitsui Trading Company, 4
Miyazaki (Maj.-Gen.), 185
Mochizuki (Reverend), 197
Mogul Emperors, 122; rule of, 200, 202
Mohan Singh, 16-31, 36-38, 40-46, 52, 70, 75-77, 79, 82-99, 115, 122, 124-6, 192, 208, 211, 215; and Fujiwara, 20, 22-26, 81, 87, 93, 95, 97, 126-7, 208, 216
Mongolia, 198
Moscow, 108, 111
Moulmein, 194
Mountbatten, Lord Louis, 151, 155
Mukden Incident (1931), 58
Muslim(s), 23, 53, 72, 106-7, 112, 218
Mussolini, 107-9
Mutaguchi Renya (Lt.-Gen.), 126, 137, 151, 161, 164-8, 171-6, 182-9, 192
Myitkyina, 150, 153, 172

Nagai Yatsuji (Col.), 63
Nagar, G.R. (Col.), 146
Nagas, 154, 172, 177
Nair, A.M., 46
Naka Eitarō (Lt.-Gen.), 167, 169, 171, 184-6
Nakado (Rear Admiral), 141
Nakano Gakkō, see *Rikugun Nakano Gakkō*

Nanking (Government), 75, 91, 129-30, 205
National Front, 106
Nazis, 108
Nazi High Command, 108-9
Nee Soon, 38-39
Nehru, Jawaharlal, 23, 42, 48, 59, 96, 105-6, 113, 121, 124, 200-2, 209, 216, 218
Nehru Brigade, 83
Nehru Regiment, 175-6
Nepal, 48, 71-73
Netaji, 107, 122-6, 128, 131, 137-9, 142, 164, 174-5, 178-81, 190, 195-200, 202; see also Bose, Subhas Chandra
New Britain, 29
New Guinea, 98
New Order (in Greater East Asia), 25, 27, 31, 45
Nicobar Islands, 66, 132-3, 145, 191, 203, 214-6
Nishiura Susumu (Col.), 173
Nogi (Gen.), 53
Noguchi Yonejirō, 55, 142

Ōbata Eiryō (Lt.-Gen.), 158
Ōbata Shinryō (Gen.), 165
Ogawa Saburō (Maj.), 68, 83, 92, 179
Oikawa Koshirō, 143
Okakura Kakuzō (or Tenshin), 55-57, 110, 212
Okamura (Lt.-Col.), 30
Okamoto (Maj.-Gen.), 50, 63
Ōkawa Shūmei, 49-50, 57-58
Okazaki (Consul-General), 60-61
Operation 21, 161, 164, 167
Operation U, 120, 172, 180-1, 187, 191-2
Osaka, 44
Ōshima Hiroshi (Lt.-Gen.), 61, 110-4
Osman, 72; group, 71
Ōta Saburō, 205
Otaguro, 43-44
Ozeki Masaji (Maj., Lt.-Col.), 26-27, 50-51, 63, 178

Pacific, 66, 85, 111, 139, 142, 157, 163, 210-1; war in, 2, 20, 48, 50
Pacific War, 58-59, 62, 111, 116, 149, 162, 165, 187, 192, 215
Pakistan, 209
Palel, 166, 171, 179, 188
Pan-Asianism, 48, 54-55, 58, 63, 132
Pashto (language), 107
Pathan, 107-8
Patna, 208
Pattani, 12

Pearl Harbour attack, 12, 43
Pearl's Hill Prison, 86, 98
Peking, 165, 198
Penang Island, 16, 27, 42, 68, 71-74, 98-99, 114, 125; harbour, 113
Pegu, 95
Perak, 9, 16, 23; River, 20-21
Permanent National Government (of Azad Hind), 128
Peshawar, 107
Phibun Songgram, 11-12, 75, 131
Philippines, 29, 75, 119, 129-31, 205, 216
Port Blair, 134-5
Potsdam Proclamation, 195
Prasad, Baleshwar, 100
Pratap, Raja Mahendra, 47-48, 51-52
Prince of Wales, 12
Pritam Singh, 18-22, 24-27, 30, 36-43, 82, 126, 195; and Fujiwara, 4-7, 10, 12, 14-15, 19-20, 22, 126
Provisional Government of Free India, see Free India Provisional Government
Punjab, 71; Regiment, 16, 38

Quebec, 163

Raffles, Sir Stamford, 34
Raffles College, 36
Raffles Hotel, 69
Raghavan, N., 41-43, 71, 73-74, 76-79, 85, 90-91, 94-95, 98-99, 125
Rai, Lala Lajpat, 48, 54
Raju, D.S. (Col.), 39
Raju (Dr), 124-5
Ram Swarup (Capt.), 28, 69, 85
Rama Murti, 144, 197
Ramakrishna, 103
Ramakrishna Mission, 39
Rangoon, 6, 46, 68-69, 72, 85-86, 90, 122, 136, 138-9, 144-7, 161, 167-9, 190-1, 200, 204
Rani of Jhansi Regiment, 121, 138, 147, 181, 191
Ravenshaw Collegiate School, 103
Red Fort, 200, 202, 207-8
Rahman, Habibur (Maj., Col.), 98, 141, 146, 195, 197
Repulse, 12
Retsu Division, 185
Ribbentrop, 108, 112
Rikugun Nakano Gakkō (Army Intelligence School), 69, 71, 80, 212
Rome, 105, 108

Rommel, 150
Rōnin, 58
Rowlatt Bill (1919), 104
Roy, Rammohan, 102
Royal National War Institute, 62
Russia (Soviet), 63, 108, 111, 141, 150, 194-6, 198, 211-2
Russo-Japanese War (1905), 53, 117

Sabang Island, 114
Sahay, Anand Mohan, 46-47, 50-52, 196
Sahgal, P.K. (Maj., Capt.), 98, 146, 203-4
Saigon, 28, 43, 68, 81, 95, 114, 144, 187, 194-6
Saipan, 140
Saitō Jirō (Col.), 68
Sakaguchi (Col.), 185
Salween River, 153, 170-2
Samarkand, 108, 141
Samurai, 58
Sandhurst, 85-86
Sanno Conference, 40-42, 45-48, 51-52, 68, 70, 75
Sanskrit, 102
Santiniketan, 56
Sapru, Sir Tej Bahadur, 202
Satō Kenryō (Lt.-Gen.), 143
Satō Kōtoku, 184-5, 189, 192
Satyananda Puri (Swami), 41-43, 75
Sawada Renzō, 205
Scottish Church College, 103
Seletar, 38, 97, 123; Naval Base, 32, 35-36
Sen, Keshab Chandra, 102
Sen, P.K., 202
Senda, 90-91, 95, 126, 208
Sen Gupta, 49
Shah Nawaz Khan (Maj., Lt.-Col.), 38-39, 65-66, 83-84, 98, 122, 124-5, 146-7, 170, 174-9, 192, 198, 203, 206
Shadhid (Martyr) Island, 134
Shanghai, 43-44, 72, 75, 123, 144, 196
Shibata Uichi (Lt.-Gen.), 184
Shidei (Gen.), 196-8
Shigemitsu, 63, 67, 114, 116, 130, 141-4, 164, 196, 206, 214
Shillong, 168
Shimada, 206
Shōnan, 81, 139
Sikh(s), 4-6, 14, 22-25, 71-72, 87, 122-4, 211, 218; in Bangkok, 4-6, 41; in Malaya, 19; in Shanghai, 123
Singapore, 8-9, 26, 28-29, 34-35, 39-42, 68-69, 81, 83, 86, 89, 97, 100, 111, 118, 120-6, 128, 130, 136, 144, 159,

165, 169, 172, 176, 179, 191, 194, 209; battle of, 27, 29, 32, 35-36; defences of, 7, 27, 32, 34-35; Japanese capture of, 7, 111, 149, 211; as headquarters of IIL, 100
Singora, 17, 21; airfield attack, 12
Singora Indian Association, 14
Singh, Dalip, 202
Sittaung, 166, 178
Sivaram, M., 100
Slim (Lt.-Gen.), 155
Slim battleline, 26-27
Solomon Islands, 173
Sōma Aizō, 49
Sōshi, 58
South Manchuria Railway Company, 57
Southeast Asia, 2, 35, 39-41, 45-46, 52, 60, 62-65, 69-70, 79-81, 100, 107, 109, 113, 119, 125, 128, 130, 132, 135-6, 144-5, 155-7, 162, 176, 191, 200, 206-7, 210, 212-3, 217-9; Command, 151
Southern Army, 10, 27, 29, 40, 65, 67-68, 70, 81-82, 85, 123, 126, 136, 158-9, 161-2, 164-8, 171, 173-4, 185-8, 194, 206
Soviet Union, *see* Russia
Stalingrad, 109-10, 112, 163
Schenkl, Fraulein, 113
Stilwell (Gen.), 153, 172
Sugawara Michio (Lt.-Col.), 158
Sugita Ichiji (Col.), 185-6
Sugiyama Gen (Gen.), 3, 30, 50, 62-63, 67, 114-6, 135, 138, 143, 158, 161, 164, 211, 214, 217
Sukarno, 131
Sumatra, 7, 23, 27, 40, 75, 98, 114
Sumatra Youth League, 25
Sun Yat-sen, 48-49, 54
Sungei Patani, 16, 21
Supreme War Conference, 144
Swaraj (newspaper), 104
Swaraj (Independence) Island, 134
Swaraj Institute (Freedom Institute), 71, 73-74
Swaminadhan, Lakshmi (Capt.), 121

Tagore, Debendranath, 102
Tagore, P.S., 48
Tagore, Rabindranath, 54-56, 59, 102, 142, 212
Taipei (Taihoku), 144, 195, 197
Taiping, 23
Taiwan, 114, 143, 195-7, 199
Takaoka Taisuke, 68
Takeda, Prince, (Col.), 167

Takeshita, 160
Tamu, 171, 178
Tamura (Col.), 3, 10-12, 25, 50; and Fujiwara, 4, 6
Tanabe, 158, 161
Tanaka Nobuo (Lt.-Gen.), 183
Tanaka Shin'ichi (Gen.), 30-31, 40, 172
Tani Yutaka, 8-10
Tatsumi Eiichi (Col., Lt.-Gen.), 62
Tazoe (Lt.-Col.), 182
Tegnoupal, 179
Terauchi, Count, (Gen., Field-Marshal), 10, 29-30, 65, 123-4, 135, 137, 144, 161, 166-7, 172-3, 192, 194-5, 206
Thailand, 1, 3, 5, 8-10, 12, 16-17, 27, 29, 32, 34, 40-42, 46, 69, 75, 79, 131, 149, 217; Foreign Ministry, 11; Government, 4, 10-11, 41, 129; Japanese occupation of, 7, 10-12, 149, 211; relations with Japan, 4, 10-12
Thai Army, 4
Thai-Bharat Cultural Lodge, 41
Thai-Indochinese relations, 4
Thais, 8, 9, 79
Thakin Party, 28
Thimmayya, K.P. (Lt.-Col.), 122
Third Airborne Division, 26
Third Reich (Army), 1
Tiddim, 175
"Tiger of Burma", 160
"Tiger of Malaya", 8-10
Togo (Admiral), 53
Togo Shigenori, 76
Tōjō (Gen.), 30, 43, 45, 52, 61-67, 79-82, 91, 110, 112, 114-8, 120, 124, 130, 133, 135, 137-8, 142, 151, 158, 162-4, 173, 186-8, 192, 206, 211-2, 214; Cabinet, 7, 140
Tokyo, 1-3, 7, 10-11, 22, 27, 32, 40-45, 48-49, 51-52, 54, 60, 65-68, 70-71, 75, 79-83, 86, 90, 92-98, 100-1, 111-8, 124, 129-33, 135-8, 141-2, 144-5, 149-50, 157-62, 164, 166-7, 169, 171, 173, 181, 185-6, 188-9, 191, 195-8, 205-6, 211-4; Sanno Conference in, 40-42, 45-48, 51-52, 68, 70, 75; School of Foreign Languages, 59; Imperial University, 57, 59; War Crimes Tribunal, 62
Tominaga (Gen.), 30, 40
Tonzang, 182
Total War Research Institute, 62
Tourane, 196
Tōyama Mitsuru, 49-50, 54, 58, 63, 117, 142

Trincomalee, 73
Tripuri, 106
Tsubokami (Ambassador), 11, 76
Tsuchimochi (Capt.), 19, 69, 88
Tsunematsu, 185
Turkey, 47
Twenty-fifth Army, 10, 12, 22, 27-30, 32, 37, 67, 158
Twenty-eighth Army, 145
Tyersall Park, 38

Ubin Island, 35-36
Uchida Ryōhei, 54
Ukhrul, 178
Umezu Yoshijirō, 143
United States of America, 11, 47, 64, 130, 150, 153; American Army, 1, 155, 157, 163, 170, 207; Americans, 2, 195
Urdu, 59
Ushiro Masaru (Maj.), 186-8
Uttam Chand, 108

Van Vaidyakorn, Prince, 131
Vivekananda, 103
Voice of Asia, The, 50
Voice of India, 47

Wang Ching-wei, 130
Washington, 7; Naval Conference, 34, 43; peace talks, 80
Wavell (Gen.), 34, 124, 151, 194

West, the, 102
Western Europe, 56
Western colonialism/imperialism, 37, 53, 58, 60, 62, 69, 76, 79, 210, 212
Wingate, Orde (Brig.-Gen.), 150, 164, 182
World Federation Centre, 47-48
World Federation Volunteer Corps, 48
World War II, 56, 58, 212

Yamada, 167
Yamaguchi (Lt.), 87-88, 183, 186
Yamamoto Bin (Col., Maj.-Gen.), 61, 110-2, 114-5, 117-8, 123, 135-7
Yamashita (Lt.-Gen.), 22, 24, 27, 29, 32, 35
Yamashita Hirokazu, *see* Fujiwara Iwaichi
Yamauchi (Lt.-Gen.), 184
Yonai Mitsumasa, 114, 130, 143
Yanaihara Tadao, 59
Yanagita (Lt.-Gen.), 183-4
Yokohama, 46
Yoshida Shōin, 2
Young Malays Association (YMA), 25, 40
Yunnan, 153, 172
Yutani, 89
Yūzonsha (Society of the Remaining), 57

Zeawaddy, 203
Zebyu (mountains), 154

About the Author

Joyce Chapman Lebra received her B.A. and M.A. in Asian Studies from the University of Minnesota and her Ph.D. in Japanese History from Harvard/Radcliffe. She is the first woman Ph.D. holder in Japanese History in the U.S. She was Professor of Japanese History and Indian History at the University of Colorado until her retirement.

Professor Lebra received many awards, including an Honorary Doctor of Humane Letters degree from the University of Minnesota in 1996, two years Fulbright fellowship in Japan and one and a half years Fulbright fellowship in India. Other fellowships include a Japan Foundation fellowship, a National Endowment for the Humanities fellowship, and fellowships from the American Association of University Women, Australian National University, and others. She is noted in Who's Who in America, Who's Who of American Women, and Who's Who in American Education. She has lectured widely at the University of Hawai'i, Oxford University, the London School of Economics, Tokyo University, Waseda University, Nagoya University, Hong Kong University, the Institute of Southeast Asian Studies in Singapore, the Netaji Research Bureau in Calcutta, Melbourne and Monash Universities, Macquarie University, Sydney University, Brisbane University, and Australian National University in Canberra. She delivered the Harmon Memorial Lecture at the U.S. Air Force Academy in 1991.

Professor Lebra has authored twelve previous books, including two historical novels, *Durga's Sword* and *Sugar and Smoke*. She led three research teams to Asia to research on women's roles in the workforce, each of which resulted in a book: *Woman in Changing Japan*, *Chinese*

Women in Southeast Asia, and *Women and Work in India.* Her other books include: *Jungle Alliance: Japan and the Indian National Army, Japanese-trained Armies in Southeast Asia: Independence and Volunteer Forces in World War II, Okuma Shigenobu: Statesman of Meiji Japan, The Rani of Jhansi: A Study in Female Heroism in India,* and *Shaping Hawai'i: The Voices of Women.* She also edited *Japan's Greater East Asia Co-prosperity Sphere: Selected Readings and Documents.* She has written chapters in three books and some fifty articles in scholarly journals.

www.ingramcontent.com/pod-product-compliance
Lightning Source LLC
Chambersburg PA
CBHW030109010526
44116CB00005B/162